OFFICE MATTERS

3RD EDITION

Englisch für kaufmännische Büroberufe

von
Isobel Williams

in Zusammenarbeit mit
der Verlagsredaktion

Cornelsen

Verfasserin:	Isobel Williams
Beraterinnen:	Karin Cerny, Wien Irene Eckart, Flensburg Gloria Matzig, Aachen
Projektleitung:	Andreas Goebel
Außenredaktion:	James Abram
Redaktionelle Mitarbeit:	Oliver Gascoigne, Oliver Busch (Wörterverzeichnisse)
Bildredaktion:	Gertha Maly
Umschlaggestaltung, Layout und technische Umsetzung:	vitaledesign, Berlin
Illustrationen:	Thomas Malangeri (www.tausendschwarz.de) Oxford Designers & Illustrators

Erhältlich sind auch:	**Handreichungen für den Unterricht mit CD-ROM und Audio-CD** **ISBN: 978-3-06-450605-3**
Online-Ergänzungen unter:	**www.cornelsen.de/matters**

www.cornelsen.de

1. Auflage, 5. Druck 2020

Alle Drucke dieser Auflage sind inhaltlich unverändert und können im Unterricht nebeneinander verwendet werden.

Druck: Firmengruppe APPL, aprinta Druck, Wemding

ISBN: 978-3-06-450604-6 (Schülerbuch)
ISBN: 978-3-06-450743-2 (E-Book)

PEFC
PEFC/04-32-0928

PEFC zertifiziert
Dieses Produkt stammt aus nachhaltig bewirtschafteten Wäldern und kontrollierten Quellen.
www.pefc.de

VORWORT

Office Matters – 3rd Edition ist die komplett aktualisierte Neubearbeitung des bewährten Lehrwerks für kaufmännische Büroberufe und wurde für die Ausbildung in Berufsschulen sowie die innerbetriebliche Aus- und Weiterbildung konzipiert. Das Lehrwerk basiert auf den Lehrplänen der Bundesländer für Berufsschulen.

Es ist auf Lernende zugeschnitten, deren Englischkenntnisse den Anforderungen eines mittleren Bildungsabschlusses bzw. eines durchschnittlichen gymnasialen Grundkursabschlusses entsprechen (A2–B1). Darüber hinaus gibt es in den Rubriken *Extra Material* auch anspruchsvolleren Lernstoff für fortgeschrittene Schüler/innen (B2). Neu an der *3rd Edition* ist auch die durchgängige Vorbereitung auf die KMK-Zertifikatsprüfung in Englisch (Stufe II). Dies geschieht anhand prüfungsbezogener und mit einem KMK-Symbol gekennzeichneter Aufgaben im Schülerbuch, einer KMK-Seite pro Unit sowie einem *KMK mock exam* im Anhang.

Office Matters – 3rd Edition enthält 12 Units, in denen unterschiedliche Bereiche der Arbeit von Bürokaufleuten behandelt werden. Unit 12 befasst sich mit einer Bewerbung im Ausland (einschließlich Lebenslauf und Bewerbungsschreiben). Die Units sind in sich geschlossen und können in beliebiger Reihenfolge oder auch unter Auslassung einzelner Kapitel bearbeitet werden. Dennoch wird empfohlen, die vorgegebene Reihenfolge einzuhalten, um einen kontinuierlichen Aufbau des Fachvokabulars zu gewährleisten.

Das Lehrwerk zielt in erster Linie darauf ab, kommunikative Kompetenzen zu vermitteln. Dazu werden in fallstudienartigen Units Gesprächssituationen wie Telefonate oder Direktgespräche mit englischsprachigen Geschäftspartnern geübt. Das nötige Fachvokabular und wichtige Redewendungen, die in *Language boxes* sowie in erweiterter Form im Anhang aufgeführt sind, werden in Rollenspielen und Partnerübungen gefestigt. Neben der rein fachlichen wird dabei auch die soziale Komponente des Arbeitsalltags berücksichtigt. Außerdem werden das Lese- und Hörverständnis sowie das eigenständige Verfassen englischsprachiger Geschäftskorrespondenz (E-Mail, Brief, Fax) trainiert.

Das praxisorientierte Lernen wird durch authentische Texte wie Internetseiten, Zeitungsbeiträge und Geschäftskorrespondenz sichergestellt. Vielfältige Übungen vermitteln das notwendige sprachliche Hintergrundwissen. Die Lehrer-CD-ROM enthält ein breites Spektrum an Zusatzmaterialien zur Erweiterung der Arbeit mit dem Schülerbuch.

Neben der Aufarbeitung des Fachvokabulars und der spezifischen Redemittel werden auch Grundlagen der Grammatik zur Wiederholung angeboten. Sie werden in deutscher Sprache mit Hilfe von Beispielen erklärt und im handlungsbezogenen Kontext geübt. Der Anhang enthält *Partner files* mit Vorlagen zu Rollenspielen. Zwei Wörterlisten – alphabetisch sowie nach Units gegliedert – ermöglichen das schnelle Auffinden von Vokabeln, während die wichtigsten Wortfelder zum Nachschlagen und Lernen in einem kurzen deutsch-englischen Glossar zur Verfügung stehen.

Office Matters – 3rd Edition vermittelt die englischsprachigen Grundlagen, auf denen sicheres Auftreten und korrektes Handeln im Büro beruhen. Wenn die Lernenden sich dabei mit Vergnügen der englischen Sprache bedienen, hat dieses Werk sein Ziel erreicht.

2 — Dialog bzw. Hörtext auf der Audio-CD

KMK — Übungen zur Vorbereitung auf die KMK-Zertifikatsprüfung

WEBCODE **OMU0101** — Die Webcodes weisen auf Zusatzmaterial zur selbstständigen Weiterarbeit hin und können unter **www.cornelsen.de/matters** abgerufen werden.

UNIT 1

Getting started

- introducing yourself and other people
- describing daily routines
- taking a telephone call

1 Warm-up

A **Work in a group of three. Introduce yourself to the two other people in your group.**

My name is …

I'm from …

I'm an office assistant / a trainee / from Berlin.

B **Introduce one of the people in your group to the rest of the class.**

This is …

He's/She's from …

He/She is …

! I'm **a** trainee. / I'm **an** office management assistant.

C **Work in a new group. Use some of the phrases above to introduce yourself in a formal way.**

D **Now introduce your partners to another group.**

LANGUAGE

Making introductions

Greeting people you do not know

A	Good morning/afternoon/evening. I'm …	**B**	How do you do? My name is …
A	Nice to meet you.	**B**	Nice to meet you, too.
A	Excuse me. Are you … ?	**B**	Yes, I am. / No, I'm not. I'm …
A	Welcome to …	**B**	Thank you. It's nice to be here.

Introducing people

This is … ■ These are my colleagues, John and Mary. ■ I'd like to introduce …

2 Working as an office management assistant

"Your Office Matters" is an online magazine for office workers.

Read the information for trainee office management assistants and then do the tasks.

Mozilla Firefox
Your Office Matters
www.yourofficematters.com/trainee_office_management_assistants
Google
Facebook Meistbesuchte… Erste Schritte Aktuelle Nachr… Lesezeichen

Are you thinking of working in an office? Perhaps you're considering a career as an office management assistant or "office assistant", as people say? Here is some information which might help you make up your mind.

A Office assistants work in small, medium and large companies and organizations. They work in every type of industry, including manufacturing and service.

B Office assistants usually don't have any problems finding work. The work is interesting and full of variety, so you'll never be bored. You're busy all day.

C An office assistant provides support for managers and other members of staff in the workplace. For this reason, you should enjoy working with people and be a good communicator.

D You need computer skills and excellent organizational skills.

E Do you think you would make a good office management assistant? Talk to a careers officer about the qualifications you need. Your local job centre has information about training.

F Advertisements for office management assistants appear in the press or online every day.

A Match the FAQs (1–6) to the paragraphs (A–F). KMK

1 I need more advice. Who can I ask?
2 What do I have to do as an office assistant?
3 Where will I work?
4 How do I find a position as an office assistant?
5 Why should I choose this kind of work?
6 What skills do I need when I work as an office assistant?

B Work with a partner. Without looking back at the website on page 7, correct the incorrect statements below. Check your answers together.

1. Office assistants only work in the service industry.
2. An office assistant's job is sometimes monotonous.
3. Not many firms employ office assistants these days.
4. Office assistants don't have to do a lot of work.
5. An office assistant doesn't have much contact with other people at work.
6. It's difficult to find information about training for office assistants.

3 Things you do at work

Replace the highlighted tasks in the text with phrases from the box below.

do data processing • handle the mail • keep records • order office supplies • organize files • work with spreadsheets

If you're going to work as an office assistant, you'll have to do a lot of different things at work. Every day you will put away paperwork or documents[1] after you or someone else has worked with them, make sure that the office has enough paper, envelopes and other stationery[2] and take round the post[3]. Some office assistants help with financial planning[4]. You might also produce material on the computer[5] or write down things so that people can check them later[6].

GRAMMAR

The simple present and the present progressive

1. Office assistants usually **work** hard.
2. Abdi **goes** to classes once a week.
3. **Is it** fun to work in an office?
4. **Do** you **think** you would make a good office assistant?
5. Office assistants **don't have** problems finding work.
6. We **are setting up** a new office at the moment.
7. **Are** you **working** in a team this week?

- Die einfache Gegenwart (*simple present*) wird für anhaltende Zustände (1) oder sich wiederholende Ereignisse (2) verwendet.
- Fragen und Verneinungen bildet man, außer bei *be* (3), mit dem Hilfsverb *do* (4, 5).
- Die einfache Gegenwart wird oft mit folgenden Signalwörtern verwendet: *always, hardly ever, never, normally, often, sometimes, usually.*
- Die Verlaufsform der Gegenwart (*present progressive*) beschreibt Handlungen oder Vorgänge, die zeitgleich mit dem Sprechen/Schreiben ablaufen (6, 7).
- Die Verlaufsform der Gegenwart wird oft mit folgenden Signalwörtern verwendet: *at the moment, just, now, this week/month/year.*
- Beide Formen können mit zukünftiger Bedeutung verwendet werden (siehe S. 17).

4 Practice

A Complete the questions and negative sentences in the simple present using the verb in brackets. Be careful with the word order.

Example: What / the company? (sell)
What does the company sell?

1. Where / the trainees? (be)
2. He / his own desk. (not have)
3. I / a lot of time today. (not have)
4. you / your office? (like)
5. She / her work. (enjoy)
6. Where / the new photocopier? (be)
7. Laura / hard? (work)
8. He / a good communicator. (not be)

B Use the verbs in brackets to make sentences and questions using the simple present or the present progressive. Explain your decisions.

1. The assistant … (talk) to his boss just now.
2. She always … (work) carefully.
3. Peter … (produce) a spreadsheet this morning.
4. She never … (meet) her colleagues after work.
5. … (he/make) coffee for his colleagues every day?
6. Mike … (not know) the name of the new office assistant.
7. … (you/speak) English at work with your colleagues?
8. … (she/write) a report in English at the moment?

> **!** Don't forget!
> ***He, she, it,***
> *das* **s** *muss mit!*

5 Talking about training

KMK

2

An interviewer from the "Your Office Matters" website is talking to Abdi and Beatrice about their training.

Hören Sie sich die zwei Interviews an und ergänzen Sie diese Notizen mit den entsprechenden Informationen über Abdi und Beatrice.

- *Warum macht er/sie die Ausbildung zum Bürokaufmann/-frau?*
- *Was gefällt ihm/ihr am Besten an der Ausbildung?*
- *Was gefällt ihm/ihr nicht? Warum?*
- *Wie kommt er/sie mit dem Problem zurecht?*
- *Welche Fertigkeiten benutzt er/sie bei der Arbeit?*

6 Why are you training to be an office assistant?

Work with a partner. Interview each other about your training.

- Why are you planning on an office career?
- What skills do you have?

7 Country codes and contact details

A Match the countries (1–10) to the country codes (a–j) to produce a list of international telephone codes.

1	Austria	**6**	Russia
2	France	**7**	Switzerland
3	Germany	**8**	Turkey
4	Ireland	**9**	United Kingdom
5	Poland	**10**	United States/Canada

a	1	**f**	44
b	7	**g**	48
c	33	**h**	49
d	41	**i**	90
e	43	**j**	353

TIP

Telephone numbers

Say each digit separately, except for double digits, e.g. 01233 4567899 = "oh (AE zero) one two double-three four five six seven eight double-nine".

country code = *Vorwahl*
extension = *Durchwahl*
mobile phone (*AE* cell phone) = *Handy*
landline = *Festnetz*

B Work in a group of three and dictate the given contact details to each other.

Partner A: Look at this page.
Partner B: Look at File 1 on page 118.
Partner C: Look at File 10 on page 121.

While you are listening, if you don't understand something, you can ask, "Can you spell that, please?" or, "Could you repeat that, please?"

Partner A: Dictate these contact details to Partners B and C. Check B and C's answers.

1 Ms Leena Suominnen
Koivisto Kirja Kauppa OY
Kirkkokatau 28
20100 Turku
FINLAND

Telephone +358 22 84 73 61

2 the contact details of your firm or your own contact details

TIP

Telephoning in English

Preparation – Think about what you want to say before you start. Note down a few English phrases you could use during the conversation.

Making contact – Say your name and the name of your company clearly.

During the phone call – Make sure that you note down all proper names correctly. Ask the person on the other end to speak more slowly or to repeat something if you haven't understood it.

Small talk – English-speakers often chat about a general topic, such as the weather, at the beginning of a conversation.

Names – If you are talking to someone of higher "status", you should use their surname unless they specifically ask you to use their first name.

Bad news – English-speakers usually begin bad news with phrases such as *I'm afraid (that) … or I'm sorry, but … .*

LANGUAGE

Making a phone call

Identifying yourself
Good morning. My name's …
Good afternoon. This is … from (company).

Making small talk
How are you?
How's the weather today?

Explaining the reason for your call
I'm enquiring about …
I'd like some information on …
Could you tell me about … ?

Asking for a person/department
I'd like to speak to Mr/Ms …
Could you put me through to the … department, please?

Saying what you want to do
Can I leave a message?
I'll call again later.

Ending the call
Thank you for your help.
Goodbye.

8 Could you repeat that, please?

Match the English sentences (1–10) to the German equivalents (a–j).

1 Could you repeat that, please?
2 I'm afraid the line is engaged.
3 I'm sorry, (person's name) is unavailable at the moment.
4 Please hold the line.
5 Who's calling, please?
6 Would you like to speak to someone else?
7 Would you like to leave a message?
8 I'm trying to connect you.
9 I'll put you through.
10 Could you spell your name, please?

a Bleiben Sie bitte dran. 4
b Der Anschluss ist besetzt. 2
c Ich stelle Sie durch. 8
d Bitte wiederholen Sie. 1
e Buchstabieren Sie bitte Ihren Namen. 10
f Möchten Sie mit jemand anderem sprechen? 6
g Ich versuche, Sie zu verbinden. 9
h Möchten Sie eine Nachricht hinterlassen? 7
i Die Person, die Sie sprechen möchten, ist im Moment nicht da. 3
j Wie ist Ihr Name bitte? 5

9 Please hold the line

WEBCODE **OMU0101**

Abdi is taking a telephone call in English.

Complete the dialogue using phrases from the sentences in exercise 8.

A Can I speak to Ms Schmidt, please?
B May I ask …[1] ?
A Of course. This is Liam Donnelly.
B I'm sorry, could you …[2], please? Spell your name
A It's L I A M, D O double-N E double-L Y. I'm calling from Dublin, from Donnelly's Paper Mill.
B Sorry? Donnelly's Paper? Could you …[3], please? repeat that
A Sure. Donnelly's Paper Mill, in Dublin.
B Donnelly's Paper Mill, Dublin. Thank you, Mr Donnelly. I'll try Ms Schmidt for you. Please …[4]. hold the line
A Thank you.

B Mr Donnelly? Are you still there?
A Yes. I am.
B Sorry, this is taking a bit longer than it should. I'm still …[5].
A Thanks.

B Mr Donnelly. I'm afraid Ms Schmidt is …[6] at the moment. unavailable
Would you like to speak to …[7] ? Someone else
A Yes. Is Mr Müller in the office today?
B Yes, he is. I'll …[8]. put you throgh

B I'm sorry, Mr Donnelly. Mr Müller's number …[9]. Would you like to …[10] ?
A No, thanks. I'll try again later.

TIP

International spelling alphabet

It is useful to know the international spelling alphabet when you are telephoning in English.

A	Alpha	H	Hotel	O	Oscar	V	Victor
B	Bravo	I	India	P	Papa	W	Whiskey
C	Charlie	J	Juliet	Q	Quebec/Queen	X	X-ray
D	Delta	K	Kilo	R	Romeo	Y	Yankee
E	Echo	L	London/Lima	S	Sierra	Z	Zulu/Zed
F	Foxtrot	M	Mama/Mike	T	Tango		
G	Golf	N	November	U	Uniform		

CAN DO

After working through this unit I can …	Check …
▪ introduce myself and others.	Ex 1, page 6
▪ understand people talking about their training.	Ex 5, page 9
▪ give and receive contact details.	Ex 7, page 10
▪ connect a telephone caller to my company.	Ex 9, page 12
▪ take a telephone message.	Ex 10, page 13
▪ make a telephone call in English.	Ex 11, page 13

10 Rezeption – Hörverstehen

Beatrice is taking a telephone call in English.

3

A Hören Sie sich das Telefongespräch an und machen Sie sich Notizen, indem Sie folgende Informationen ergänzen:

Name des Anrufers
Woher ruft er an?
Was möchte der Anrufer?
Was sagt Beatrice?

4

B Listen to the second part of the telephone call and choose the most appropriate endings to complete the sentences.

1 Ms Frey can't talk to the caller because she is …
a talking on another line.
b writing a report.
c just leaving the office.

2 Beatrice …
a puts the caller through to someone else.
b gives the caller Ms Frey's private telephone number.
c takes a message.

3 The caller would like Ms Frey to call him …
a in the office.
b on his mobile.
c at home.

4 The last three digits of the caller's number are …
a 292.
b 922.
c 229.

11 Interaktion

Arbeiten Sie mit einem Partner / einer Partnerin. Führen Sie ein möglichst freies Telefongespräch mit Hilfe dieser Angaben.

Partner A

Nehmen Sie einen Anruf an. Nennen Sie Ihren eigenen Namen.

Partner B

Grüßen Sie. Sagen Sie, wer Sie sind und halten Sie etwas Smalltalk.

Antworten Sie entsprechend. Fragen Sie, wie Sie behilflich sein können

Bitten Sie darum, mit einer bestimmten Person verbunden zu werden.

Die Person ist nicht erreichbar. Nennen Sie den Grund. Bieten Sie an, eine Nachricht anzunehmen/weiterzuleiten.

Hinterlassen Sie eine Nachricht.

Notieren Sie die Nachricht.

Bedanken und verabschieden Sie sich.

12 Small talk

Read the text and then do the tasks below.

How to improve your small talk skills

Many people think that making small talk at work is a waste of time. But is it? Making small talk with colleagues and business partners helps people get to know each other better. It also helps to break the ice before meetings or other business events.

Making small talk can be difficult for some learners. Small talk means talking about almost anything. Even though someone has excellent vocabulary in specific areas, they may have difficulties discussing topics they are unfamiliar with. They do not know which words to use, so they slow down or stop speaking completely.

These tips will help you improve your small talk skills

- **Think about small talk in your own culture**
  Make a list of the things people discuss when making small talk in your own culture. Learn the vocabulary you need to make small talk about those subjects in English.
- **Do research about the culture or country of the people you'll be talking to**
  Search the Internet, read magazines, or watch TV programmes. If you know where your small talk partners are from, find out something about their city and have a question ready for them. Your partners will be happy that you're interested in where they're from. If you ask the first question, then your business partners will do most of the talking and you'll have time to relax.
- **Use the Internet to collect specific vocabulary**
  Most businesses and interest groups use words specifically related to their business or activity. Learn the vocabulary the others are likely to use.
- **Find common interests**
  Try to find a subject that interests both of you, for example, travel or a current film you have both seen. You might want to compare your culture with your partner's culture. Don't make judgements, though. Saying something like: "The food in my country is better than the food here in England" will sound very rude.
- **Listen**
  Let others talk. Listening carefully will help you understand the people you are speaking to. Listening will also give you time to think of an answer.
- **Remember**
  Small talk shouldn't touch on taboo subjects like death or divorce. Stay away from controversial subjects like sexual orientation. Even though you believe in something very strongly, making small talk about your own religious or political beliefs is not good. Never try to convince the other person that your ideas are "correct".

1 Explain why it is useful to be able to make small talk in business.
2 Describe the difficulties some learners might have when they make small talk.

13 Mediation

KMK

Lesen Sie den Text „How to improve your small talk skills" und machen Sie sich Notizen auf Deutsch. Fassen Sie die Tipps auf Deutsch kurz zusammen.

Making arrangements

- writing emails
- making and confirming arrangements
- changing arrangements

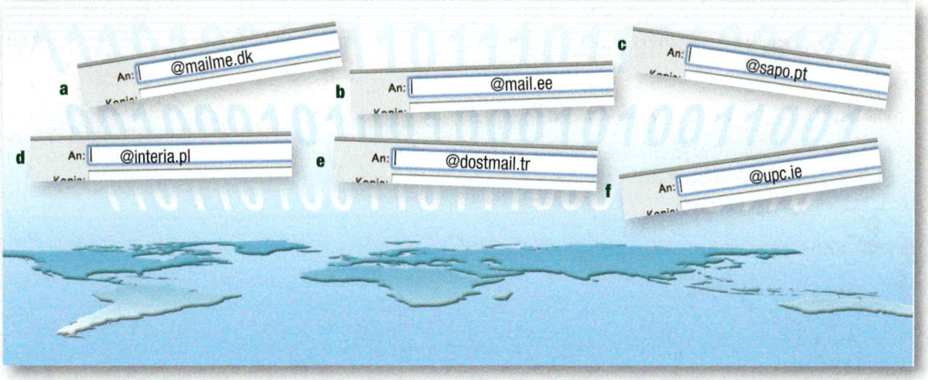

1 Warm-up

A Match the countries (1–6) to the email providers above (a–f).

1	Ireland	**3**	Estonia	**5**	Poland
2	Denmark	**4**	Turkey	**6**	Portugal

B Match the symbols (1–8) to the words (a–h) which can be used to give email addresses over the phone.

1	+	**5**	-	**a**	at	**e**	plus
2	_	**6**	.	**b**	capital letter	**f**	number
3	@	**7**	3	**c**	dot	**g**	small letter
4	A	**8**	b	**d**	hyphen	**h**	underscore

C Work with a partner and dictate email addresses to each other.

Partner A: Look at File 2 on page 118.
Partner B: Look at File 9 on page 121.

2 Email etiquette

A Work in groups. Discuss the email etiquette tips below. Which of these things do you always/sometimes/never do when you write business emails?

1. Check your email for spelling mistakes before you send it.
2. Make sure that the subject line of your email is as clear as possible.
3. Include your name and contact information at the end of your email.
4. Attach documents when you say you will and make sure they are correct.

B Add more tips to the list, then report back to the class.

3 Making arrangements

Swiss Pharma is participating in the Pharmaceutical Fair in Basle again this year. Beatrice Kuhn is making arrangements for her boss, Franziska Frey.

A Match Beatrice's emails (1–3) to the correct replies (a–c) below.

Betreff:
Von: Signatur: Ohne

Swiss Pharma is going to be at the Pharmaceutical Fair this year as usual. Ms Frey has asked me to invite you for a working breakfast in the meeting room at our stand (Hall 1, Stand 101) from 9.30 till 12.00 on Saturday, 24 September.

Could you let me know if the date is suitable for you?
1 If it is, then I would book a hotel.

Betreff:
Von: Signatur: Ohne

What time do you think you will arrive in Basle? Shall I arrange for someone to collect
2 you?

Betreff:
Von: Signatur: Ohne

I'm writing to let you know that Tony Miller, from the Research Department, can't be with us on Friday morning so I'm afraid we will have to change the time of the presentation.

The presentation of the test results will now take place after lunch, at 14.00.
3

a My train arrives at 8.15. I won't need anyone to pick me up as there are always plenty of taxis at the station.
I expect I'll arrive just after 8.30. Please confirm that someone will be at the stand at that time.

b Thank you for the information about the postponement.
We look forward to seeing the results on Friday afternoon.

c This is just to let you know that the date is fine. There might be a problem as far as my hotel is concerned. I'm flying in from New York and my plane lands at 23.00. Please inform the hotel that I'm going to arrive late.

B Which pair of emails deals with a) making arrangements, b) confirming arrangements, c) changing arrangements?

C Complete these sentences using words from the emails above.

1. Are these plans definite? Please write to … that you will be here next week.
2. Send the invitations by email so that they will … in time.
3. This is the third … this month. Will the meeting ever take place?
4. There are 25 participants so I'll … the big conference room.
5. I'm sorry, but I can't come tomorrow. I hope it isn't too late to … our plans.
6. I'll … your flights so that you have a stop-over in London.

D Work with a partner. Use the missing words from task C to write sentences which you might use when a) making arrangements, b) confirming arrangements, c) changing arrangements.

GRAMMAR

Future forms

1 I think the meeting **will take** about two hours.
2 I'**ll (will) organize** the paperwork tomorrow.
3 We **won't (will not) invite** him to speak again.

- *Will* wird verwendet, um Vorhersagen zu machen oder Vermutungen über die Zukunft auszudrücken (1). In diesem Fall steht *will* häufig nach *expect, hope, think, I'm certain/ sure/afraid*.
- *Will* wird für spontane Entscheidungen, Angebote und Versprechen verwendet (2).
- Im gesprochenen Englisch lautet die Verneinung *won't*, ansonsten *will not* (3).

4 We'**re going to open** at 12.00 on Friday.
5 The flyers **are going to help** us create interest in the product.
6 We'**re having** a meeting later this week.

- *Be going to* (+ Grundform des Verbs) wird verwendet, um über Pläne oder Absichten zu sprechen (4), oder wenn die Gewissheit (oder ein Anzeichen dafür) besteht, dass etwas geschehen wird (5).
- Die Verlaufsform der Gegenwart *(present progressive)* kann auch mit Zeitangaben der Zukunft verwendet werden, um über feste Absprachen und Pläne für die Zukunft zu sprechen (6).

7 The train **arrives** at 10.25.
8 The fair **starts** on 14 March.

- Für Stunden- und Fahrpläne bzw. Veranstaltungsprogramme verwendet man die einfache Gegenwartsform *(simple present)* (7, 8).

4 Practice

Work with a partner. Choose the correct form of the future to complete the dialogue. Say why you chose each form.

A What are you doing / do you do[1] next week?

B I will start / 'm starting[2] my practical training at Swiss Pharma in Basle on Monday. I work / 'm going to work[3] in the accounts department for the first two weeks.

A Where do you work / will you work[4] after that?

B I don't know where I'm going to be / am[5] then. I expect that I move on / will move on[6] to another department.

A How do you travel / are you going to travel[7] to work?

B I'm going to go / go[8] by train. It isn't taking / won't take[9] long.

A I heard that the train drivers are planning / plan[10] a strike on Monday.

B Oh dear. How will I get / do I get[11] to work?

A Well, I drive / 'm driving[12] to Basle on Monday. I'll take / take[13] you if you like.

TIP

Writing emails

The subject line

The first clue to the content of an email is in the subject line. This must say clearly what the email is about.

Structuring an email

Your email should get your message across as clearly and concisely as possible. Most emails are read on-screen, so keep them as short as possible.

Salutation / Complimentary close

If you do not know your business partner, use a formal salutation.
If you know your business partner well, it is enough to sign off with your first name. If you do not, add your position and the name of your company under it.

The body of the email

Start the email with a capital letter and write in paragraphs separated by a free line.
Do not write in CAPITALS; do not use exclamation marks!

Formal or less formal language

Emails can use formal language or be less formal. Short forms are fine in less formal emails (*I'll, we'll, he'd*, etc.); long forms are more formal.

5 What's it all about?

A Read the subject lines (a–f) in Franziska Frey's inbox and find an email which …

1 is a request for information.
2 gives information about a meeting.
3 asks for assistance.
4 contains new information.
5 announces a change of plan.
6 is a covering letter to accompany some material.

Nach Datum sortieren ▾

- **a** Need your help with English
- **b** New location for event on Saturday
- **c** Flyer (attached)
- **d** Meeting 25.03. Starting time?
- **e** Update on project
- **f** Agenda

B **Work with a partner. Write suitable subject lines for the following emails in Beatrice's inbox.**

1 Sorry, I have to change the date of the meeting to Friday 12 July.
Postponement of the meeting (date)

2 Could you send me information about the presentation, please?
Request for information

3 I am on holiday from 21.03 till 04.04 inclusive and will answer emails when I return. Automatic reply / Notification of absence

4 I am writing to confirm your application for a stand at the Pharmaceutical Fair. The stand number is C208. Update for the pharmaceutical fair
Application confirmation

5 As promised, here is the link to the website: www.tipsformails.com Link to „tipsformails" / Requested link

6 This is just to let you know that I have booked a table for lunch in the restaurant. I suggest we meet there at 12.30. restaurant reservation
Invitation for lunch

LANGUAGE

Writing emails

	Salutation	Complimentary close
Formal	Dear Ms/Mrs/Miss/Mr Smith	Regards Best wishes Yours sincerely Cordially (*AE*)
Less formal	Dear Paul Good morning, Paul Dear Paul and Paula Hi/Hello Paul/Paula	Regards Best regards Best wishes All the best

Opening sentence

Formal	I'm writing to …
Less formal	Just a quick note/line to …

Conclusion

Formal	I look forward to your reply.
Less formal	I hope to hear from you soon.

TIP

Polite language in emails

As a relationship becomes more friendly and your business partner begins to use less formal words and phrases in their emails, you should do the same. However, always continue to use polite language like *please*, *thank you*, *could* and *would like*:

Can you let me know by Monday? → *Could you let me know …*

I need the information today. → *I would like the information …*

We want to have a meeting. → *We would like to …*

6 Using a friendly tone

A Match the formal words and phrases below with the less formal ones from the box.

to answer • to ask • to be sorry • to check out • to get in touch • to help • to set up • to tell • to say that sth is OK • to be quick

1 to arrange
2 to assist
3 to confirm
4 to contact
5 to enquire
6 to inform
7 to look at in detail
8 to be prompt
9 to regret
10 to reply

B Read the latest email exchange between a customer, John Brown, and Beatrice Kuhn. Use words and phrases from task A to rewrite Beatrice's email in the same tone as John's email. You may have to change the form of some of the words.

Subject: **Hotel accommodation 23/24 Sept.**
From: JohnBrown@bigpound.net.uk Signature:

Dear Beatrice

Thanks for booking the hotel. I've checked it out online and it looks really good.

There's a notice on the web site about check-in times. I'm sure you told the people at reception that I'll be arriving late. Could you let me know if that's organized?

Thanks and best wishes.

John

PS – It'll be nice to meet you in person at last.

Kopie:
Blindkopie:
Betreff: **AW: Hotel accommodation 23/24 Sept.**
Von: beatrice-kuhn@swiss_ph... Signatur: Ohne

Dear Mr Brown

Thank you for replying so promptly to my email. I am pleased to hear that you are happy with the hotel accommodation.

I would like to confirm that I have contacted the hotel and informed them that you are going to arrive after 10 pm.

I look forward to meeting you, too.

Regards
Beatrice Kuhn

7 Apologizing

WEBCODE **OMU0201**

The day before John Brown is supposed to fly to Basle, he writes to Franziska Frey to say that he cannot come to the meeting.

Read his email below and find the words and phrases he uses to …

1. explain why the date is no longer convenient.
2. apologize.
3. suggest meeting at a later date.
4. suggest a time.

Subject: Cancelling 24 Sept. meeting
From: JohnBrown@bigpound.net.uk **Signature:**

Dear Franziska

I'm afraid I won't be able to meet you in Basle on Saturday as planned. Negotiations with the company in New York are taking longer than expected, so I have to stay on for another day.

I'm sorry about this, but I know you'll understand.

How about postponing our meeting till next week?

Would 30 September be all right? Would some time in the afternoon suit you? If not, then the following Monday (3 October) would be OK for me. I hope that one of these dates is suitable.

I'd like to invite you out for a meal after our meeting. How about going to that Italian restaurant where we were last time?

Wishing you loads of success at the Pharmaceutical Fair,

John

8 Making alternative suggestions

KMK

Franziska has other plans for the dates John has suggested. She forwards John's email to Beatrice and asks her to write a reply.

Read Franziska's email to Beatrice and then write Beatrice's reply to John Brown.

Betreff: Fw: Cancelling 24 Sept. meeting
Von: franziska-frey@swiss_phr… **Signatur:** Ohne

Dear Beatrice

Please read John's email below and get back to him for me.

Tell him that neither of the dates he suggests suit me. I have an all-day meeting on 30 September and I'm on holiday the following week.

Suggest that we bring our meeting forward and have it in his office in London on 21 September in the morning.

Ask him to get back to you by tomorrow at the latest to confirm that meeting.

Thanks.
Franziska

LANGUAGE

Prepositions of time

definite times, holiday periods
at 9 o'clock / 2 pm / noon / the weekend
at the end of the week/month/year
at Easter/Christmas

! **at** the moment
(NOT ~~in~~ the moment)

time periods
in the morning/afternoon/evening
in February/March, etc.
in the first/second/third/fourth quarter
in a minute / five minutes

on Monday, Tuesday, etc.
between 9 am **and** twelve noon
between Monday **and** Thursday

deadlines
by Monday / (the) close of business / this evening / the weekend (at the latest)

by / until (till)
I'd like this done **by** this evening. *(= spätestens bis heute abend)*

My notebook is broken. Could I borrow yours **until/till** I get it fixed? *(= solange es repariert wird)*

In less formal situations, we often use *till* instead of *until*.

9 Practice

Complete the sentences with the correct prepositions of time.

1 What are you doing in the time … our breakfast meeting and your presentation?
2 Ms Frey has to stay at the stand … 7 this evening.
3 Beatrice has to hurry. She has to be at the Fair … 8.30.
4 He has a meeting at the Pharmaceutical Fair … Wednesday.
5 Ms Frey is really busy … the moment.
6 We're attending another fair … 24 April.
7 Could you have the report about the presentation ready … Tuesday at the latest?
8 I'm sorry but we can't start the demonstration … everyone has arrived.

10 Setting up a meeting

You work for a British company in London. Your boss, Susan Hall, has asked you to arrange a meeting with Gary Doyle, an important client from Belfast.

Write an email to Gary Doyle using Susan's notes.

I'd like to have a meeting with Gary Doyle to finalize the contract.
My suggestion: we meet at the Industrial Fair in Frankfurt next week.
I have two free dates: Thursday, 26 at any time in the morning until 13.00
Friday, 27 between 12.30 and 18.30
We'll probably need about 3 hours.
Ask him to get back to you by tomorrow as you'll need time to organize a conference room.

Thanks.
Susan

LANGUAGE

Making arrangements by email

Inviting sb to a meeting

I/We Ms Smith	would like to invite you to	a meeting lunch/dinner a working breakfast	on (day, date). at (time).
The meeting will take place at		my office our premises the (name of fair)	in (town/city).
We have chosen the	(name of restaurant)	for our breakfast/lunch/dinner.	

Accepting the invitation

Formal	Thank you for your invitation	to	meet you participate in discussions	at (place)	at (time). on (date).
Less formal	I am pleased We are delighted	to accept		your invitation/offer.	

Saying no

Formal	I regret	I cannot attend I cannot come to	the meeting lunch/dinner	on the date at the time	you suggest.
	I am sorry to have to tell you that …				
Less formal	I'm sorry, but I can't because		I'm (reason)	on that date. at that time.	

Making an alternative suggestion

Formal	I/We would like to	suggest postpone the meeting until	(date/time).	
Less formal	How about	meeting (for dinner) having a discussion getting together	on (day) at (time)	instead?

Conclusion

Formal	I look forward to your reply.
Less formal	I hope to hear from you soon.

CAN DO

After working through this unit I can …	Check …
▪ give email addresses over the phone.	Ex 1, page 15
▪ understand emails about arrangements.	Ex 3, page 16
▪ write a clear subject line for an email.	Ex 5, page 18
▪ understand when to use less formal English in a business email.	Ex 6, page 20
▪ understand an email postponing a meeting.	Ex 7, page 21
▪ write an email suggesting alternative arrangements.	Ex 8, page 21
▪ arrange a business meeting. (formal language)	Ex 10, page 22
▪ re-arrange a business meeting. (less formal language)	Ex 11, page 24

11 Produktion

Schreiben Sie Gary Doyles Antwort an Susan Hall (Übung 10) auf Englisch. Beziehen Sie die unten stehenden Punkte mit ein.

- Dank für die E-Mail.
- Terminvorschlag für das Treffen mit Frau Hall auf der Industrial Fair am Donnerstag, 26., um 9.30 Uhr bevorzugt/lieber.
- Konferenzraum wird nicht benötigt, weil es am Firmenstand von Doyle eine geeignete Möglichkeit gibt.
- Geben Sie den Standort an: Halle 3, Stand 75.
- Sie freuen sich, Frau Hall wiederzusehen und den Vertrag abzuschließen.

12 Produktion

Wegen des gerade vereinbarten Treffens mit Frau Hall muss Herr Doyle einen geplanten Frühstückstermin mit seinem schottischen Geschäftsfreund Paul absagen.

Schreiben Sie Herrn Doyles E-Mail an Paul auf Englisch und nutzen Sie dabei die unten stehenden Kalendereinträge.

Beziehen Sie die folgenden Punkte mit ein:

- Sie müssen absagen, da leider ein wichtiger Vertragsabschluss dazwischen kam.
- Bieten Sie einen Alternativtermin an.

Mon 23	Bank holiday		
Tue 24	Meeting: 10.00 Blair	Lunch: TB 12.30 – 14.30 Quentins	
Wed 25	AL 134 07.20 → London (ETA 08.50) LH 921 09.50 → Frankfurt (ETA 12.20)		Dinner: Hans Treder 19.00 (Hotel Restaurant)
Thur 26	~~Working breakfast: Paul 9.00 – 11.30~~ Ms Hall! 9.30 – 12.30	Presentation: 14.00 – 16.00	
Fri 27	Stand: 10.00 – 12.00		LH 918 19.15 → London (ETA 20.45) AL 142 21.20 → Belfast (ETA 22.30)
Sat 28	Golf: Harry Jones 11.00		
Sun 29			

13 "Subject-is-the-email" messages

The subject line of an email should state clearly what the email is about, but some people use the subject line of their emails to give the complete message.

Read this blog entry, then answer the questions which follow.

Mozilla Firefox

Your Office Matters Blog

www.your-office-matters.com/blog

Facebook Meistbesuchte... Erste Schritte Aktuelle Nachr... Lesezeichen

Your Office Matters Blog

Last week, I received the following message by email.

Subject: Please book the conference room for 7 May, 9.30–12.00. Thx. Trudi
(The body of the message was empty.)

The message, which came from my boss, was typical. Trudi is always very busy, so she often fires off a "subject-is-the-message" email like this. She always takes the time to write her name at the end of the message, and I appreciate that.

On the same day, John, who works at Reception, sent me an almost complete message in the subject line of an email.

Subject: Rebecca Erler has arrived …
The body of the message read: " … and is waiting for you at Reception. John"

I was on the phone when Ms Erler arrived, so John couldn't reach me. As soon as I saw in the subject line of the email that popped up on my screen, however, I could end my phone call quickly and run downstairs.

I know that some people don't like the idea, but if you can say what you want in one sentence, then it's OK to do it like this. Using the subject line as a kind of instant messaging medium is very practical. It takes subject line efficiency to a new level, and I like that. Why waste people's time making them read more than they need to read? As long as the condensed messages suit the circumstances, their speed and efficiency can help me be more efficient too.

Alice: I don't think this is acceptable email etiquette. When I got a "subject-is-the-email" message, I thought that the sender had forgotten to write a message. I mailed him back and asked, "What's the message?" It was a real time-waster, not a time-saver.

Ben: It's important to sign off at the end of a message so that the reader knows that's all there is. You can use your name, or your initials, or use the abbreviation EOM at the end of a subject-line message. EOM stands for "end of message".

1 Say why the blogger accepts "subject-is-the-email" messages from the boss.
2 John sent an almost complete message in his subject line. Why was that a good idea?
3 Describe what happened when Alice received a "subject-is-the-email" message.
4 What does Ben say is important? Do you agree with all of his tips? Why/Why not?

14 Mediation

KMK

Sie diskutieren mit einer Kollegin über verschiedene Möglichkeiten, den Arbeitsablauf effizienter zu gestalten. Erzählen Sie ihr auf Deutsch, was Sie gerade im Weblog gelesen haben.

UNIT 3

Starting to write letters

- talking about office items
- writing business letters
- writing and saying dates

1 Warm-up

A **Match the photos above (a–j) with these items of office stationery (1–10).**

1	envelope	**6**	pens
2	highlighters	**7**	stapler
3	labels	**8**	Post-its©
4	notepad	**9**	printer paper
5	paper clips	**10**	staples

B **Make two lists, sorting the items under the headings "Paper" and "Other items".**

C **Which of the things on the lists do you use in your office regularly?**

2 The parts of a business letter

Match the parts of this business letter (1–11) to the labels below (a–k).

1 **Event Planning**
Alberner Hafen 17/12
A–1110 Vienna

Tel. +43 (01)12 34 56 70
dandie@eventplanning.at
www.eventplanning.at

2 Ms Hannah Craig
Craig Office Supplies
189 Sighthill Industrial Estate
EDINBURGH
EH11 4QH
UNITED KINGDOM

3 29 April 20..

4 Your ref: HC/EOS
Our ref: DD/AS

5 Dear Ms Craig

6 **5th European Office Supplies Trade Fair**

We received your letter of 18 April enquiring about the 5th European Office Supplies Trade Fair which will take place in Vienna from 11–14 August. We are pleased to note that you are interested in participating in the Fair as a member of the trade.

7 *Event Planning* is responsible for co-ordination of the infrastructure of the Fair, including the allocation of stands.

Please find enclosed our Information Pack which covers all the points you need to help you plan your participation at the Fair.

Please get in touch with us if you require more information.

8 Yours sincerely

Daniel Diehl

9 Daniel Diehl
Assistant Organizer

10 cc Alice Schiller, Manager

11 Enc: Information pack

a address
b body of the letter
c complimentary close
d copies
e date
f enclosure
g inside address
h reference
i salutation
j signature
k subject line

3 A jumbled letter KMK

Bringen Sie die Teile dieses Briefes in die richtige Reihenfolge.

1 Yours faithfully

2 Enc

3 On your website you offer a six-month practical work placement in your firm for an office assistant.

I am a 21-year old trainee at Mossmann GmbH, a printing firm, in Berlin. Once a week, I attend a vocational school where I am studying office communication. My training period ends in July. As I am keen to improve my English skills in an English-speaking country, I would like to apply for an unpaid work placement position in your company.

Enclosed is my curriculum vitae and copies of my school-leaving certificates and recommendation letters.

I look forward to hearing from you soon.

4 c/o Mossmann GmbH
Breitestr. 388
D–14197 Berlin / Deutschland

5 Marks & Co
HR Department
11 Lamppost Close
NOTTINGHAM

6 December 9, 20…

7 *Lena Hess*
Lena Hess

8 **Practical Training**

9 Dear Sir or Madam

LANGUAGE

Writing business letters

	Salutation	Complimentary close
To a firm	Dear Sir or Madam (*BE*)	Yours faithfully (*BE*)
	Gentlemen (*AE*)	Yours very truly / Cordially yours (*AE*)
To a person	Dear Mr Brown	Yours sincerely (*BE*)
	Dear Sharon	Sincerely yours / Best personal regards (*AE*)

! Be careful with dates. In Europe *12.9.2014* means "12 September 2014", but in the USA and many parts of Asia it means "9 December 2014".

4 Writing the date

A Write out these European dates, then read them to a partner.

Example: 17.9.2022 *17 September 2022*

1	6.1.2015	**4**	9.4.1999
2	2.3.2012	**5**	5.7.1919
3	3.10.2019	**6**	2.11.2020

B Write out these American dates in European form.

Example: 4.2.2011 *2 April 2011*

1	12.5.2016	**4**	9.10.1970
2	6.8.2014	**5**	7.2.1917
3	2.11.2021	**6**	5.4.2039

TIP

Writing a paragraph

Paragraphs are used to separate main ideas. Generally, a paragraph should only deal with one main topic. A useful structure to remember is:

1 topic sentence – expresses the main idea of the paragraph,
2 supporting sentences – details which explain the main idea,
3 concluding sentence – summarizing what has been said or drawing a conclusion.

A new paragraph signals to the reader that they are going to read about a new topic. To start a new paragraph, leave a whole line and start at the beginning of the line after.

5 Dividing a letter into paragraphs

Work with a partner. Decide together where the ideas in the letter below should be divided into paragraphs then re-write the letter.

I am interested in applying for a period of practical training in an English firm. The description of your firm on the Internet and the details about practical training which are given there match my abilities and interests very closely. I am about to complete my training as an office management assistant in a German distribution company. My duties include writing memos, faxes, emails and letters, planning meetings, telephoning and taking and passing on messages. I sometimes work as an interpreter when English-speaking visitors come to the company. I also attend a vocational school where I am studying English, word-processing and bookkeeping. This training leads to a certificate which every country in Europe recognizes. Please find enclosed my CV and photocopies of my qualifications. As I am particularly keen to improve my English skills in an English-speaking country, I would appreciate the opportunity to discuss this application with you. I look forward to hearing from you soon.

TIP

Abbreviations

An abbreviation is a shortened form of a word or phrase. We use abbreviations in business correspondence to save time. Abbreviations do not normally have a full stop after them in British English.

6 Abbreviations in business correspondence

WEBCODE
OMU0301

A **Use your monolingual dictionary to find out the meanings of the abbreviations in the business letters on pages 27 and 28. Write them in your notebook with the German equivalent alongside.**

B **Match the German words and phrases (1–9) to their English equivalents (a–i).**

1	Kopie an	**a**	please reply
2	das heißt	**b**	department
3	so schnell wie möglich	**c**	copy to
4	Freiumschlag	**d**	for example
5	zum Beispiel	**e**	and so on
6	Abteilung	**f**	that is
7	und so weiter	**g**	personal assistant
8	bitte um Rückantwort	**h**	as soon as possible
9	persönlicher Assistent	**i**	stamped addressed envelope

7 Practising the layout of a letter

KMK

This letter is complete but the parts are in the wrong order.

Schreiben Sie den Brief in der richtigen Reihenfolge und Form. Benutzen Sie das heutige Datum.

Ian McKenzie, Office Stationery Suppliers, 22 High Street, Edinburgh EH1 1TF, United Kingdom

cc Peter Armbruster

Yours sincerely

My enquiry for practical training placement

Dear Mr McKenzie

Enc

Lettenstrasse 501, CH-6343 Rotkreuz, Switzerland.
Tel. +41 41 1234567
olitell@gmx.ch

Your ref: IM/OT/01

Oliver Tell

Oliver Tell

Thank you for your reply to my application for a practical training placement in your firm.

As requested, I enclose my CV and copies of my certificates.

My current employer, Peter Armbruster, Satz und Druck AG, will be happy to supply references.

I look forward to hearing from you soon.

8 Writing good business letters

The "Your Office Matters" website offers tips for office assistants.

Read these tips about how to write business letters, then do the tasks below.

Mozilla Firefox

Your Office Matters

www.yourofficematters.com/writing_business_letters

Facebook Meistbesuchte... Erste Schritte Aktuelle Nachr... Lesezeichen

Every office assistant should be able to write good English. Whether it's an email or a business letter, a short newspaper announcement or an online advertisement, whatever you write, you must produce texts which any reader can understand.

Let's start with writing good business letters. Here are some things to keep in mind.

First, make notes on what you're going to write about. Write down everything which should go into the letter. ... **a**

Next, prepare a framework for your letter. A business letter usually has three parts, as follows:

- Introduction (reason for writing)
- Body of the letter (main point or points)
- Conclusion (what will, might or should happen next)

Sort your notes under the headings above. While you are doing this, make sure that every point in your letter is relevant. ... **b**

Now that you have a framework, you can start to write. Go through the points one by one and build up your letter. ... **c**

When you've finished, you should always proof-read your letter. ... **d**

Last but not least, the person you are writing to might have a lot of correspondence to read so always remember – KISS* and DRY**. ... **e**

* Keep it Short and Simple ** Don't Repeat Yourself

A Some bits of advice are missing from the webpage. Choose one of the sentences below (1–5) to complete the gaps (a–e).

1. Read it several times, each time looking for different mistakes.
2. Stick to the point and don't use long, complicated sentences.
3. Tick each point as you deal with it.
4. You don't have to list the points in a logical way.
5. Delete what isn't necessary.

B Make a checklist of things you should do before starting to write a letter. What should you check before you send the letter?

GRAMMAR

Modal verbs and their substitutes

- Hilfsverben (*modal verbs*) sind Wörter wie *may*, *can*, *must*, *should*. Sie drücken, z. B. eine Fähigkeit, eine Erlaubnis oder ein Verbot aus.
- Hilfsverben stehen normalerweise in der Gegenwartsform, manche auch in der Vergangenheit. Ersatzverben (*substitutes*) werden benutzt, um alle übrigen Zeiten zu bilden.

Hilfsverb	Ersatzverb	Entsprechung
can	*be able to*	können
could		konnten/könnten
may	*be allowed to*	dürfen
might		dürften
must	*have to / had to*	müssen/müssten
need not	*don't have to*	nicht müssen
shall		sollen
should/ought to		sollten
must not	*not be allowed to*	nicht dürfen

9 Practice

A Choose one modal verb from the brackets to complete the sentences.

1 She has passed her exams so she (can/could/must) start looking for work now.
2 (May/Must/Should) I borrow your dictionary?
3 Why (can/should/shall) I proofread the letter?
4 We are behind with the order so we (can/must/need not) work overtime.
5 The meeting's at 10. It's only 9 o'clock now so you (can/could/need not) hurry.
6 You (could/might/ought to) have some questions prepared for the interviewer.
7 (Can/Might/Must) I ask someone to help me with the letter?
8 They (ought to/might/must) go to the Trade Fair if they have time.

B Replace the German words in the sentences below with a modal verb or a suitable substitute.

1 Last year, I *konnte* take time off work to attend further training seminars. Now my boss says that I *muss* concentrate completely on my work.
2 He *musste* work hard on his English grammar when he started his training. Now he *kann* write and speak perfect English.
3 You *solltest* get up early in the morning. If you arrive late tomorrow, you *darfst nicht* take the examination.
4 I *musste nicht* speak German when I went to Germany. All our German business partners *konnten* speak good English.

TIP

Capital letters

Not only the names of countries (Italy, Germany, etc.) and their languages and inhabitants (Italian, German, etc.), but also the adjectives that describe them have capital letters in English:

eine deutsche Stadt	a German city
italienische Geschäftspartner	Italian business partners

10 Rezeption: Hörverstehen

5

Thorsten Lach verfolgt die wöchentlichen Podcasts der Website „Your Office Matters". Heute hört er einen Beitrag, in dem die Vor- und Nachteile von Briefverkehr und E-Mail-Austausch in der Geschäftskorrespondenz gegeneinander abgewogen werden.

Hören Sie sich den Podcast an und beantworten Sie die Fragen in Notizform in Ihrem Arbeitsheft.

1. Was könnte dafür sprechen, dass E-Mails weniger professionell als Briefe wirken?
2. Welche Ratschläge werden gegeben?
3. Warum möchten viele Leute vertrauliche Informationen nicht per E-Mail verschicken?
4. Wie lässt sich das Problem der Vertraulichkeit lösen?
5. Wie ist es um den rechtlichen Aspekt bestellt?
6. Welche praktischen Vorteile einer E-Mail werden herausgestellt?
7. Wie ist es um die Umweltverträglichkeit bestellt?

11 Mediation

Ihr Vorgesetzter, der fest von den Vorzügen eines herkömmlichen Geschäftsbriefes überzeugt ist, möchte von Ihnen hören, was Sie im aktuellen Podcast (Übung 10) erfahren haben.

Verwenden Sie Ihre Notizen um zu erklären, warum eine E-Mail genauso professionell wie ein Brief sein kann. Beschreiben Sie die Vorzüge einer im E-Mail-Verkehr durchgeführten Korrespondenz.

CAN DO

After working through this unit I can ...	Check ...
▪ identify and talk about items we use in an office.	Ex 1, page 26
▪ identify the parts of a business letter.	Ex 2, page 27
▪ put items in the correct order to compose a business letter.	Ex 3, page 28
▪ understand the differences between American English and British English dates and use both forms correctly.	Ex 4, page 29
▪ divide the body of a letter into paragraphs.	Ex 5, page 29
▪ compose a business letter using the correct layout.	Ex 7, page 30
▪ understand a text describing how to write business letters.	Ex 8, page 31
▪ understand in a short podcast and describe what I have heard.	Ex 10, page 33

12 Business letters

Business letters are written from one firm or organization to another. The normal course of business correspondence between a buyer and seller starts with an enquiry.

A **Study the flow chart, which shows the most common types of business letter, then match each step to one of the descriptions (a–h).**

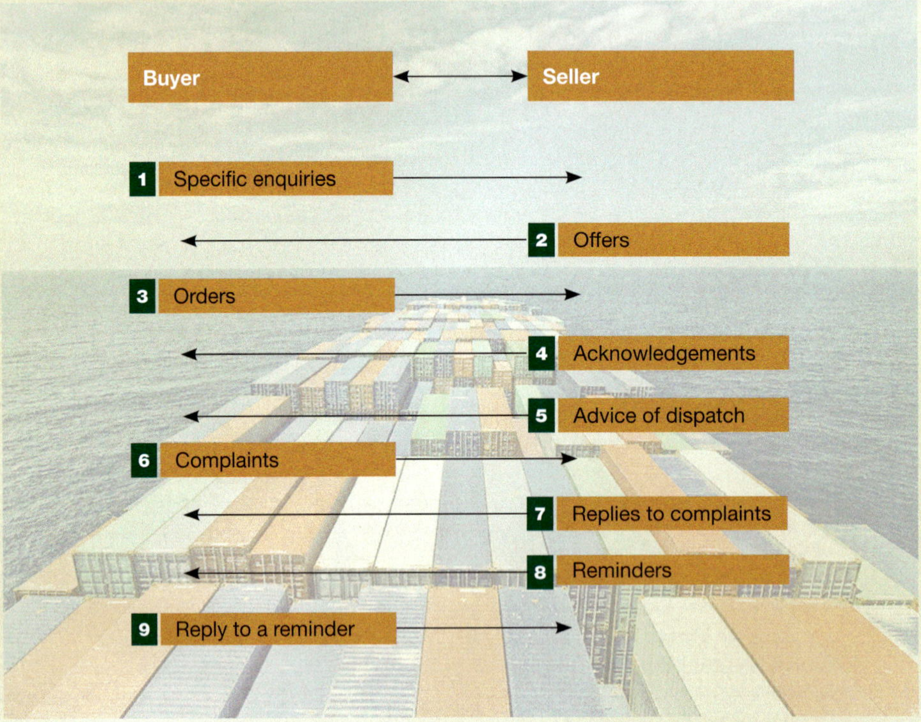

a requesting payment of overdue invoices
b acknowledging that a mistake has occurred, giving an explanation for what has gone wrong and saying how things will be made right
c requesting goods or services
d describing something that has gone wrong and requesting the addressee to do something about it
e telling the customer that the goods have left the seller's store and are now on the way
f making initial contact
g answering enquiries about specific products
h explaining why a payment is overdue
i confirming an offer without repeating all the details

6

B **Listen to four people explaining why they are writing a specific business letter. What type of letter are they writing?**

C **Work with a partner. Imagine you are writing some business letters. Compose short speeches like the ones you have just heard. Try out your speeches on two other people and ask them to guess which type of letter you are writing.**

Describing a company

- welcoming visitors to the company
- describing a company layout
- giving directions

a

b

c

d

e

f

1 Warm-up

A Match the names of the companies (1–6) to the logos above (a–f).

1 Apple
2 Best Western Hotel Group
3 Audi
4 Ernst and Young
5 Hochtief
6 GLS

B Which of the sectors below does each company belong to? There are two more sectors than you need.

a information technology
b light industry
c manufacturing
d building industry
e industry and technology
f service industry
g transport and logistics
h financial services

C Which sector does your company operate in? What type of business is it?

TIP

Forms of business organization

Ltd (UK) Limited Company (*GmbH*)
A (private) limited company is owned privately by shareholders.

plc (UK) Public Limited Company (*AG*)
A plc sells shares to the public.

Inc or **Corp** (USA) Incorporated/Corporation
An incorporated business is registered as a legal entity with the Registrar of Companies. These companies may be "closed corporations" (*GmbH*) or "open corporations" (*AG*).

2 About a company

In the year 2000, Tom Fischer took a risk and started a small business. The firm has grown steadily since day one and has recently won an important contract.

Read the article below, then do the tasks which follow.

German Computer Company Wins Schools Contract

Fischer Computer AG, a small computer hardware company based near Stuttgart, has won a contract to supply hardware and support to schools in the UK over the next five years. The contract is worth approximately €37 million.

Thomas Fischer, CEO, Fischer Computer AG

When he was a student, Tom Fischer, took a summer job at a computer factory. Today, he runs his own firm, Fischer Computer AG. The firm develops and manufactures computer hardware.

Tom Fischer was born in a small town near the German/Swiss border. He left school in 1998 and went to vocational college where he did an apprenticeship as an office management assistant.

In the same year, Fischer took a summer job at a local factory. He worked in the office where he processed orders. One of the main activities at the factory was building computers. One day, when he was walking across the factory floor, Fischer realized that he wanted to run his own computer hardware company.

In the year 2000, soon after he graduated, he set up Fischer Computer.

The company started small. At the beginning, Fischer rented an old warehouse. He employed three people to work on the assembly line on an hourly basis.

Success came early when Fischer won the "European Young Entrepreneur" prize in 2001. Other awards followed.

Over the years, Fischer Computer has grown and developed. Today, over 1100 people work for Tom Fischer.

The company went public two years ago and, since then, Fischer Computer AG has expanded into eastern Europe. Fischer Computer AG has been in its own, custom-built premises on an industrial estate near Stuttgart for six months now.

Last year, Fischer Computer AG achieved a turnover of almost €450 million.

A Answer these questions based on the article.

1 What is the "important contract"?
2 How long will the contract run?
3 How much is it worth?

B Which of the following statements are incorrect? Correct them using your own words. The information may be in different parts of the article. KMK

1 Tom Fischer started work at a factory as soon as he left school.
2 He was a management trainee when he was at vocational college.
3 His first job was building computers on an assembly line.
4 After he finished his course, Tom Fischer started his own company.
5 Only a few people worked for the company at the beginning.
6 Fischer Computer AG has won three prizes.
7 The company sells shares to the public.
8 The firm specializes in computers for schools.

C **Complete the text using words from the article. Some gaps require two words.**

When Grit Simon was a student, she worked for Tom Fischer. Tom ran a computer hardware …[1]. He needed people to work on the … …[2], putting the parts of the computers together. The area where Grit worked was cold and noisy. Even though, she enjoyed working on the … …[3]. While she worked, Grit often thought about her future. One day, she decided to look for work in the import/export sector. She applied for an apprenticeship in a …[4]. The owners stored goods there before they sent them to other parts of the world. Today, Grit works as a manager for In & Out, a small import/export company in Hamburg. She has an office in some modern …[5] on an … …[6] near the edge of the city.

3 The structure of a company

A **Study this organization chart of Fischer Computer AG and find the English words for these parts of the company.**

1 *Einkauf*
2 *Rechnungswesen*
3 *Forschung und Entwicklung*
4 *Produktion*
5 *Marktforschung*
6 *Personalabteilung*
7 *Rechtsabteilung*
8 *Verkauf*

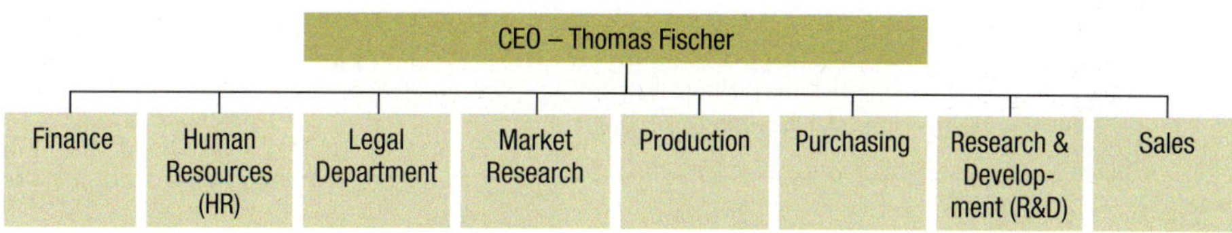

B **Say which of the departments above deals with the following things.**

1 accounts
2 bringing in revenue
3 buying raw materials
4 finding out what goods/services customers want
5 contracts and agreements
6 designing new products
7 employment possibilities
8 manufacturing of goods

C **Make sentences using the job titles (1–6) and the job descriptions (a–f).**

1 An accountant …
2 A managing director or Chief Executive Officer (CEO) …
3 A personal assistant …
4 A customer relations manager …
5 A receptionist …
6 A sales representative …

a answers the phone and welcomes visitors to the company.
b presents and sells products to customers.
c deals with customer enquiries.
d supports an employee in a higher position.
e is responsible for the whole company.
f processes everything to do with accounts.

Explaining what someone does at work

assists	is in charge of	manages	takes care of
is head of	is responsible for	reports to	works with

D **Draw an organization chart of your company and name some of the people. Which department do they work in? What is their position and job title?**

GRAMMAR

The simple past and the present perfect

1 He **started** his own business when he was 22 years old.
2 Last week, the company **built** its millionth computer.
3 **I have just ordered** a new laptop.
4 He **has visited** the company a few times.

simple past
- Das *simple past* verwendet man für Handlungen in der Vergangenheit, die bereits abgeschlossen sind (1, 2).
- Bei regelmäßigen Verben bildet man das *simple past*, indem man *-(e)d* an den Infinitiv (1. Form) des Verbs anhängt (1).
- Unregelmäßige Verben haben für die Vergangenheit eine eigene Form (2).
- Unregelmäßige Verben muss man auswendig lernen. Siehe Liste auf S. 176.
- Signalwörter zum *simple past* sind, z. B.: *yesterday*, *last week*, *last month*, *ago*.

present perfect
- Das *present perfect* verwendet man für Handlungen, die:
  – soeben geschehen sind und Auswirkung auf die Gegenwart haben (3).
  – sowohl die Vergangenheit als auch die Gegenwart betreffen (4).
- Das *present perfect* wird mit *have/has* und dem Partizip (3. Form) des Verbs gebildet (3, 4).
- Signalwörter für das *present perfect* sind z. B.: *since*, *for*, *already*, *just (now)*, *now*, *(not) yet*.

since/for/ago, S. 81

4 Practice

A Re-write these sentences using the simple past.

1 She always *writes* her bills at the end of the month.
2 He usually *visits* the electronics shop at the weekend.
3 Sonja *works* on the assembly line.
4 John *flies* to London on business regularly.
5 They *are* at the computer club.
6 *Do* you *know* anything about the company?

B Make sentences using the present perfect form of the verbs in brackets.

Example: *he / already / his homework (do)*
He has already done his homework.

1 she / just / work (finish)
2 I / never / a contract (write)
3 you / ever / a deadline? (not meet)
4 he / recently / very busy (be)
5 Sally / yet / her new job? (start)
6 Jim / a computer / yet? (buy)

C Complete the sentences with the simple past or the present perfect form of the verb in brackets. Say what helped you decide which form to choose.

1 Mark (download) some software yesterday.
2 She never (have) any money since she started buying goods online.
3 Things (improve) for the company in the last few years.
4 Julian (be) at the computer centre a few years ago.
5 (you/see) Pete recently?
6 We (finish) our training last week.

TIP

How can I improve my listening skills?

The more you listen to English speakers, the easier it is to understand them. Listen to ...

- English radio and TV programmes (also online)
- podcasts in online editions of English magazines
- DVDs in English

Before you start to listen make sure you know what the text is about. What is the topic? What can you learn from the title of the exercise? Read the questions carefully so that you know what to listen for.

Always listen twice. First, try to understand the gist of the text. Listen a second time to pick out the details.

5 Welcoming two visitors to Fischer Computer AG

KMK

7 Colin King and Sara Cheung have just arrived for a meeting with Tom Fischer. Andreas Berger meets the visitors at reception.

Hören Sie sich das Gespräch an und beantworten Sie folgende Fragen.

1. Welche Stelle besetzt Andreas Berger in der Firma?
2. Wie war der Flug der Gäste?
3. Warum ist Herr Fischer (noch) nicht anwesend?
4. Was bietet Andreas den Besuchern an?

6 Describing the layout of an office building

Andreas and the visitors have taken the lift upstairs. He is describing the layout of the offices.

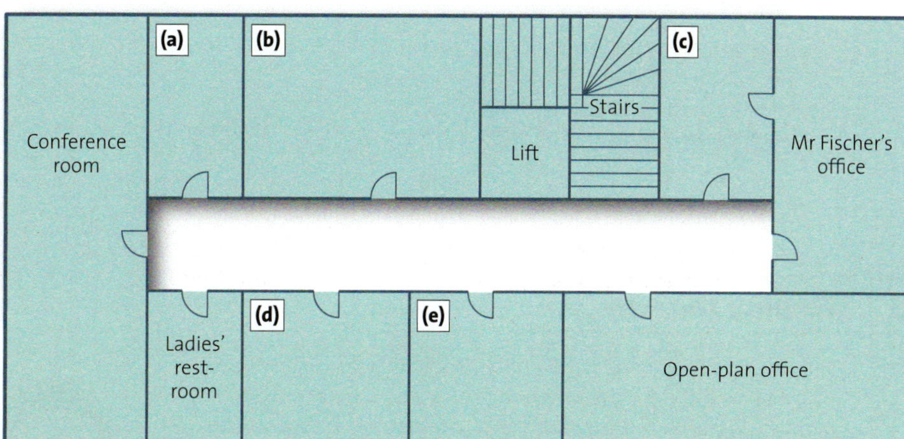

8 **A Study the floor plan and the list of places below, then listen to Andreas' description. Find the places on the floor plan.**

1. Accounts Department
2. Andreas Berger's office
3. Sales Department
4. Human Resources
5. the men's restroom

B **Read the list below, then listen again. Which words and phrases do you hear?**

8

LANGUAGE

Describing where things are

above the photocopier

beside the shelves

between the filing cabinets

behind the sofa

in front of the screen

opposite the filing cabinet

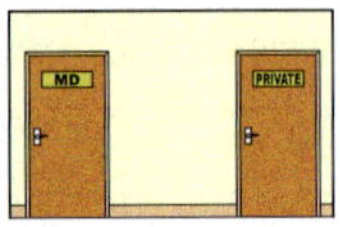

next door to each other

near the door

over there

on the top floor
on the first floor

on the ground floor
in the basement

on the right/left
downstairs

at the end
(of the corridor)

7 Describing the layout of your company premises

WEBCODE **OMU0401**

Work with a partner.

Partner A

Draw a plan of the building you work in. Do not show your plan to your partner. Describe the plan of the building to your partner using some of the words above .

Partner B

Listen to Partner A's description. Draw the plan on a sheet of paper.
When you have finished, compare your drawings. After that, swap roles and repeat the task.

8 Finding the way

One of Sara Cheung's school friends, Mike Blair, works in another company on the industrial estate where Fischer Computer AG is based. Sara has made an appointment to see him after lunch. Mike phones to give Sara instructions about how to get to his premises from Fischer's.

9

A **Study the map of the industrial estate on page 41 then listen to the phone call. Follow Mike Blair's instructions as he speaks. Where does Mike work?**

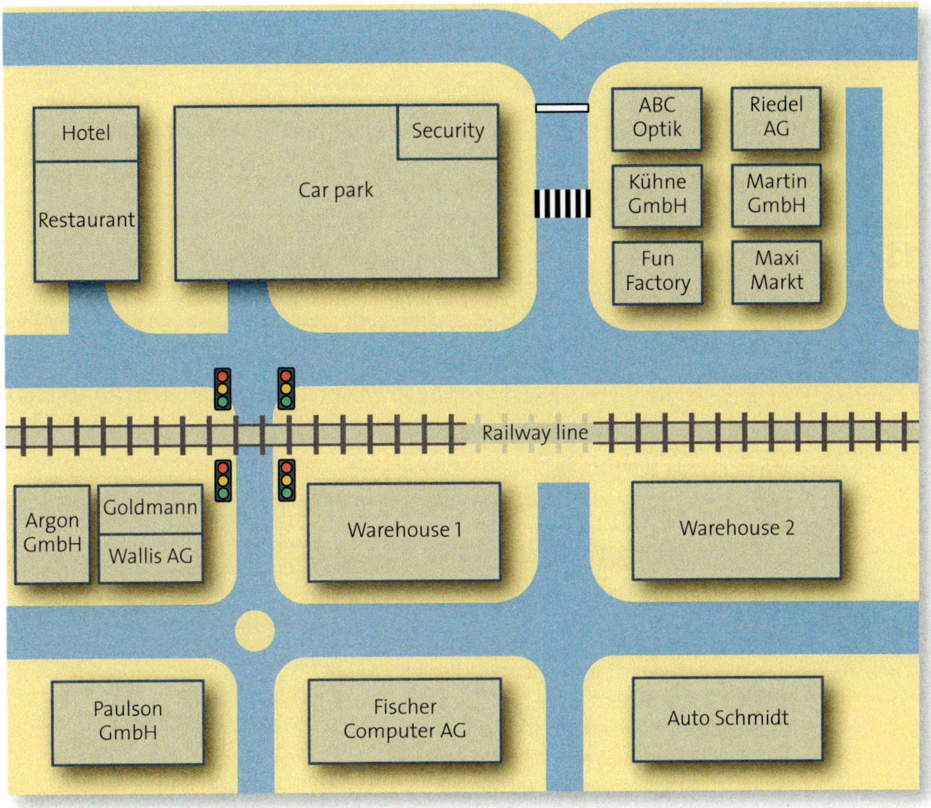

9

B Read the list below, then listen again. Which words and phrases do you hear?

LANGUAGE

Giving directions

Go over …
Go across the …
Go straight ahead.
Keep going on …
It's just after/past/outside the …
Keep to the right/left.

Stay on the right/left.
Turn left/right.
Take the first right/left.
in the middle of the …
in the distance
on the right-hand / left-hand side

On the road

car park	entrance gates	railway crossing	t-junction
crossroads	pedestrian crossing	roundabout	traffic lights

9 Giving directions

Work with a partner. You are at the entrance gate of the industrial estate. Take turns to give each other directions to different places on the estate. Do not tell your partner the name of the company or place he/she is going to. He/she should find the way and name the building or place.

Start like this: *We're at the entrance gate. Go past the security office, then …*

10 Produktion

Ein Freund aus Großbritannien möchte mehr über Ihr Arbeitsumfeld wissen.

Beschreiben Sie in einer E-Mail den Aufbau Ihrer Firma. Nennen Sie Namen und die Position von zwei oder drei wichtigen Beschäftigten. Erklären Sie, in welcher Abteilung Sie arbeiten und wem Sie direkt unterstellt sind.

11 Mediation

Ein Kollege möchte die Räumlichkeiten, in denen das Online-Magazin „Your Office Matters" produziert wird, besichtigen. Er weiß nicht, ob er per Flugzeug oder mit der Bahn kommen soll.

Verwenden Sie die Hinweise und den Lageplan der Website „Your Office Matters" und erklären Sie auf Deutsch, wie Ihr Kollege am besten zum Verlagsgebäude findet.

Mozilla Firefox
Your Office Matters
www.yourofficematters.com/trainee_location
Google
Facebook | Meistbesuchte... | Erste Schritte | Aktuelle Nachr... | Lesezeichen

How to find us

Arriving by plane
Take the airport bus heading towards Central Station. Get off the bus at the Big City roundabout and walk back towards the traffic lights. Turn left into Broad Street until you come to the Long Lane crossroads. Go over the crossroads and continue along Broad Street. Our offices are half-way down Broad Street, on the right.

Arriving by train
Take the Metrolink tram heading towards the airport. Travel along the High Street until you get to the Big City roundabout. Get off the Metrolink there and walk towards Long Lane. Turn left into Long Lane and go straight ahead until you come to Broad Street. Turn left into Broad Street and you'll see our offices, half-way down Broad Street, on the right.

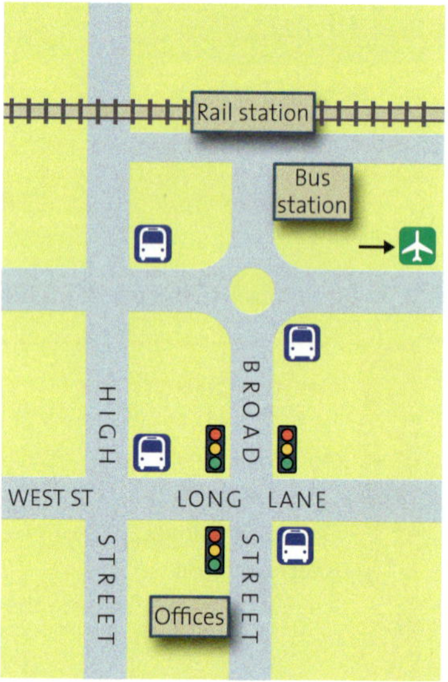

CAN DO — After working through this unit I can ...	Check ...
▪ describe the type of company and sector I work in.	Ex 1, page 35
▪ understand a short text about the history of a company.	Ex 2, page 36
▪ describe the structure and departments of a company.	Ex 3, page 37
▪ give directions on where to find departments and premises.	Ex 6–9, pages 39–41
▪ write a personal email describing the department I work in.	Ex 10, page 42
▪ use a website to explain how to get to a specific destination.	Ex 11, page 42

12 An online retailer

Read this text about Amazon.com then do the tasks below.

Amazon is one of the world's largest online retailers. It is the number one online retailer in America and sells nearly three times as many goods as its nearest rival, Staples Inc.

Jeff Bezos (photo) launched Amazon.com in 1994. They say that he dreamed up the idea of the online bookstore on a long drive across America. At the beginning, he ran the company from his parents' garage in Washington State.

The business soon came to the attention of two successful entrepreneurs, Nick Hanauer, a local businessman, and Tom Alberg, a member on the board of directors of many high-powered companies. At the end of 1995, both men put money into Amazon.com. Bezos used some of the invested money to improve the Amazon website.

It wasn't long before Amazon.com was delivering books to all parts of America but Bezos realized that he had to offer more if he wanted people to come back as customers. He decided to ask buyers to write their own book reviews. The idea worked. People who wrote reviews felt involved with the company. They started to see Amazon as more of an online community and not just a place to buy things.

In 1997, Amazon generated $15.7 million in revenue. The company went public and Bezos added CDs and films to the goods on offer. In 1998, Amazon started to sell software, electronics, video games, toys and domestic appliances.

At the end of 1999, Amazon registered over a billion dollars in sales but then the company began to lose money. In 2000, Amazon laid off more than 200 people. One year later, over 1000 workers had to go. It looked as if Bezos' dream was coming to an end.

Determined to save the site, Bezos invited other companies to sell their products through Amazon.com. Today you can buy all kinds of goods on Amazon.

Although Amazon.com is not directly responsible for what other firms sell on their platform, the company receives part of the money the other retailers have taken in with their Amazon sales. With the help of this extra revenue, Amazon.com was able to get back on its feet.

A Use information from the text to put these facts into chronological order. Then make a time-line showing the development of Amazon.com.

1. Amazon starts to sell other goods.
2. Jeff Bezos started to sell books online.
3. The company began to lose money.
4. Other companies began to sell their products through Amazon.com.
5. People first bought shares in Amazon.com.
6. Some successful entrepreneurs put money into Amazon.com.

B A trainee who is interested in Amazon.com has asked you to describe the development of the company. Use the time-line you created above.

UNIT 5

Making enquiries and offers

- finding information about suppliers
- writing enquiries
- writing offers

1 Warm-up

A **Where can a potential customer find information about suppliers and their goods or services?**

B **What information might a potential customer ask for before buying a product or choosing a service?**

2 A letter of enquiry

A **Read the letter of enquiry on the opposite page. Find examples of the things you discussed in exercise 1.**

B **Which of the following statements are incorrect? Correct them using your own words.** KMK

1. Alois Baum found information about Wooden Furniture on the Internet.
2. Möbel Baum GmbH is a manufacturing company.
3. Alois Baum is familiar with the goods Wooden Furniture manufactures.
4. He knows how the goods will be sent and how he should pay.
5. Möbel Baum is not sure if they will order regularly from Wooden Furniture.
6. Wooden Furniture can ask the GLS bank for information about Möbel Baum's creditworthiness.

Möbel Baum GmbH
Breite Gasse 2
D-79106 Freiburg i. Breisgau

Tel.: +49 (0)761 7654321
info@moebel-baum.de
www.moebel-baum.de

Wooden Furniture Ltd
29 Dryden Street
LONDON SE 92 BS
UNITED KINGDOM

Our ref: DD/AS

27 January 20..

Dear Sir or Madam

Enquiry about office furniture

We have seen your advertisement in this month's edition of the trade magazine "Furniture and More". We note that your company manufactures office furniture.

Our company is a leading German importer of household furniture. We are planning to extend our range of goods to include office furniture.

We would be grateful if you sent us a catalogue showing your line of products.

Please let us have details of your terms of delivery and payment.

If your company's goods meet our requirements, we may be prepared to place regular orders.

The GLS Bank in Freiburg, Germany will be happy to supply references.

Many thanks for your attention to our enquiry.

We look forward to hearing from you soon.

Yours faithfully

Alois Baum

Alois Baum
Managing Director

C **Match these German phrases and sentence to the English equivalents in the letter.**

1. Wir haben Ihre Anzeige … gesehen.
2. Unsere Firma ist ein führender deutscher Importeur …
3. Wir haben vor, …
4. Wir wären Ihnen dankbar, wenn …
5. Bitte nennen Sie uns Einzelheiten …
6. Wenn die Dienstleistungen Ihrer Firma unsere Voraussetzungen erfüllen, …
7. Die … Bank wird Ihnen gerne Referenzen zukommen lassen.
8. Vielen Dank …

GRAMMAR

Conditionals 1 and 2

1 If you **order** in bulk, you usually **get** a discount.
2 If the company **contacts** the bank, they **will learn** that we are creditworthy.
3 You **would get** a discount if you **settled** your account by the 15th of the month.

- Ein Bedingungssatz (*if*-Satz) besteht aus zwei Teilen: einem Nebensatz mit *if* und einem Hauptsatz (1–3).
- Sätze des Typs 0 drücken eine zwangsläufige Folge aus (1). Sie beschreiben eine allgemein gültige Wahrheit.
- Sätze des Typs 1 drücken Bedingungen aus, die leicht erfüllt werden können (2). Die Folge dieser Bedingung ist sehr wahrscheinlich.
- Sätze des Typs 2 drücken Bedingungen aus, die unwahrscheinlich erfüllt werden können (3). Die Folge dieser Bedingung ist ungewiss.
- Der Satz kann mit dem *if*-Teil oder der Folge beginnen. Geht der *if*-Teil voran, hängt man ein Komma an (1, 2).

3 Practice

A **Work with a partner. Use the words to make complete type 1 and type 2 conditional sentences. Remember to place the comma in the correct position.**

Example: we order goods today / they arrive Friday
If we order the goods today, they will arrive by Friday.
If we ordered the goods today, they would arrive by Friday.

1 your offer satisfactory / we place order
2 you phone sales manager / he give information
3 how long / you hold prices / we order today
4 we not get confirmation / we cancel order
5 you fax invoice / I transfer money
6 we place order / you reduce price

! Don't use *will* in the *if*-clause!
*If I ~~will~~ **need** more goods, I **will call** you.*

B **Complete the sentences with the correct form of the verb in brackets.**

1 If you (increase) the quantity of items, we would be able to offer you a discount.
2 If you (reduce) the price of the goods, we would buy more.
3 We would be pleased if you (send) samples.
4 Alois Baum will choose another supplier, if they (offer) better terms.
5 If we (order) more goods, we would get a larger discount.
6 We will send the goods by express delivery, if you (sign) the contract by tomorrow.
7 If we (not order) new stock soon, we won't be able to deliver to our customers.
8 We (not pay) the extra cost if the quality of the goods wasn't so high.

TIP

Enquiries

Introduction: Explain where you got to know about the company you are writing to.

Main part of the enquiry (two or more paragraphs):
- Information about your company.
- What you would like to know, e.g. type of goods, amount and cost of the goods you are interested in; enquire about discounts, terms of delivery and payment, date of delivery.
- Offer information from a bank or a business partner if you are a new customer.

Close:
- Express your interest in ordering goods.
- Complimentary close.

LANGUAGE

Writing an enquiry

Source of address		
We saw your	advertisement/advertising leaflet brochure/catalogue	in …
We have your name from	the chamber of commerce our business partners, (firm),	in …
We visited your	stand presentation	at the trade fair in …

About your firm		
We are	a small/medium-sized/well-known company/firm.	
	distributors/manufacturers/suppliers of …	
	a wholesaler/retailer	for … to the … trade.
We are interested in	your … (products). expanding our range of …	

What you require		
Please	send us	samples of your … your latest catalogue.
Please	give us let us have	a quotation for … details of all discounts.
Full details of your terms of delivery and payment would be appreciated.		
References		
References can be obtained from (name of bank/company).		

Polite ending		
If your goods/products	find our (customers') approval,	…
… we will	be able to place consider placing	a sizeable order very soon.
We look forward to	hearing from you receiving your reply/offer	soon. within the next few days.

4 Writing a letter of enquiry

You are an office assistant at Büroland, an office supplier in Munich. Your boss has asked you to write a letter of enquiry to a potential supplier in Belfast, Northern Ireland.

Work with a partner and write the letter. Include the following points:

- Source of address: local chamber of commerce
- Own company: well-known supplier of office stationery (outlets all over Germany); planning to extend operations into Austria
- What you require: price list, details of terms of delivery and payment
- References: Deutsche Bank, Munich
- Polite ending
- Address your letter to Belfast Office Supplies, Kennedy Way Industrial Estate, Belfast BT11 9DT, Northern Ireland

Keep your letter at hand as you will need it again for a later exercise.

5 An offer

Carole Davis, Sales Manager at Wooden Furniture Ltd, sends a reply to the enquiry from Alois Baum (page 45). In his letter, Alois Baum has requested two things.

A Read the reply and find the responses to Alois Baum's requests.

1 February 20..

Dear Mr Baum

Enquiry about office furniture

With reference to your enquiry of 27 January 20.., we are pleased to hear that you are interested in our products and are planning to include them in your range of products.

As requested, we enclose our latest catalogue. We are pleased to inform you that everything shown in the catalogue is currently in stock.

We would like to take this opportunity to draw your attention to the latest addition to our range, the Executive Conference Table (page 4).

Our prices are quoted EXW and our terms of payment are within 10 days 2.5 % cash discount.

Our products are packed individually in strong cardboard boxes. We deal with orders immediately and offer an efficient and reliable service.

We feel sure that a trial order will convince you of the quality of our goods.

Please contact us if we can be of any further assistance. We look forward to hearing from you soon.

Yours sincerely

Carole Davis

Carole Davis

B **Answer the following questions about the letter.** KMK

1. If Alois Baum places an order soon, will Wooden Furniture Ltd be able to deliver everything he orders?
2. Wooden Furniture Ltd is offering a new product. What is it?
3. Who is going to pay transport costs, insurance and customs duties?
4. How can Alois Baum save his firm money?
5. How does Wooden Furniture Ltd make the goods ready for transport?
6. What can Alois Baum do if he needs more information?

C **The sentences below (1–8) are from a reply to an enquiry which Alois Baum wrote to a German company. Find the English equivalents in Carole Davis' letter.**

1. Bei Zahlungen innerhalb von 10 Tagen gewähren wir einen Rabatt von 2,5 %.
2. Bitte nehmen Sie Kontakt mit uns auf, wenn Sie weitere Einzelheiten benötigen.
3. Ich freue mich, dass Sie sich für unsere Produkte interessieren.
4. Unsere Preise verstehen sich ab Werk.
5. Unsere Produkte sind einzeln verpackt.
6. Wir bearbeiten Aufträge sofort und garantieren Effizienz und Zuverlässigkeit.
7. Wir möchten diese Gelegenheit wahrnehmen, Ihre Aufmerksamkeit auf … zu lenken.
8. Wir sind sicher, dass ein Probeauftrag Sie von der Qualität unserer Ware überzeugen wird.

TIP

Incoterms® 2010

Before they sign a contract, a buyer and seller have to agree on who pays the costs of transport and insurance and who is responsible for customs duties. It is also important to agree at what point the risk of loss of the goods or of damage to the goods passes from the seller to the buyer and at what point the goods become the property of the importer.

In international trade, exporters and importers can rely on the international Incoterms® 2010, which are rules that are recognized throughout the world. For example, the Incoterm **EXW** (Ex Works, *ab Werk*) states that the buyer is responsible for the goods as soon as they leave the seller's premises (see page 52).

6 Writing an offer

WEBCODE **OMU0501**

You work in the Sales Department of Belfast Office Supplies, Kennedy Way Industrial Estate, Belfast BT11 9DT, Northern Ireland. Your boss has asked you to reply to the enquiry from Büroland, an office supplier in Munich (see page 48).

Work with a partner and write the letter, including the following points:

- Thank customer for the enquiry (give the date)
- Thank for the interest in your company's products
- Say that your are enclosing a price list as requested
- Give details of terms of delivery and payment
- Add further information about your products or service, e.g. environmentally-friendly packaging; delivery within one week.
- Express hope that you will hear from Büroland soon.
- Address your letter to Büroland, Bavaria Weg 17, 80801 Munich, Germany

TIP

Offers

Introduction: Thank the customer for the enquiry.

Main part of the offer (two or more paragraphs):
- Refer to your catalogue, price lists, samples, etc. which you are sending.
- Describe the goods, give order numbers.
- Draw attention to anything special, e.g. new items.
- Give details of amounts ordered, price, rebates, date of delivery, terms of delivery.
- Say how long the offer lasts.
- Respond to individual questions.

Incoterms® 2010 rules, S. 52

Close:
- Focus on the plus points of your firm (quality goods/service, reliability, ability to deliver orders quickly).
- Assure the customer that you will deal with the order carefully and quickly.
- Complimentary close.

LANGUAGE

Writing offers

Reference to enquiry

Many thanks for We refer to	your letter of (date) enquiring your enquiry of (date)	about … *(general enquiry)* for … *(specific enquiry)*
We are pleased to note from your letter of (date) that you are interested in …		

Reference to information, samples, etc.

Enclosed (please find) our latest	brochure / catalogue. leaflet / price list.
We are sending you a selection of samples.	
We would like to draw your attention to our	latest special offer. new products/range.

Terms

We would like to point out that our/all prices are quoted … (Incoterms® 2010 rule).		
We draw your attention to the fact that our	guarantee warranty period	extends over … is valid for …
Terms of payment: we offer a cash discount for payment within … days.		
For orders over … we offer a discount of … %.		
We have pleasure in offering you …% discount on/off the net price for …		

Further information

Our delivery date is approximately Delivery time is about	… days/weeks after receipt of your order. … weeks/months.
We can guarantee immediate delivery.	

Polite ending

We hope that the enclosed samples meet with your approval.
We look forward to receiving your order and assure you that we will give it our prompt and careful attention.

7 Produktion

A Sie sind Kaufmännische/r Assistent/in einer deutschen Druckerei (*printer*). Ihr Vorgesetzter bittet Sie, eine Anfrage an eine britische Papierfabrik zu schreiben, die als Lieferant infrage käme.

Verfassen Sie die Anfrage. Berücksichtigen Sie die folgenden Punkte:

- Quelle der Anschrift des Unternehmens, z. B. Internet, Fachzeitschrift
- Informationen zum Betätigungsfeld Ihrer Firma, z. B. führende Druckerei von Fachzeitschriften (*trade magazines*)
- Bitte um Warenproben verschiedener Papiersorten der infrage kommenden Qualitätsstufen
- Auskunft zu Liefer- und Zahlungsbedingungen
- Referenzen
- Freundliche Bitte um baldige Antwort

Geben Sie Ihrem Unternehmen einen Namen und eine Anschrift. Schreiben Sie dann die Anfrage an Campbell's Papermill, 2 River Bank, Penicuik EH26 7TP, United Kingdom. Verwenden Sie die korrekte Briefform und das heutige Datum. Unterzeichnen Sie den Brief.

B Sie arbeiten in der Verkaufsabteilung von Campbell's Papermill in Penicuik. Heute haben Sie die Anfrage (A) einer Druckerei aus Deutschland erhalten.

Verfassen Sie ein Angebot. Berücksichtigen Sie folgende Punkte:

- Danken Sie für die Anfrage
- Nennen Sie Besonderheiten Ihres Papieres, z. B. umweltfreundliche Herstellung *(ecological production methods)*; altpapierhaltiges Papier *(recycled fibre-based paper)*
- Reagieren Sie auf die in der Anfrage geäußerten Wünsche, z. B. nach Warenproben
- Teilen Sie Liefer- und Zahlungsbedingungen mit
- Geben Sie weitere Informationen, z. B. dass die sofortige Lieferung nach Anfrage möglich ist
- Bitten Sie freundlich um baldige Antwort.

8 Mediation

Ein neuer Kollege / eine neue Kollegin möchte von Ihnen wissen, warum die „Incoterms® Rules" für den internationalen Güterverkehr so wichtig sind. Lesen Sie den Text auf Seite 52 und den „Tip" auf Seite 49 und erklären Sie ihm/ihr auf Deutsch, was diese sind, welche Teile des Kaufvertrags sie abdecken und was sie nicht abdecken.

(„Incoterms" ist die Abkürzung für „International Commercial Terms". Die deutsche Bezeichnung dafür ist „Internationale Handelsklauseln".)

CAN DO

After working through this unit I can ...	Check ...
▪ talk about where customers might find information about suppliers.	Ex 1, page 44
▪ read and understand commercial correspondence and identify standard vocabulary, phrases and sentences.	Ex 2, page 45 Ex 5, page 48
▪ write a guided enquiry.	Ex 4, page 48
▪ write a guided offer.	Ex 6, page 49
▪ compose and write an enquiry; reply to the enquiry with an offer.	Ex 7, page 51

9 Incoterms® 2010 rules

Study the text and diagram, then answer the questions below.

The International Chamber of Commerce (ICC) has produced a set of definitions for the most commonly used terms in international trade. These terms are known as Incoterms® rules. The ICC published the first Incoterms® rules in 1936 and they are updated regularly. As of 2010 there are eleven Incoterms® rules.

The Incoterms® rules make it easier for traders in different countries to conduct business with one another. They are a voluntary set of rules and do not take precedence over any mandatory laws. Using the rules provides business partners with the legal certainty upon which a contract can be based, however.

Once they are included in a contract (and are accepted by the other party), the Incoterms® rules which have been stated apply to both parties.

Incoterms® are one part of the contract but not the whole contract. They say nothing about the price to be paid or the method of payment. They do not deal with the transfer of ownership of the goods, breach of contract, or product liability; all of these issues need to be considered in the contract of sale.

Incoterms® 2010 rules – reference chart

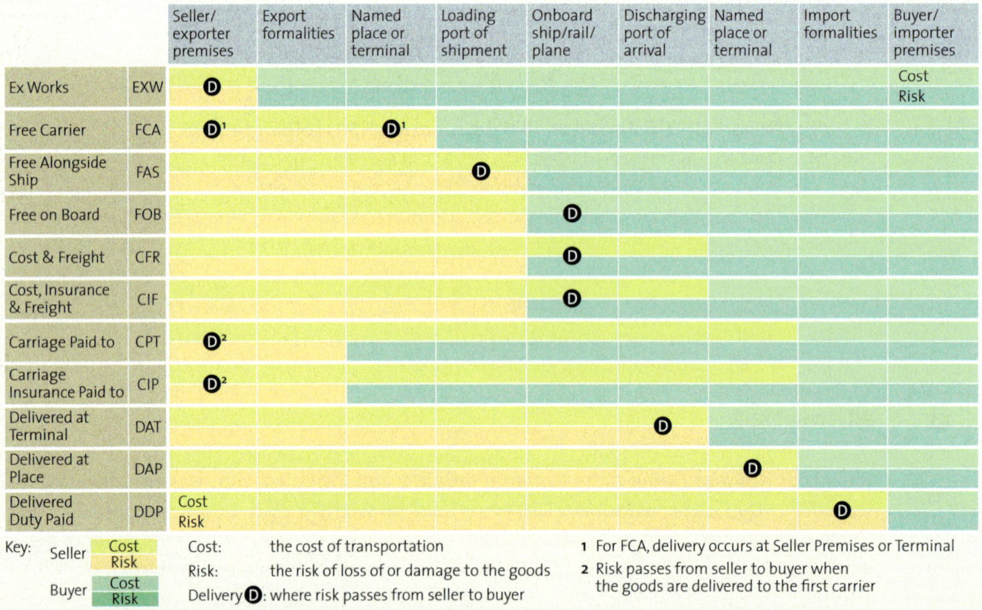

1. Which Incoterms® 2010 rule represents the minimum obligation for the seller?
2. Which rule states that the seller pays all costs in delivering the goods to the destination, including import duties and taxes?
3. Which rule states that the seller pays for the goods to be delivered to the carrier at an agreed place?
4. Which rule states that the seller must pay all costs as far as the port of destination, excluding insurance?
5. Which rule states that the seller pays for the goods to be delivered to the ship, but not loaded onto it?
6. Four of the rules are aimed at trade where transportation is entirely conducted by water. Two of these are CFR and CIF. What are the other two terms?

Placing and acknowledging orders

UNIT 6

- placing orders
- discussing prices
- acknowledging orders

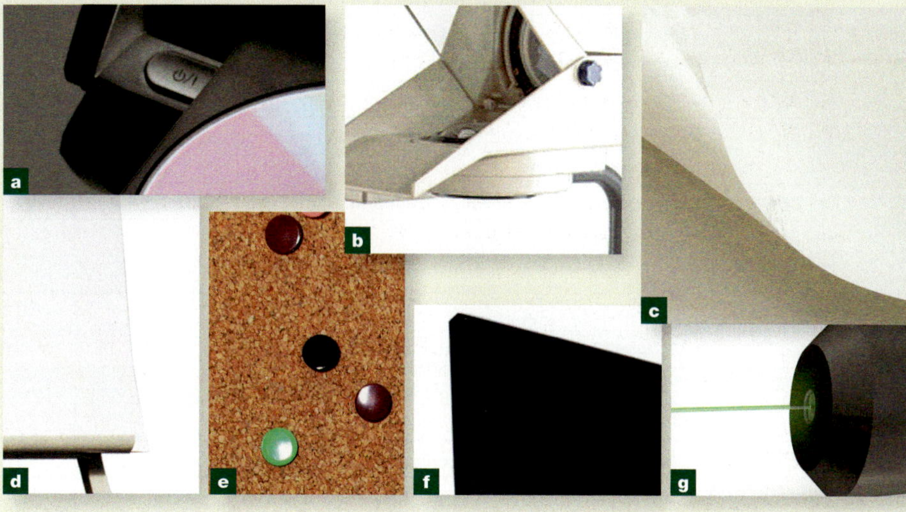

a b c d e f g

1 Warm-up

Work with a partner. Look at the close-up photos of parts of business equipment and decide together what the things are. You will find the English words for the items in the catalogue on page 54.

2 Ordering by phone

KMK

10

Katrin Troll is doing her work placement at A to Z Logistics in London. She calls Good Business Equipment and places an urgent order.

Listen to the telephone conversation. Copy the order form and complete it with the missing information.

Good Business Equipment **Order form**

Customer Details		
Name	Katrin Troll	
Address	A to Z Logistics, North Park Industrial Estate, London N7 9EJ	
Phone	020 71594783	
Email	Katrin@A2Z.co.uk	

Order		
Item number	…	
Description	…	
Quantity …	Price …	Total …

Method of payment	
Bank transfer	Cheque COD
Credit card:	Amex Mastercard Visa

Good Business Equipment

In a hurry?
For quick delivery, phone 0800 13 24 59 76
Free delivery in the UK on orders over £100

Display		
01FC	Moveable flip chart	£62.42
02FC	Moveable flip chart (four stainless steel legs)	£149.00
03FC	Flip chart paper, 40 unlined sheets with 2 red permanent markers and 2 green permanent markers	£18.99
04CB	Square cork board 60 cm x 60 cm	£5.50
05CB	Rectangular cork board 88 cm x 60 cm with 100 multi-coloured, round-headed pins	£8.90
06WB	Electronic white board with built-in printer	£820.00
07LP	Laser pointer (10cm long)	£6.99
Projection		
08OP	Overhead projector	£320.55
09DP	Multi-media projector with stable plastic case	£2,160.90
TV/DVD		
10TV	Flat-screen television	£749.99
11TV	Flat-screen television with integrated DVD/Blueray player	£2,400.00
12BR	Blueray player	£460.50
13WB	Wall bracket for flat TV (width: 7 cm; height: 4 cm; length: 78 cm; weight 0.7 kg)	£146.50

3 Choosing business equipment

You work in the purchasing department of your company. You have been asked to buy equipment for the new conference room. You can spend up to £3,500.

Work in groups. Study the catalogue above and decide together what you would like to buy. Make notes, including item numbers, description, size, quantity and price. You will need these notes for exercise 5.

LANGUAGE

Making choices

I think we should buy/order a/an …
Let's get the …
How about buying/getting/ordering a/an/the … ?
That one is too big/small/expensive.
Should we choose/order a different/another one/model?
I prefer the other one/model.

! €13,000 (NOT ~~€13.000~~) 3.5 % (NOT ~~3,5 %~~)

GRAMMAR

Adjectives and adverbs

1 It's an **urgent** order. We need it **urgently**.
2 It's an **up-to-date**, **multi-media** machine.
3 It's a **good** piece of equipment. It does the job **well**.
4 How **fast** can you deliver? **Fast** delivery costs extra.
5 He **seems** happy. / She **looks** angry.

- Im Englischen werden die meisten Adverbien von einem Adjektiv abgeleitet, indem man *-ly* anhängt (1). Das ist auch bei den meisten Adjektiven der Fall, die auf *-e* enden, z. B. *safe* → *safe**ly***.
- Viele Adjektive werden gebildet, indem man zwei (oder mehr) Wörter durch Bindestrich zusammenfügt (2).
- Das zu *good* gehörende Adverb ist *well* (3).
- Die Adverbien *hard*, *fast*, *early* und *late* sind identisch mit dem Adjektiv (4).
- Adjektive beschreiben, wie jemand oder etwas ist, und beziehen sich auf ein Nomen (*order*, *machine*, *piece of equipment*).
- Adverbien bezeichnen, wie etwas gemacht wird, und beziehen sich auf ein Verb (*need*, *do the job*).
- Auf Verben, die einen Zustand beschreiben (*be*, *seem*, *become*, *stay*, *remain*), und Verben, die eine Eigenschaft beschreiben (*look*, *sound*, *feel*, *taste*, *smell*), folgt ein Adjektiv, kein Adverb (5).

4 Practice

A Decide whether to use an adjective or adverb in the following sentences.

1 There is a fan in the computer so it stays cool/coolly.
2 The projector is good/well made.
3 The Internet is very slow/slowly today.
4 You can use a laser pointer to point to things accurate/accurately.
5 Are the prices in the catalogue correct/correctly?
6 The goods will certain/certainly arrive tomorrow.
7 Please handle the new equipment careful/carefully.
8 My English is good/well but if someone speaks fast/fastly, I have problems.
9 Katrin works quick/quickly but she is always very accurate/accurately.
10 The CD player sounds strange/strangely.

B Work in groups. Look around the room and describe objects and people using adjectives and adverbs. Who can guess what/who you are describing?

Examples
A: *Tall, wearing a pink pullover. Speaks English well.*
B: *The teacher.*
A: *Correct.*

B: *Small, black, plastic. Makes a loud noise sometimes.*
C: *Is it your running watch?*
B: *No, that's not correct. It has a blue display.*
D: *It's your mobile phone.*
B: *Yes. That's right.*

5 Telephoning your order

You are going to practise placing a telephone order using the notes you made while doing exercise 3.

Work with a partner from another group.

Partner A: You will take the order. Prepare an order form before you start.
Partner B: Use your notes to place the order.

LANGUAGE

Ordering by phone

Placing the order
I'd like to place an order for …
I'm phoning with a repeat order.
Do you have the details of our last order?
Can you take my order? / supply us from stock?
How soon can you deliver? / dispatch the goods?
Shall I repeat that?
Could you read that back to me, please?

Taking the order
As this is a repeat order, we can give you a discount.
We can dispatch/send out the goods immediately/tomorrow / next week.
Can I confirm these details? / read it back to you?
Could you repeat that, please?

Describing size and dimensions		
How long is it?	It's 000 cm long.	The length is 000 cm.
How wide is it?	It's 000 cm wide.	The width is 000 cm.
How high is it?	It's 000 cm high.	The height is 000 cm.
How big is the television?		It's 00 by 00 by 00.

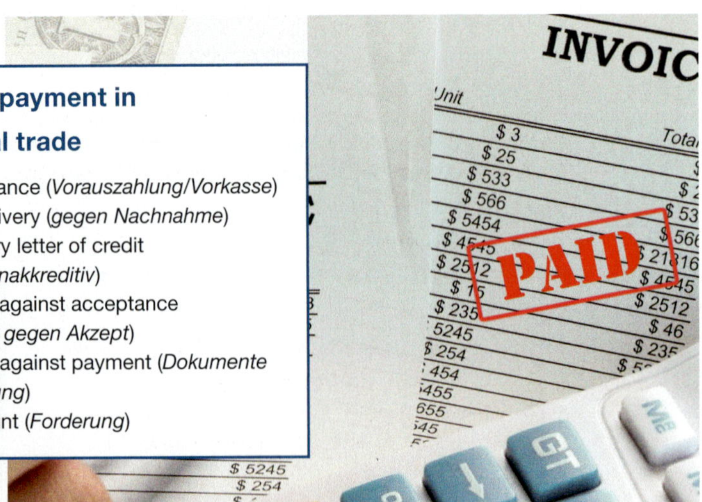

TIP

Methods of payment in international trade

1 Cash in advance (*Vorauszahlung/Vorkasse*)
2 Cash on delivery (*gegen Nachnahme*)
3 Documentary letter of credit (*Dokumentenakkreditiv*)
4 Documents against acceptance (*Dokumente gegen Akzept*)
5 Documents against payment (*Dokumente gegen Zahlung*)
6 Open account (*Forderung*)

6 Payments in international trade

A Match each of the methods of payment in the box on page 56 with one of the definitions below (a–f).

a An arrangement by which the importer pays for the goods as soon as they arrive.
b Using this method of payment, the goods are shipped and delivered before payment is due (usually in 30 to 90 days).
c An arrangement between the exporter, a bank and the importer. The exporter sends the shipping documents to the bank; the bank only releases the documents to the importer after he has paid for the goods.
d In this case, the importer pays before the goods are dispatched.
e An arrangement by which shipping documents will not be released to the importer until he has signed a bill of exchange for the value of the goods.
f This is a guarantee given by a bank that payment will be made to the exporter after he has presented shipping documents which confirm that the goods have been shipped.

B Which method of payment is most/least attractive to the exporter?

7 An order for office furniture

Last week, Alois Baum from Möbel Baum in Freiburg received a catalogue from Wooden Furniture Ltd in London (see pages 45 and 48). Mr Baum has decided to place a trial order.

Complete Alois Baum's order using words and phrases from the box on page 58.

Order no. AB 6822
7 February 20..

Dear Ms Davis

Trial order for office furniture

Thank you for your …[1] of 1 February.

We agree to your …[2] and are pleased to …[3] for office furniture as follows:

Catalogue number	Item	Quantity	Item price	Total price
02	Computer desk	2	£350	£700
03	Square table	1	£800	£800
03	Round table	1	£1,000	£1,000
03	Rectangular table	1	£1,200	£1,200
05	Desk chair	2	£137	£274
07	Small pine shelf	1	£150	£150
07	Medium pine shelf	1	£160	£160
				£4,284

We understand that …[4] are FOB.

…[5] will be made by bank transfer within 30 days of …[6].

Please …[7] this order.

We look forward to receiving the …[8] as soon as possible.

Yours sincerely

TIP

Orders and acknowledgements

An order should include the following items:

- order number
- details of quantity, packing, product order number and price
- terms of delivery, discounts and terms of payment

When **confirming receipt** of an order for **standard items**, it is enough to simply confirm your original offer without repeating the details.

When **acknowledging** an order for **non-standard items**, repeat all the details of the order, i.e. details of the product, including colour, size and model number; details of methods of payment and delivery.

LANGUAGE

Placing and acknowledging orders

Placing orders
Thank you for your quotation of …
Many thanks for your quotation.

We agree to your terms and are pleased to give you an order for …
We enclose / are enclosing order no. …

We understand that all prices are (Incoterms® 2010 rule) / include VAT.
Payment will be made by (method of payment) on delivery of the goods.
Payment will be made within … days of receipt of the goods.

Please acknowledge this order by return of post.
We look forward to receiving the goods as soon as possible.
We trust you will give this order your prompt/careful attention.

Acknowledging orders
Thank you for your order of (date) for (goods).
We were very glad/happy/pleased to receive your order.

We are pleased/happy to confirm your order.
We are sure that the items/goods will arrive in good condition.

We will execute your order to your complete/full satisfaction.
We look forward to doing business with you again / further orders in the future.

WEBCODE
OMU0601

CAN DO

After working through this unit I can …	Check …
▪ read and understand information in a catalogue	Ex 1, page 53
▪ understand a telephone call and complete an order form.	Ex 2, page 53
▪ discuss prices and descriptions of business equipment.	Ex 3, page 54
▪ telephone an order for business equipment.	Ex 5, page 56
▪ identify words and phrases which are used in an order.	Ex 7, page 57
▪ write an order for office furniture using details from a catalogue.	Ex 8, page 59
▪ write an acknowledgement.	Ex 9, page 59

8 Produktion

Sie arbeiten für ein deutsches Unternehmen. Ihr Vorgesetzter hat sich den Katalog der Firma Wooden Furniture Ltd angeschaut und fordert Sie nun auf, neue Büromöbel zu bestellen. In Ihrem Büro arbeiten vier Angestellte.

Schauen Sie diesen Katalog durch und entscheiden Sie, was sie an Büroeinrichtung bestellen möchten. Danach schreiben Sie Ihre Bestellung und adressieren diese an Carole Davis, Wooden Furniture Ltd, 29 Dryden Street, London SE9 2BS, United Kingdom. Ihr Vorgesetzter hat Ihnen keine Obergrenze für die Ausgaben gesetzt.

01 Executive desk *New!*

Dark red English cherry wood.
A beautifully made desk. **£1,955**
(height 60 cm, length 160 cm, depth 82 cm)

02 Computer desk

An inexpensive desk. Put together carefully by our craftsmen. Pull-out keyboard shelf extends depth to 90 cm. **£350**
(length 130 cm, height 72 cm, depth 74 cm)

03 Square, rectangular, round tables

Solid English oak. 78 cm high. Different shapes fit nicely into any size of office. State shape required when ordering.

Square table (80 cm x 80 cm) **£800**

Round table (90 cm diameter) **£1,000**

Rectangular table (140 cm x 80 cm) **£1,200**

04 Traditional chair

English walnut with comfortable leather seat. **£487**

05 Desk chair

Good design. Well made.
Excellent value for money. **£137**

06 Storage cabinets

with or without steel locks.
(height 104 cm, width 48 cm, depth 63 cm)

£360 (without locks)

£420 (with locks)

07 Pine shelves

in three sizes, small, medium and large. Made from high quality pine. State size required when ordering.

small (length 120 cm, height 60 cm, depth 20 cm) **£150**
medium (length 240 cm, height 80 cm, depth 20 cm) **£160**
large (length 300 cm, height 100 cm, depth 20 cm) **£170**

08 Container with wheels

Extend your storage space with a compact container with wheels for your files. Fits easily under any desk.
(height 60 cm, width 48 cm, depth 72 cm)

£190

Larger size also available.

9 Produktion

Sie arbeiten für die Firma Wooden Furniture Ltd in London.

Schreiben Sie eine Bestätigung an Alois Baum und danken Sie ihm für seine Bestellung vom 7. Februar (Übung 7).

10 Mediation

KMK

Im Zusammenhang mit der Neugestaltung Ihres Arbeitsplatzes kam auch die Frage auf, was man mit dem Elektroschrott machen sollte, der im Büro anfällt. Nachdem Sie dazu einen wichtigen Beitrag in einer Fachzeitschrift gefunden haben, möchten Sie nun Ihren Kollegen die wichtigsten Punkte vorstellen.

Lesen Sie den Zeitschriftenartikel. Machen Sie sich Notizen, dann fassen Sie den Inhalt kurz auf Deutsch zusammen. Orientieren Sie sich dabei an den Fragen, die auf den Text folgen.

Recycling

Intelligent Recycling of Used Electronic Equipment

Environmental experts estimate that electronic equipment makes up about 2% of solid waste. This may not sound like much, but electronic waste is full of toxic materials which sink into the ground, contaminate water and, eventually food. Recycling old electronic equipment is a must if we want to slow down the build-up of dangerous waste all over the planet.

All electronic equipment and material, for example computers, monitors, terminals, printers, fax machines, modems, copy machines, clocks, calculators, telephones, mobile phones, components, batteries and various other pieces of equipment made of plastic and/or metal can be recycled.

Here are some tips about how to recycle electronic equipment:

Computers

Many computer manufacturers have their own recycling or trade-in schemes. Check the instruction booklet which comes with the equipment, or check online whether you can send your old hardware back to the manufacturer.

If not, take your computer to a specialist to be dismantled. Don't do this yourself. You have to know how to dismantle the equipment properly to obtain the usable parts and materials.

If the computer is still functioning, you could donate it to a local school or non-profit organization.

Printer cartridges

Some recycling companies pay for ink jet and/or laser toner cartridges which are in good condition, i.e. with a case which is not broken or has any cracks. Always check which cartridges are accepted before you send them in as some recycling companies will charge you to take in cartridges that are not accepted.

Ribbon cartridges are not accepted by paying recycling companies.

Batteries

Most electronics retailers have a box near the check-out where customers can put in batteries for recycling.

It is important that you dispose of batteries properly and safely. Never put a battery into a fire or an incinerator. Burning a battery will cause it to explode.

Intelligent recycling of used equipment is a must for all of us. Follow the rules above and help keep our planet healthy. ▪▪▪

1. Warum ist das Recyceln von Elektroschrott wichtig?
2. Was kann recycelt werden?
3. Wie kann man alte Computer, Druckerpatronen und Batterien umweltverträglich entsorgen?

Preparing for meetings

UNIT 7

- writing invitations to a meeting
- preparing an agenda
- opening a meeting

1 Warm-up

A Look at the photos above and answer the following questions.

1. How often do you attend meetings at work?
2. What types of meetings do you attend?
3. How are you involved in the meetings?
4. Do you enjoy going to meetings? Why/Why not?

B What makes a meeting successful? Brainstorm ideas in groups then copy this mindmap and add your own ideas.

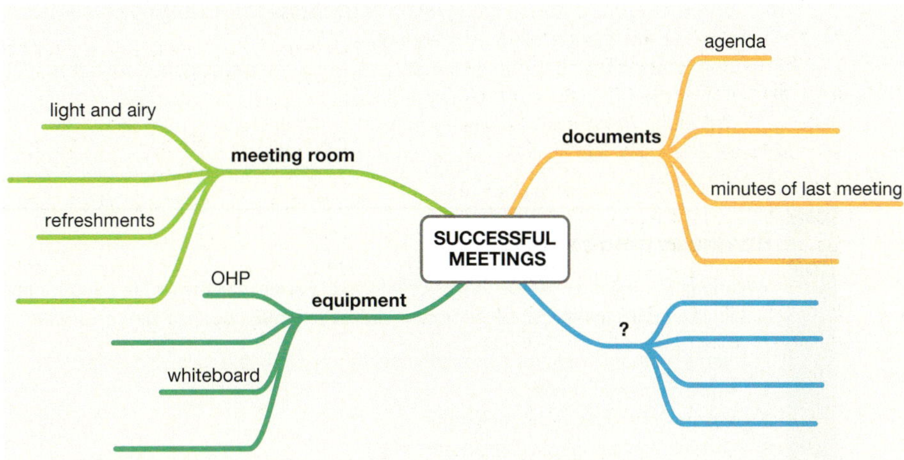

C Share your ideas with the class and decide together on a list of five essential ingredients for successful meetings.

2 Two invitations to meetings

Paul Müller and Johanna Pflüger are doing a work placement at Best plc, an international company based in Brighton. On page 63 you can see two invitations to meetings which will take place at Best plc soon.

A Look quickly at the invitations. Which invitation is formal? Which is informal?

B Use the invitations to find the English equivalents of these German words.

1 Treffen
2 Protokoll
3 Tagesordnung
4 Abwesenheit
5 Sonstiges
6 Bericht

C Read the invitations carefully, then answer these questions.

1 Which of them is an internal meeting? Which is an external meeting?
2 How often do they take place?
3 Who is going to attend?
4 What will happen at the trainees' meeting? Use your own words to write a short description.

D Match the list of items on the formal agenda (1–8) to the descriptions (a–f).

a This is when the participants discuss any issues relating to the last meeting.
b This is the time in the meeting when participants can discuss any other business which is not mentioned on the agenda.
c This is when the chairperson announces when the participants will next meet.
d This is the time when someone reads out the notes from the last meeting.
e These are the three main points to be covered at the meeting.
f At this point, the chairperson will report who (if anyone) is unable to attend.

TIP

Business meetings

Invitations to meetings can be formal or informal. Formal invitations are used for important events like board meetings. Most other invitations to meetings are sent as emails.

The items on the agenda for a meeting usually appear in the following order:
1 Apologies for absence;
2 Minutes of the previous meeting;
3 Questions relating to the minutes;
4 New items for discussion.

Most meetings finish with Any Other Business (AOB) and the date of the next meeting.

To: paul.mueller@best.com.uk; johanna.pflueger@best.com.uk
Copy:
Subject: trainees' meeting
From: sally.owen@best.com.uk
Signature:

Hi Johanna, hi Paul

This is just to let you know that I've decided to have our weekly get-together on Friday afternoon this week. I plan to start at 3 p.m. I know that we all dislike having meetings on a Friday afternoon but I think we should manage to cover everything in around 90 minutes so we can finish at 4.30.

Here are the points we'll be talking about:

Feedback on the trip to the logistics centre
Your presentations next month
How to take the minutes of a meeting

If you have any questions, please let me know before the meeting.

Best wishes
Sally

Invitation to the Board Meeting, 29 September 20..

Head Office, Brighton

Good, better, BEST plc

We are pleased to invite you to the above-mentioned monthly meeting.
The meeting is planned to run from 9 to 12 a.m.

Agenda

1 Apologies for absence
2 Minutes of last meeting
3 Matters arising from the minutes of the last meeting
4 Progress report on search for an agent in Eastern Europe (Robin Best, 10 minutes)
5 Short presentation on consumer preferences in Eastern Europe (Gabi Wendring, 20 minutes)
6 Action plan for entry into Eastern Europe (discussion, 60 minutes)
7 AOB
8 Date of next meeting

We look forward to seeing you.

GRAMMAR

Gerund (-ing form) or infinitive after verbs

1 I **expect to see** her at the meeting.
2 We **gave up inviting** him to meetings years ago.
3 He said he would **start to write** / **start writing** the minutes this morning.
4 **There's no point in doing** something you don't want to do.

- Nach einigen Verben steht der Infinitiv (*to* + Grundform des Verbs) (1).
- Nach anderen Verben steht das Gerundium (*-ing*-Form) (2).
- Nach einigen Verben kann sowohl der Infinitiv als auch die *-ing*-Form stehen (3).
- Nach bestimmten Ausdrücken steht immer die *-ing*-Form (4).

Eine Liste der Verben, nach denen das Gerundium steht, und der Verben, nach denen der Infinitiv steht, finden Sie auf Seite 175.

3 Practice

Use the list of verbs on page 175 to complete the following sentences.

Example: I look forward … (meet) you on Tuesday.
I look forward to meeting you on Tuesday.

1 Paul enjoys … (attend) meetings.
2 Sally offered … (chair) the meeting.
3 Johanna has promised … (arrive) early next time.
4 It's not worth … (discuss) this point any longer.
5 Robin has decided … (not/use) the new projector when he gives his report.
6 Could you stop … (talk) please? Johanna wants … (begin) her presentation.
7 Sally plans … (ask) Paul to take the minutes at the next meeting.
8 Some people dislike … (have) meetings at Head Office.
9 There's no point in … (start) the meeting until everyone has arrived.

4 Writing an invitation to a meeting

KMK

Best plc is looking for a distribution agent in Eastern Europe. At a recent trade fair, Robin Best met a Polish agent, Andrzej Kowalski, and now he would like to ask him to meet the members of the board at their next meeting at Head Office in Brighton.

Write the invitation, using the following information:

The object of the meeting is to discuss the possibility of Mr Kowalski's acting as an agent for Best plc in Eastern Europe. Suggested date and time: 21 October from 9.00 until 12.30, including lunch. During the meeting, Robin Best will present some of the firm's products (15 minutes) and Gabi Wendring, Head of Marketing, will give a talk about consumer preferences in Eastern Europe (30 minutes). After lunch, Mr Kowalski will be given a tour of the Best premises (30 minutes).

If the date and time are suitable, Best plc will organize a flight and accommodation for Mr Kowalski.

!

19 Uhr = 7 (o'clock) **in the evening** / 7 p.m.
The twenty-four hour clock is only used in timetables in English.

LANGUAGE

Invitation to a meeting

The	monthly quarterly annual	meeting of the	team staff group	will be held will take place	on (date) at (time) in (place).
Please	confirm let us know	that you	will are able to	attend.	

TIP

Doing business with people from other cultures

People do business differently from culture to culture. There are differences in the way people meet, how they dress and how they build relationships. Many companies offer courses in intercultural competence. If you are working in international business, it would make sense to go on such a course.

5 The start of the meeting with Andrzej Kowalski

KMK

It is 21 October. Robin Best is opening the meeting and welcoming the guests.

11

Listen to the start of the meeting, then complete the sentences below with the most suitable ending.

1 Jim Clarke …
- **a** is going to take the chair.
- **b** was going to take the chair, but he can't.
- **c** asks if he can chair the meeting.

2 Robin is going to …
- **a** leave the meeting early.
- **b** take the minutes.
- **c** act as chairperson.

3 Andrzej Kowalski …
- **a** flew to Brighton early this morning.
- **b** will stay in Brighton tonight.
- **c** arrived in Brighton the day before the meeting.

4 Gabi Wendring …
- **a** has done research in Eastern Europe and is happy with the results.
- **b** worked as a Marketing Manager in Eastern Europe.
- **c** will help Andrzej Kowalski set up distribution in Eastern Europe.

5 The tour of the premises …
- **a** will take place earlier than planned.
- **b** has been cancelled.
- **c** will take longer than planned.

6 Phrases for starting a meeting

KMK

11

A Copy the headings (a–g) into your notebook, then listen again and note down phrases which belong with these headings.

- **a** Asking an attendee to introduce themselves
- **b** Getting people's attention
- **c** Introducing an attendee
- **d** Reporting apologies
- **e** Starting the meeting
- **f** Stating the aims of the meeting
- **g** Welcoming attendees

B Now sort the headings (a–g) into chronological order as they appear in the meeting, then add the sentences below under the correct headings.

1. This is Victoria Oswald. Victoria is in charge of Logistics.
2. Kevin Dawes sends his apologies.
3. We have a lot to cover today, so I'd like to begin by looking at the data.
4. Thank you all for coming.
5. Can we settle down, please?
6. Mark, this would be a good point for you to tell us about yourself and your position in the firm.
7. Today, we're going to discuss last month's figures and see where we can make an improvement.

7 Practising opening a meeting

WEBCODE **OMU0701**

Johanna and Paul are practising opening a meeting. They have made some notes about what they would like to say.

Work with a partner. Using Johanna's and Paul's notes, take turns to practise opening a meeting. The words and phrases you learned in exercise 6 will be useful.

Paul's meeting

- *objectives: first meeting with new advertising agency, "Artwork Design"*
- *attendees: Heinz Eikmeyer (head of "Artwork Design") and his partners*
- *apologies: David Robb (on holiday)*
- *introduce myself*

Johanna's meeting

- *aim of meeting: to talk about preparations for trade fair*
- *attendees: marketing and sales personnel*
- *apologies: Lucy Smith (ill)*
- *introduce new colleague, Isa Ocklenburg from Vienna*

TIP

Making requests

Use *would like* rather than *want* when making requests. *Would like* is more indirect and, therefore, is more polite and respectful.

8 Produktion

Sie arbeiten für Adam and Smith, ein Architektenbüro mit Sitz in Cardiff. Die Firma hofft auf den Auftrag, einen Bürokomplex in der Innenstadt für Graham Bond Investments zu entwerfen. Graham Bond und seine Partner wollen sich mit der Architektengruppe treffen, um Näheres zu besprechen. Dabei soll es auch um die Honorarvorstellungen von Adam and Smith gehen.

Ihre Vorgesetzte Helen Lamb hat Sie aufgefordert, Herrn Bond und seine Partner zu einem Treffen einzuladen, das am 17. Januar von 10 bis 12.30 Uhr im Büro von Adam and Smith stattfinden soll. Bei diesem Treffen wird Robert Adam der Firma einige Entwürfe (*designs*) vorstellen (30 Minuten). Herr Bond wird den möglichen Kostenrahmen erläutern (20 Minuten). Im Anschluss werden sich die beiden Gruppen getrennt beraten und dann wieder zusammensetzen.

Schreiben Sie eine formelle Einladung an Graham Bond. Schlagen Sie eine Tagesordnung vor, die die oben genannten Punkte umfasst.

9 Produktion

Helen Lamb sollte das o.g. Treffen am 17. Januar leiten, musste jedoch wegen Krankheit absagen. Sie bittet Sie die Sitzung zu leiten.

Verwenden Sie die Informationen aus Übung 8 und notieren Sie, was Sie zu Beginn des Treffens sagen werden. (Nicht vergessen: Begrüßung, Vorstellung, Abwesenheit Frau Lamb.)

CAN DO

After working through this unit I can ...	Check ...
▪ talk about what makes a business meeting successful.	Ex 1, page 61
▪ understand invitations to meetings and a formal agenda.	Ex 2, page 62
▪ write invitations to business meetings.	Ex 4, page 64 Ex 8, page 67
▪ understand details I hear at the start of a business meeting.	Ex 5, page 65
▪ open a meeting using given notes.	Ex 7, page 66
▪ prepare a written opening for meeting.	Ex 9, page 67

The "Your Office Matters" website also has some tips on how to take the minutes of a meeting.

Mozilla Firefox

Your Office Matters

www.yourofficematters.com/taking_the_minutes

Facebook Meistbesuchte... Erste Schritte Aktuelle Nachr... Lesezeichen

Taking Minutes – FAQs

What are minutes?

Minutes are a written description of a meeting. After the minutes have been written, they are sent out to the people who attended the meeting. The minutes do not become an official part of the record of the meeting until they are approved by the attendees.

Who takes the minutes?

They are normally taken by one person. This can be anyone; it might be you.

How can I prepare to take minutes?

Have a look at the minutes from previous meetings, the names of the attendees and the items on the agenda.

Make sure you know the names of the attendees. During the meeting, if you can't remember someone's name, take a brief note of their seating position and find out their name after the meeting.

What should I include when I write up the minutes?

Minutes usually start by giving the title, date, time and place of the meeting.

They continue with a list of attendees. After that, they give a short review of each agenda item and a record of any vote or decision taken for each item.

Note the finishing time of the meeting and include the date and time of the next meeting.

Write the minutes immediately after the meeting so that nothing is forgotten.

Today's Tip – Taking minutes

Always draw up an outline before you go to a meeting. Include the following:

- the title of the meeting
- the location of the meeting
- a blank space to write the time the meeting started and ended
- the name of the chairperson
- a list of attendees that you can tick (or a blank list for attendees to sign)
- a blank space for the names of any attendees who arrive late or leave early

Leave space underneath to make notes on discussions and further actions.

If you know that a vote is to be taken, write the heading: Vote on (topic). Leave space to fill in the result of the vote.

10 Mediation

KMK

Lesen Sie die Webseite und machen Sie sich Notizen auf Deutsch. Erklären Sie einem anderen Auszubildenden, wie man bei einer Besprechung Protokoll führt.

Giving a presentation

- preparing a presentation
- describing graphs
- talking about figures

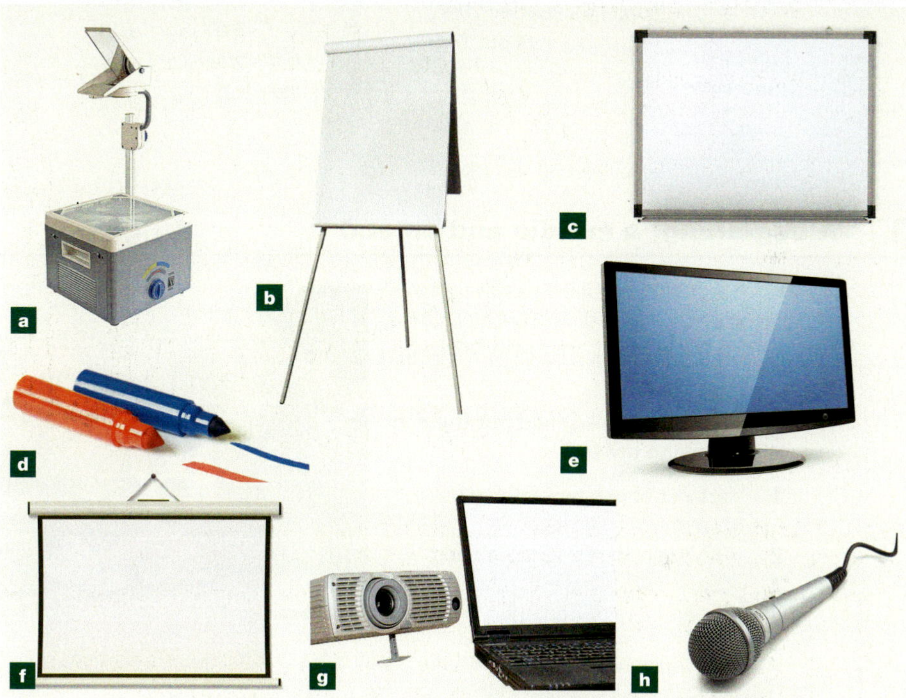

1 Warm-up

A Think of the last presentation you attended. What made it good or bad?

The last presentation I attended was bad. The presenter just stood at the side of the room and read out what was written on the PowerPoint® slides.

I was at a good presentation last week. The visuals were excellent and we got them as handouts with written explanations on them. That was really useful.

B Match the items of equipment which can be used in a presentation (1–8) to the photos at the top of the page (a–h).

1 flipchart
2 laptop and digital projector
3 microphone
4 overhead projector
5 marker pens
6 screen
7 TV
8 whiteboard

2 Equipment for a presentation

Work with a partner. Read these notes about what is going to happen at two presentations. What items of equipment might the presenters need?

Johanna

- present graphics (draw on them)
- brainstorming session (collect the ideas where everyone can see them)
- show examples of websites

Paul

- show DVD
- PowerPoint® slides

Remember! It's a large audience in a big conference room.

3 A beginning, a middle and an end

Trainees at Best plc (see Unit 7) always attend a course on presentation skills. Chris Hands, the presentations skills coach, starts the course by showing some slides.

A Read the slides (a–d) and put them in the following order:

1 Introduction to presentations skills course
2 The beginning of a presentation
3 The middle of a presentation
4 The end of a presentation

Presentation Skills Course | **Good, better, BEST plc**

Make it memorable

- The last thing they hear may be the only thing people remember.
- Summarize your main points.
- Give people a "takeaway" in the form of an understandable handout.

a

Presentation Skills Course | **Good, better, BEST plc**

Guidance and simplicity

- Guide the audience through your argument step by step. Use clear signals to show that you're going to move on to the next point.
- Use graphics to illustrate and support your points.
- Use simple language but always keep in mind that there is nothing worse than "talking down" to an audience.

b

Presentation Skills Course	Good, better, BEST plc

Why give presentations?

To
- inform people.
- persuade people to do something.
- sell a product or service.
- train people.

Why do people attend presentations?

To
- get information.
- learn something useful.
- find new ideas.

How can I give good presentations?
This course will help you deliver the best presentations possible.

c

Presentation Skills Course	Good, better, BEST plc

Awaken interest as soon as possible

- Use an interesting visual element or a surprising fact to grab your audience's attention.
- Get your audience involved immediately by asking them for an answer to a thought-provoking question.
- Give the topic or objectives of your presentation. Remember to repeat this information at a later point.

d

B Work with a partner. Complete this handout together using words from the slides in exercise A.

Presentation Skills Course	Good, better, BEST plc

What makes a successful presentation?

The beginning is the most important part of the presentation so start with an …[1] opener. Build a relationship with the people you are talking to …[2] by asking them to respond to a question. Don't forget that your …[3] would like to know what you're going to talk about or what your …[4] are. Tell your audience what the structure of your presentation will be.

Once you've got started, …[5] your listeners logically through your presentation. Always use …[6] when you move on to the next point. Remember that a picture can be more useful than a spoken explanation so use …[7] where appropriate. Use the simplest …[8] you can without being patronising.

At the end of your presentation, it's vital that your listeners …[9] what you've told them so …[10] your message in short words. If you've used illustrations, pass them out as a …[11]. Make sure that your audience is aware that they've heard useful …[12] which they can put to good use immediately.

C Übertragen Sie den Inhalt des Texts „What makes a successful presentation?" ins Deutsche. Vermeiden Sie eine wortwörtliche Übersetzung, aber verfassen Sie ganze Sätze. KMK

4 Paul's presentation

WEBCODE **OMU0801**

Paul Müller is giving his first presentation to the other trainees at Best plc.

A In which order should he deliver the following stages of his presentation?

1. *answer questions from the audience*
2. *conclusion*
3. *deliver the main points of the presentation*
4. *give an outline of the presentation*
5. *give a summary of the presentation*
6. *greetings – say hello to the audience*
7. *introduce yourself*

12

B Listen to Paul's introduction and check the way he has organized his presentation. Say what he is going to do at the very end of his presentation.

C Listen again. Which of the words and phrases below does Paul use?

LANGUAGE

Language for presentations

This morning, I'm going to talk about …
Our topic today is …

I've divided the presentation into three main parts, as follows: …
First/Firstly, …; Second/Secondly, …
Next/Now, … ; After that / Then, …

Now I'd like to move on to …
The next topic I'm going to talk about is …

Before I finish my presentation, I'd just like to mention …
Finally / In conclusion / To conclude / In summary, …

5 Feedback on Leon's presentation

After every trainee has given his/her presentation, Chris invites the other trainees to give feedback. During this feedback session, the coach gives the trainees some tips. Leon Jahn has just finished his presentation.

13

A Hören Sie sich die Diskussion nach Leons Vortrag an und notieren Sie Tipps zu folgenden Themen: KMK

» *Körpersprache*
» *Stimme*
» *Vorbereitung/Struktur des Vortrags*
» *Grafiken und Unterlagen*

B Listen again and focus on the aspects above. Judging by the feedback, how many points do you think Chris and the students will award Leon for his presentation?
(1 point = needs improvement, 2 points = good, 3 points = very good)

GRAMMAR

Comparatives and superlatives

1 This projector is **easy** / **easier** / **(the) easiest** to use.
2 This statistic is **surprising** / **more surprising** / **(the) most surprising**.
3 This information is **less interesting** / **(the) least interesting**.
4 This screen is **as big as** the other one.
5 This laptop is **lighter than** / **more powerful than** the other one.
6 This presenter is **as tall as** me / **taller than** me.

- Alle einsilbigen und alle zweisilbigen Adjektive mit der Endung *-y*, *-er*, *-le*, *-on* oder *-ow* werden mit *-er*, *-est* gesteigert. (1) Die Endung *-y* wird zu *-i*, z. B. *easy* → *easier*.
- Die meisten zweisilbigen und alle Adjektive mit mehr als zwei Silben werden mit *more/most*, *less/least* gesteigert (2, 3).
- Ausnahmen: *good*, *better*, *best*; *bad*, *worse*, *worst*; *little* (wenig), *less*, *least*.
- Vergleicht man zwei gleiche Dinge miteinander, verwendet man *as … as* (4).
- Vergleicht man zwei Dinge, von denen eines größer, besser usw. ist als das andere, muss man …*(e)r* / *more … than* verwenden (5).
- Nach *as* und *than* stehen alleinstehende Personalpronomen in der Objektform (6).

6 Practice

Write a short description of someone in the room using comparatives and superlatives. Read out your description and ask your colleagues to guess who it is.

Example: *The person I have chosen is the same age as me but is taller than me. He/She always gets good marks and is one of the friendliest people in the class.*

7 Graphs

A Work with a partner and choose the most suitable graph for describing the growth in a company's turnover. Explain your choice to the class.

Presentation Skills Course | **Good, better, BEST plc**

Which type of graph should you use?

▪ simplicity more important than precision:	pie chart, bar chart
▪ precision more important than simplicity:	line graph
▪ comparing development/changes in one item over time:	line graph, bar chart
▪ comparing several items:	pie chart, bar chart

Remember – these are only general suggestions; every case is different.

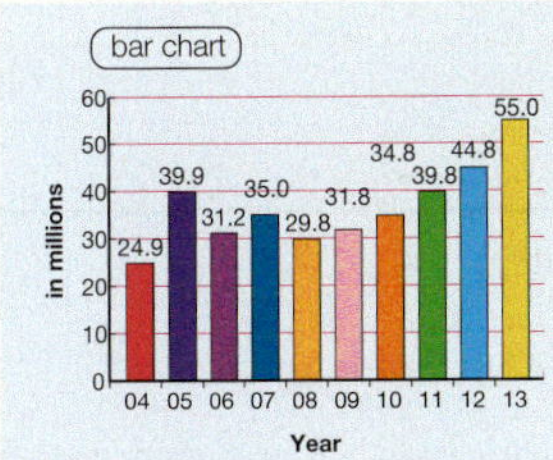

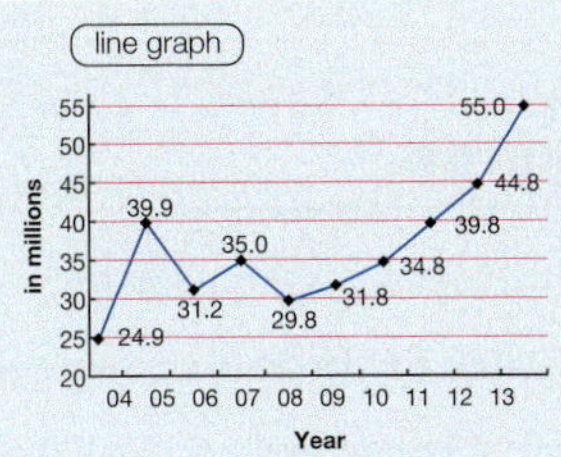

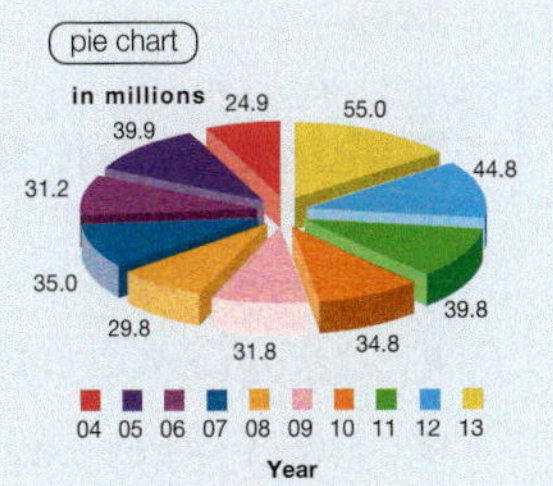

B Which type of graph would you use to illustrate the following statistics?

1. Currency exchange: euro-dollar rates over three years
2. Average income in the UK and Germany over five years
3. The contribution of five different products to a company's annual turnover
4. Two companies' costs for TV, radio, newspaper and Internet advertising for one year

8 Describing graphs

A Match the words/phrases (1–15) to the graphs (a–h). For some graphs, several expressions can be used.

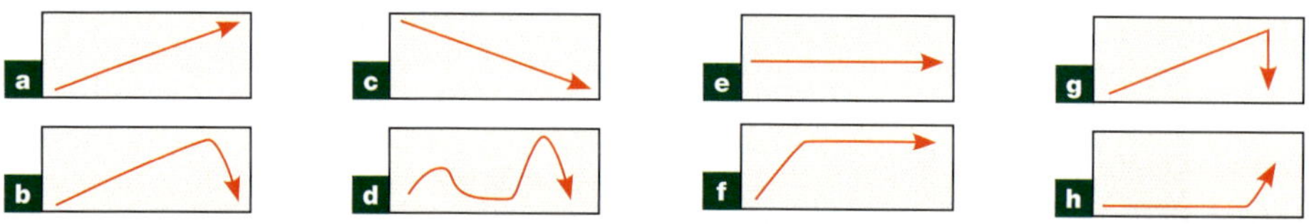

1. to remain constant / to stay the same
2. to shoot up / down
3. to go up / down
4. to increase / the increase
5. to hit a maximum / minimum
6. to flatten out / to level off
7. to decrease / the decrease
8. to drop / the drop
9. to rise / the rise
10. to fluctuate / the fluctuation
11. to fall / the fall
12. to climb / the climb
13. to recover / the recovery
14. to peak / the peak
15. to plunge / the plunge

B Work with a partner. You are each going to describe a line graph and ask your partner to draw it.

Partner A: Look at File 14 on page 123.
Partner B: Look at File 17 on page 124.

LANGUAGE

Describing graphs

The graph/chart shows …		
The horizontal/vertical axis The x axis / The y axis	represents …	
	is divided into … units/sections	each representing …
	has a scale from … to …	

9 Talking about figures

Chris Hands is using tables to describe some figures.

14

A Listen and decide which of the tables on page 75 is being presented.

B Work with a partner. Choose one of the tables on page 75 and describe the sales figures for Germany or Eastern Europe. Your partner should say which table you have described.

a

Sales of products in millions of euros				
Area	1st quarter	2nd quarter	3rd quarter	4th quarter
UK	10.3	11.4	8.2	10.5
Germany	8.9	9.3	8.6	7.1
Eastern Europe	0.2	0.8	1.7	3.6

b

Sales of products in millions of euros				
Area	1st quarter	2nd quarter	3rd quarter	4th quarter
UK	10.3	11.4	8.2	10.3
Germany	8.0	8.3	8.1	6.2
Eastern Europe	0.3	0.9	3.8	4.5

c

Sales of products in millions of euros				
Area	1st quarter	2nd quarter	3rd quarter	4th quarter
UK	10.3	11.4	8.2	10.7
Germany	8.2	7.4	8.0	9.5
Eastern Europe	0.5	1.6	2.3	2.3

10 The closing stages of a presentation

Johanna is going to give a presentation about training as an office management assistant. She has prepared the main part of her presentation and is now working on the closing stages. To help her, she has developed a flowchart and written sentences she would like to use.

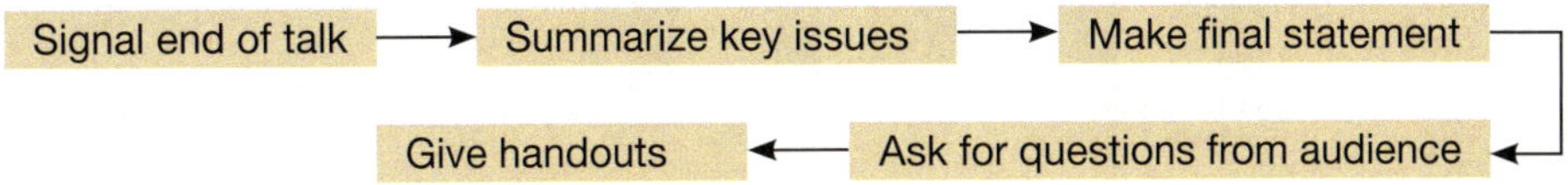

Match two of the sentences (1–10) to each stage of the close of Johanna's presentation.

1 Are there any questions?
2 Before I finish, I'd like to remind you of a few important facts and figures.
3 Finally, I'd like to say how important these issues are.
4 I'd like to go over the main points again.
5 I hope you'll find these copies of the graphics useful.
6 I'm now nearing the end of my talk.
7 I've prepared a few things for you to take away.
8 Last but not least, we have to remember that the practical experience we gain during our work placement is one of the most important aspects of training.
9 We have time for a few questions.
10 Well, that's the end of my presentation. Thank you for your attention.

11 Produktion

Verwenden Sie die Informationen der Tabelle und des Balkendiagramms[1], um Arbeitsstunden und Urlaubsregelungen in Deutschland, Frankreich, Großbritannien, Skandinavien und den USA zu vergleichen. Fassen Sie die Information für eine Präsentation stichpunktartig zusammen.

	Working hours per week	Working day[2]	Lunch break
Germany	41.1	07.30/08.30–16.00/17.30	30–45 mins 12.00–13.30
France	37.9	08.00–18.00	60 mins 12.00–14.00
GB	41.4	08.00/09.00–17.00/18.00	60 mins 12.00–14.00
Scandinavia	39.1	08.00–16.00	30 mins 11.30–12.00
USA	40+	08.00–17.00+	30 mins 12.00–13.00

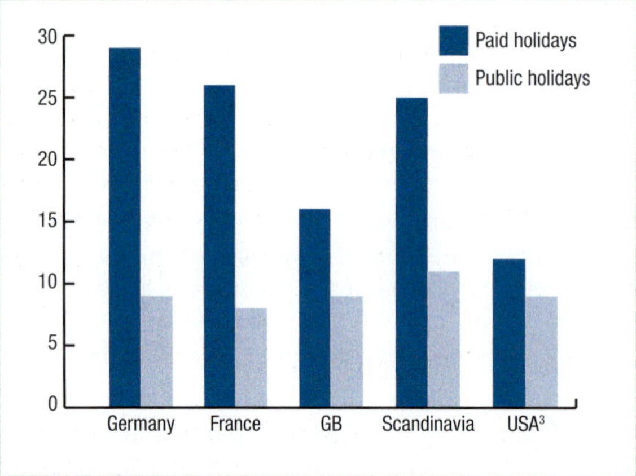

[1] Die Tabelle und das Diagramm enthalten lediglich Grunddaten.

[2] Arbeiter (*blue collar workers*) in manchen Länder beginnen/beenden ihre Arbeit eine Stunde früher als Angestellte (*white collar workers*).

[3] Nach zehn Jahren in derselben Firma nimmt die Anzahl der Urlaubstage schrittweise zu.

12 Produktion

Bereiten Sie eine kurze Präsentation über Ihre Firma vor. Schreiben Sie die Einleitung und das Schlusswort. Fertigen Sie alle benötigten Grafiken an.

CAN DO

After working through this unit I can ...	Check ...
▪ decide which equipment to use for a presentation.	Ex 2, page 70
▪ identify the parts of a presentation.	Ex 4, page 72
▪ make a list of tips for giving good presentations.	Ex 5, page 72
▪ choose suitable graphs for giving specific information.	Ex 7, page 73
▪ describe graphs and talk about figures.	Ex 8, page 74 Ex 9, page 74
▪ prepare a presentation.	Ex 10, page 75

How to give a successful presentation

You've been working on your presentation for a long time now and you think it's perfect. You're well-prepared; you've made your slides and checked your visuals. All you have to do now is walk into the room and give the presentation.
Stop! Is that really all you have to do? Have you thought about HOW you're going give the presentation? How you deliver your talk is just as important as the content.
Use these tips to give your most successful presentation ever.

First impressions count
Your audience will check out your clothes and the way you walk into the room and form an opinion of you before you even open your mouth.

TIP! Make sure that your appearance gives you a look of authority.

Dealing with nervousness
It's normal to be nervous. Even experienced speakers feel a bit nervous until they get started.
If possible, greet your audience as they arrive and chat with them. It's easier to give a presentation to people you "know" than to speak to strangers.

TIP! When you do start, speak slowly. After a few moments, you'll relax and gain confidence.

Audience rapport
Build a friendly relationship with your audience as soon as you start your presentation.

TIP! Establish eye contact with each member of your audience. Look at everyone in turn so that they feel that you're speaking to them directly.

Body language
If possible, avoid giving your presentation from a sitting position. Stand or walk slowly from side to side. If you do want to sit, try to sit on the edge of a desk. Always try to talk to your audience from a slightly higher position.

TIP! Try to keep your body still; don't wave your hands about while you talk. (Check out "Intercultural competence" below!)

Intercultural competence
Cultural differences may influence the way you give your presentation. Differences in body language can be important, for example, using your hands when presenting to an Italian audience will probably make your presentation come over as dynamic.

TIP! Use the Internet to check the cultural points you should be aware of.

Vary your voice
You can keep your audience interested in what you're saying by changing how you speak.
Start your presentation slowly, then speed up, then talk slowly again. Pause before you make an important point. Speak at normal volume, speak loudly, then speak quietly. Change your intonation; speak in a high tone or a low tone.

TIP! Never speak in a flat, monotonous voice when giving your presentation. If you do this, your audience might fall asleep!

13 Mediation

KMK

Lesen Sie den Artikel „How to give a successful presentation" und machen Sie sich Notizen auf Deutsch. Fassen Sie die wichtigsten Punkte für eine Kollegin auf Deutsch zusammen.

UNIT 9

Making and adjusting complaints

- writing letters of complaint
- complaining by telephone
- adjusting complaints

1 Warm-up

A **In groups, talk about why customers might complain.**

B **Write short sentences to describe the reasons for complaints illustrated above.**

Example: *There is a mistake in the invoice.*

> **TIP**
>
> **Reporting a delay in delivery**
>
> Most complaints about delays in delivery are made by fax or email. This ensures that the supplier looks into things as quickly as possible. Using fax or email also avoids the risk of correspondence crossing in the post.

2 A complaint from a new customer

KMK

World Medical GmbH, based in Ludwigsfelde, sells reconditioned medical equipment to companies all over the world. The company has good business relationships with its customers, but today a new customer sends a complaint.

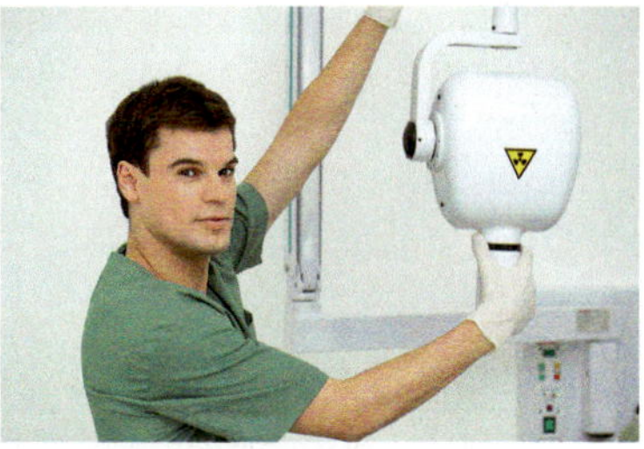

Read the fax below and answer these questions:

1 Who has written the complaint?
2 What has gone wrong?
3 What does the writer want the addressee to do?
4 Why does the writer want the addressee to do this?
5 How does the writer close his fax?

15/05/20.. Denta Dental 481 129 546 784

Denta Dental Clinic
ul. Nowogrodzka 12
00-513 Warsaw

Tel. +48 129 546 783
Fax. +48 129 546 784
Mobile +48 776 589 136

e-mail: info@denta.pl
website: www.denta.pl

Attention: World Medical, Melissa Wolf, Sales Department
Fax no. +49 3378 81 02 597

Dear Ms Wolf

Regarding our order number 942761 of 11 April for two reconditioned x-ray machines, the date of delivery was 7 May. To date, the machines have not been delivered.

Please look into the matter immediately and let us know when we can expect delivery.

We need the equipment urgently, so if you cannot deliver within the next week, we will have to look for another supplier.

As you know, this is a trial order. We feel sure you will understand that your handling of this matter will determine whether we will be able to place future orders with you.

Yours sincerely

Jerzy Adamczyk

Jerzy Adamczyk, Practice Manager

3 World Medical sends a complaint to their supplier

World Medical ships their orders in special containers made by Sheffield Metal plc, a company in England. World Medical is waiting for delivery of some containers so Melissa Wolf calls her colleague, Elisabeth Felix, in the Purchasing Department to find out what has happened.

The latest consignment of containers has not arrived, so Elisabeth Felix writes to Malcolm Ferguson at Sheffield Metal's Sales Department to complain about the delay in delivery. Elisabeth has dealt with Malcolm for several years.

Dear Malcolm

I'm sorry to inform you that Order No. 923/EF/04 for containers hasn't arrived yet. The order was sent almost one month ago, on 18 April, and delivery was promised by 3 May.

Could you please explain what has happened to the goods and let me know as soon as possible when we can expect the consignment?

As you realize, we can't fulfil our orders until we have your containers. I have heard from the Sales Department that we have, in fact, just received a complaint from a new customer who has been waiting for a delivery from us since 7 May.

We've been doing business with Sheffield Metals for over five years and we've had no cause for complaint up to now. You'll understand, however, that this current delay is causing us some problems.

Could you look into this and get back to me as soon as possible? Thanks for your help.

Best wishes
Elisabeth

Elisabeth Felix, Purchasing
World Medical GmbH

A Your colleague, whose English is not as good as yours, has written a summary of the email. Correct your colleague's statements below.

1 *Elisabeth Felix ordered containers from Sheffield Metal at the beginning of April.*
2 *The containers should have been delivered by the end of April.*
3 *World Medical GmbH does not need the containers urgently.*
4 *A new customer ordered some goods on 7 May.*
5 *World Medical and Sheffield Metals have just started to do business with each other.*
6 *This is not the first time that Elisabeth has sent a complaint to Sheffield Metals.*
7 *Elisabeth would like an explanation by the end of the week.*

B Erklären Sie der Kollegin / dem Kollegen die richtige Situation auf Deutsch. KMK

GRAMMAR

since, for **and *ago***

1 The consignment **has been** underway **for** ten days.
2 Elisabeth Felix **has been working** at World Medical **since** 2010.
3 World Medical first **bought** containers from Sheffield Metal five years **ago**.

- Man verwendet nicht die Gegenwartsform sondern das *present perfect*, wenn man sagen will, wie lange etwas schon dauert (1).
- Wenn eine Handlung in der Vergangenheit begonnen hat und bis in die Gegenwart andauert, verwendet man das *present perfect progressive* (2).
- *For* wird verwendet, um die Zeitspanne zu benennen (1).
- *Since* wird verwendet, um einen Zeitpunkt anzugeben (2).
- *Ago* wird verwendet, wenn etwas zu einem bestimmten Zeitpunkt in der Vergangenheit abgeschlossen wurde. Man verwendet immer das *simple past* mit *ago*. *Ago* steht immer am Ende der Zeitbestimmung (3).

4 Practice

A Complete these sentences with the correct form of the verb in the brackets. Then translate the sentences into German.

Example: *Elisabeth … (work) for World Medical for ten years.*
Elisabeth has worked / has been working for World Medical for ten years.
Elisabeth arbeitet seit zehn Jahren bei World Medical.

1 World Medical … (open) their factory 10 years ago.
2 The company … (have) their premises on the Brandenburg Park industrial estate since the company was founded.
3 Elisabeth … (be) in the Purchasing Department for six years.
4 Melissa … (deal with) three urgent orders since she started work this morning.
5 The Logistics Centre … (dispatch) the containers two days ago.
6 How long … (Mr Adamczyk / wait) for his equipment?
7 Malcolm … (send) a letter of apology to Elisabeth one hour ago.
8 How long … (Malcolm and Elisabeth / talk) on the phone?

! We ordered the goods **ten days ago.**
= *vor zehn Tagen* (NOT: ~~for ten days~~)

B Complete the sentences with *since, for, How long … ?* or *ago*. Then translate the sentences into German.

1 … has Elisabeth been at World Medical? – … she left vocational college.
2 She has known Malcolm … five years.
3 Malcolm has been in the Sales Department at Sheffield Metals … he was 27.
4 Malcolm did a German course two years … .
5 Elisabeth has had her own office … last Christmas.
6 Malcolm moved into an open plan office six months … .
7 Denta Dental Clinic has been waiting for the x-ray machines … a week.
8 … has the consignment been underway? – … 13 May.
9 Melissa joined the company three years … .

TIP

Complaints

Always give the details of the order number and (expected) date of delivery first, then continue with your complaint as follows:

1 Explain the situation – describe what is wrong;
2 Make a request – say what you would like the addressee to do;
3 Give a reason – explain why you would like the addressee to do this;
4 Close with a polite ending – thank the addressee for his/her help.

LANGUAGE

Making complaints

With reference to We refer to	our order number …	which arrived on … (date), … which was due on … (date), …
I'm sorry to have to inform you that …		

Situation

When we opened the	containers boxes	we	discovered saw	that …
… some of the … all of the	goods/items/parts	were	broken. missing.	
… the	bottle(s)/cask(s) container(s)/tin(s)	was were	damaged. leaking	
The goods The containers	may have been	dropped roughly handled	in transit.	
It seems that the	goods were not packed properly. packing was unsuitable.			
While testing the equipment	we saw that it was not working properly. it became apparent that it was not up to standard.			

Request

Please	investigate the matter find a solution to this problem let us know what can be done to solve this problem	as soon as possible.
Could you please explain (why) … ?		

Reason

We have a large order from a regular customer, which we have to fill quickly.
We are unable to continue production until we have the equipment.
If we do not receive the goods within the next … days, we will have to stop production.

Polite ending

We hope to receive We look forward to receiving	your answer an explanation	immediately. without delay. by … (date).
We would add that We must point out that	any further business with your company … our further business relationship …	
… will depend on how this matter is settled.		

5 Writing a formal complaint

You work for Der Verlag, Gaußstr. 223, 10589 Berlin. A delivery of recycled cardboard boxes from a Finnish supplier, FinBox, Pakkasraitti 173, FI-04360 Tuusula, Finland is overdue. You need the boxes urgently as you have to ship a big order of books to Africa. Your boss has asked you to write a letter to FinBox asking about the delay and to fax it to them straight away.

Use the details below to write your complaint to Mr Sami Virtanen, Head of Sales, FinBox.

- today's date, 6 June
- order no. BV 3877, sent 18 May
- delivery due within two weeks of date of order

6 Malcolm replies to Elisabeth's email

As soon as he received her email, Malcolm Ferguson phoned Elisabeth Felix to apologize for the delay. Later, Malcolm sent Elisabeth an email for her records.

A Read the email, then do the following tasks.

1. Describe the problem which led to the delay.
2. Say what the current state of the order is.
3. Explain what Sheffield Metals has done to ensure that the goods arrive as soon as possible.

Dear Elisabeth

I refer to your complaint of 12 May regarding order no. 923/EF/04.

We are sorry for the delay in delivery of the goods. As I explained in our phone call this morning, this was caused by late delivery of materials from one of our business partners.

I have checked and am pleased to be able to tell you that your order was dispatched two days ago. Logistics will send you an advice of dispatch by email today.

We have sent the consignment by rail this time so that transport is not interrupted by the week-end. The containers should arrive in Ludwigsfelde on Monday, 23 May.

We hope that the goods arrive safely and apologize once again for the delay.

Regards
Malcolm

B Read the email again and find the English equivalents of these German words and sentences.

1. Verspätung
2. Lieferung
3. Ihre Ware wurde vor zwei Tagen abgeschickt.
4. Versandmitteilung
5. Sendung
6. Wir hoffen, dass die Ware gut ankommt.

7 Dealing with the complaint from Denta Dental Clinic

As soon as she knows that the containers are on their way, Elisabeth gets in touch with Jerzy Adamczyk at Denta Dental Clinic.

Complete her email using words and phrases from Malcolm Fergusons's email (exercise 6, page 83).

From: Signature:

Dear Mr Adamczyk

Your …[1] about your order number 942761 of 11 April has been passed on to me.

We are sorry that you have not yet received this order. This was caused by a … … …[2] of containers from one of our … …[3].

I am pleased to be able to tell you that your order will be …[4] within the next few days.

Our Logistics Centre will send you an … … …[5] by email as soon as the …[6] is on its way.

I am sure that the …[7] will arrive safely and will be to your satisfaction.

Once again, I …[8] for the delay.

Yours sincerely

Elisabeth Felix, Purchasing

> **TIP**
>
> ### A reply to a complaint
>
> A reply to a complaint usually has four parts as follows:
>
> 1 Polite opening – acknowledge the complaint and apologize;
> 2 Reason – explain what has gone wrong;
> 3 Action taken – say what you have done to sort out the problem;
> 4 Polite ending – apologize again and close with a friendly phrase.

8 Writing a reply to a complaint

WEBCODE **OMU0901**

You are Sami Virtanen, Head of Sales at FinBox, Pakkasraitti 173, FI-04360 Tuusula.

Use the details below to write a reply to the complaint from Der Verlag, Gaußstr. 223, 10589 Berlin (exercise 5, page 83).

- today's date, 7 June
- order no. BV 3877, dispatched from FinBox factory on 30 May by road
- the delivery was then sent from Malmö (Sweden) by ship and was due to arrive four days later in Berlin by road via Travemünde
- you have contacted the transport company
- due to bad weather in the Baltic Sea, the ship could not dock at Travemünde and was diverted to Rostock
- delivery later today or by tomorrow morning at the latest

LANGUAGE

Adjusting complaints

Polite opening

We are very sorry	that to hear that to learn that	the goods arrived damaged/broken/late.		
		you have received	faulty damaged the wrong	goods.

Please accept our sincere apologies	for the inconvenience caused.
We apologize	

Reason

Unfortunately, We are sorry to say that	there was a mix-up in our sales department.
	one of our staff was ill and could not complete the order.

We have found out that the damage was caused by	bad handling in transit.
	a problem with the packing.

Our goods were damaged/lost	in transit.	
	because of	extreme weather conditions.
		an accident.

We have had	some software problems problems with new software	but these have now been solved.

Action taken

We have sent a replacement consignment	which you will receive by … at the latest.
	by courier. by express delivery.

Polite ending

We hope that we can continue our successful business relationship, despite this problem.

We assure you that we will make every effort to ensure there are no problems in the future.

9 Jerzy Adamczyk phones World Medical

The x-ray machines have arrived at Denta Dental Clinic in poor condition. Jerzy Adamczyk phones World Medical to complain. Melissa Wolf, who answers the phone is not very polite.

15

A **Listen to the phone call. Note the things that Melissa does wrong and decide how you would improve them.**

16

B **Now listen to how Melissa should have dealt with the phone call with Jerzy Adamczyk. Which (if any) of your improvements does she make?**

TIP

Writing a memorandum (memo)

A memo is an official note sent from one person to another within the same company. A memo is less formal and shorter than a letter; the information should be brief, but it should also be accurate. State the purpose of your memo clearly at the beginning. Many organizations use pre-printed memo forms.

10 Writing a memo

Copy and complete Melissa's memo to Mia Richter using the words from the box.

complain • complaint • damaged • dented • disappointed • discuss • scratched • trial

An: *Mia Richter*	Von: *Melissa Wolf*	Datum: *19/05*	Betreff: *Telephone ...*[1]
Caller: *Jerzy Adamczyk, Denta Dental Clinic, Warsaw*			Order number: *942761*

Message:

X-ray machines arrived ...[2]
- the glass on one of the machines is ...[3]
- the metal casing on the other machine is ...[4]
The customer is ...[5]*. This is a ...*[6] *order and he had to ...*[7] *about a delay in delivery last week.*
Mr Adamczyk would like you to call him tomorrow at home to ...[8] *the problem. His number is 00481 129 546 993.*
MW

11 Complaining by telephone

KMK

Arbeiten Sie mit einem Partner / einer Partnerin. Führen Sie ein möglichst freies Telefongespräch auf Englisch mit Hilfe dieser Angaben.

Partner A: Machen Sie sich zuerst Notizen:

- Name Ihrer Firma; Auftragsnummer; Liefertermin
- Grund der Beschwerde (falsche Lieferung, Lieferverzögerung, usw.)
- Ziel des Gespräches

Partner B: Nehmen Sie den Anruf an. Nennen Sie Ihren Namen und den Namen Ihrer Firma.

Partner A: Nennen auch Sie Ihren Namen und den Namen Ihrer Firma. Sagen Sie Partner B, dass es ein Problem mit der Lieferung gibt. Erklären Sie das Problem.

Partner B: Reagieren Sie höflich und gehen Sie auf das Anliegen von Partner A ein.

Partner A: Falls Sie mit der Antwort von Partner B zufrieden sind, bedanken und verabschieden Sie sich. Falls nicht, setzen Sie den Anruf fort.

Partner B: Reagieren Sie angemessen auf Partner A.

12 Interaktion

Die britische Firma Gold plc mit Sitz in Bristol stellt Tische mit Glasplatten her (*glass-topped tables*). Es gibt ein Problem mit einer Lieferung, die heute Morgen bei der Londoner Casting-Agentur Cool Casting angekommen ist. Heute ist Donnerstag, der 26. Mai.

Arbeiten Sie mit einem Partner / einer Partnerin.

Partner A: Sie arbeiten für Cool Casting. Schauen Sie sich Ihre Rollenkarte unten an und machen Sie sich Notizen, bevor Sie Partner B anrufen.

Partner B: Sie arbeiten bei Gold plc in der Verkaufsabteilung. Schauen Sie sich Ihre Rollenkarte an (File 3, Seite 118). Machen Sie sich mit den Details vertraut, während Sie auf den Anruf von Partner A warten.

Partner A:

- Begrüßen Sie Partner B und stellen Sie sich mit Ihrem eigenen Namen vor.
- Details: Bestellung Nr. 35487 für zwei Tische mit Glasplatten, Katalognummer GTT 09; Bestelldatum: 20. Mai
- Grund der Beschwerde: Die Tische kamen heute Morgen an. Beim Auspacken der Kartons sahen Sie, dass die Glasplatte eines Tisches stark zerkratzt war.
- Teilen Sie mit, dass Sie bis spätestens morgen Nachmittag Ersatz brauchen; es soll eine Premierenparty stattfinden, bei der die Tische für das Büffet benötigt werden.
- Hören Sie Partner B gut zu.
- Akzeptieren Sie den Lösungsvorschlag.
- Beenden Sie den Anruf und bedanken Sie sich dabei für die angebotene Hilfe.

13 Produktion

Sie arbeiten für Gold plc. Heute nahmen Sie die telefonische Kundenbeschwerde der Cool Casting Agency an. Die Leiterin der Verkaufsabteilung, Julie Wilson, will über alle Beschwerden informiert werden.

Verfassen Sie ein entsprechendes Memo für Julie Wilson in englischer Sprache, in dem Sie sie über den Anruf und Ihre Vorgehensweise informieren.

CAN DO	After working through this unit I can ...	Check ...
	understand a formal written complaint.	Ex 2, page 79
	understand a semi-formal complaint.	Ex 3, page 80
	write a formal complaint.	Ex 5, page 83
	explain what has been done to adjust a complaint.	Ex 6, page 83
	write a reply to a complaint.	Ex 8, page 84
	write a memo describing a complaint made by phone.	Ex 10, page 86
	make a complaint / deal with a complaint on the phone	Ex 11, page 86
		Ex 12, page 87

Golden rules for telephoning

- Be proactive. You must put something into every telephone call to get things started and to keep the conversation going. Anticipate questions. Don't answer questions with just one or two words. Offer information ('I'm sorry but our computers are not working properly.') or help ('How can I help you?' or 'Let's see what we can do.').

- Be sympathetic. If the caller is angry, show that you understand his/her feelings. Say, 'I understand how you feel.' or, 'I'm sorry to hear that.'

- Treat the caller as an individual, not as a 'customer number'. Write down the caller's name as soon as he/she gives it to you. If you don't understand, ask the caller to repeat or spell the name. Use the name once or twice during the phone call. At the end of the call, thank the caller using his/her name.

- Be friendly and interested. Be polite. If appropriate, make small talk.

- Smile. There is only one body language signal available to us on the phone. Use it to create a positive, helpful atmosphere.

14 Mediation KMK

Lesen Sie die „Golden rules for telephoning" und machen Sie sich Notizen. Fassen Sie die „Golden rules" auf Deutsch zusammen.

Dealing with delays in payment

- writing reminders
- replying to reminders
- understanding credit enquiries

1 Warm up

A **Describe the illustrations.**

B **Work in groups. Talk about why some companies do not settle their bills. What steps can a supplier take when payment is late?**

> **TIP**
>
> **Delays in payment**
>
> If a customer is late in paying a bill, a supplier will send out a reminder. The laws regarding reminders vary from country to country. In the UK, reminders are sent out in three stages as first reminders, second reminders and final demands. Second reminders and final demands are usually sent by registered post.

2 Two written reminders

Carter & Welsh is a manufacturer of calendars and diaries based in London. Evelyn Allan, who works in the accounts department, has sent out two written reminders to Forbes Office Services, a company which has not settled an account.

A Read the two reminders on this page and on page 91 then answer these questions.

1. When was the original invoice sent? When did the original period for payment run out?
2. When was the first reminder sent? How long does Forbes Office Services now have to settle the bill?
3. What possible reason for non-payment does Ms Allan suggest? What practical step does she take to solve the problem?
4. In the second reminder, Ms Allan indicates that Carter & Welsh have carried out their part of the transaction correctly. How does she know this?
5. What do we learn about the relationship to date with Forbes Office Services?
6. What is the last date for payment now?

Forbes Office Services
Tower Offices
272 Hagley Road
Birmingham B16 8LB

6 June 20..

Dear Mr Forbes

Our invoice no. CW309

We refer to our invoice of 1 May. According to our terms, payment is due within 30 days at the latest. We are sorry to note, however, that payment is overdue.

Please let us have advice of payment or an explanation within the next ten days.

It may well be that our invoice has been mislaid so, for your convenience, we are enclosing a copy of the original invoice.

If our invoice has been paid in the meantime, we would like to thank you and ask you to ignore this reminder.

Yours sincerely

Evelyn Allan

Evelyn Allan
Accounts Department

Encl. invoice no. CW3099

1

We refer to our letter of 6 June.

Although you have received the above-mentioned reminder requesting payment of the outstanding balance of £15,000, we have heard nothing from you.

The order was carried out promptly and delivered to you by the agreed date. As there has been no complaint about the consignment, we assume that you were satisfied with the goods.

Since payment has never been delayed before, we can only think that non-payment of our invoice is due to an error. If there is a problem, please let us know. Otherwise we must ask you to arrange for payment of the invoice by 2 July at the latest.

2

B Find the English equivalents of these German words and sentences in the two reminders.

1. Rechnung
2. Die Zahlung ist innerhalb von spätestens 30 Tagen fällig.
3. Mahnung
4. ausstehender Saldo
5. Die Zahlung wurde bisher noch nie verzögert.
6. Veranlassen Sie bitte die Bezahlung der Rechnung bis spätestens … .

GRAMMAR

Passives

1. The account **has been settled**.
2. Earlier, our reminders **were sent** by post; today they **are sent** by email; in a few years they **will be sent** by an automatic computer program.
3. The bill **must/should be paid** next week.
4. The lost invoice **has been found** (by the person who lost it).
5. The sum of €6,000 **was transferred** by our accounts department this morning.

- Das Passiv wird häufig verwendet, wenn man auf eher unpersönliche Art und Weise über Fakten, Vorgänge und Zahlen berichtet (1).
- Das Passiv wird mit der entsprechenden Form von *be* + Partizip Perfekt (3. Form des Verbs) gebildet. Wie im Aktiv können alle Zeitformen gebildet werden (2).
- Das Passiv kann mit einem Modalverb + *be* + Partizip Perfekt gebildet werden (3).
- Durch den Gebrauch des Passivs wird die Tätigkeit hervorgehoben. Da die beschriebene Handlung wichtiger ist als die Person/Sache, die sie ausführt, kann der/die Handelnde oft weggelassen werden (4).
- Soll der Handelnde genannt werden, benutzt man das Wort *by* = von, durch (5).

3 Practice

Make these sentences passive. Use *by* only if it is necessary.

1. Mr Forbes has not yet settled the account.
2. They received the final demand last week.
3. The solicitor has contacted the company.
4. They transferred the money this morning.
5. The company director sent an apology.
6. Has anyone explained the new accounting software?
7. The accountant will send the next reminder on 15 May.
8. They have paid the bill.

4 Writing a first (hidden) reminder and a second reminder

You work in the accounts department at Connelly's Computer Hardware, 35 Minster Lane, York YO1 7JN. Your customer, Maybury plc, 56 Fallow Road, Sheffield S20 DN13 has not paid the invoice below. As your price list has recently been updated, you can send a copy of this with your reminder.

A Today's date is 1 July 20.. . Write a first (hidden) reminder to John Smith, Purchasing Assistant, at Maybury plc and ask for payment within the next ten days. Begin your letter with reference to the updated pricelist.

Invoice

Order No. 870076 Our ref. SL 445

Date: 25 May 20..

Quantity	Item	Price	Amount
50	modems	@ £ 200	£ 10,000
50	adapters	@ £ 220	£ 11,000
		Invoice total	£ 21,000

Less 5% discount £1,050

Total £19,950

Terms: 5% discount for payment within 2 weeks.
Thereafter net.
Payment within 30 days of date on invoice.

B Today's date is 13 July 20.. . You have heard nothing from Maybury plc. Write a second reminder and send it by registered post. Allow a further 14 days and insist on payment by 26 July at the latest.

TIP

Reminders

First (hidden) reminder
Be polite and friendly. Always include a copy of the invoice in case the customer has lost it. Some first reminder letters are referred to as "hidden reminder letters" as they often advertise a special sale or an updated version of some product or service as an excuse to be able to say at the end of the letter: *By the way, our accounts department has informed us that our invoice no. … of … has not been settled yet.*

Second reminder
Be polite and firm. For legal reasons, give a "pay by" date. Use registered post.

Third or final reminder
Remain polite but keep it short. Refer to all previous correspondence. Say you will take legal action if the account is not settled within a week. Use registered post.

LANGUAGE

Writing reminders

First reminders
We are writing in connection with the above-mentioned invoice/statement.
This is to inform you that our invoice for ... (sum) is overdue.
We are sure this must be an oversight and have included a copy of the invoice for your convenience.
If your payment of our invoice has crossed with this letter, we kindly ask you to ignore this reminder.

Second reminders
We refer to our previous letter of ... (date) with regard to the above-mentioned invoice.
Could you please inform us why you have not reacted to our first reminder of ... (date)?
We have not received any reply from you so far.
We must point out that this is our second letter to you.
Payment is now ... (length of time) overdue.

Third or final reminders
Although two previous requests have been made to you for settlement of the overdue account/balance, no remittance has been received.
We must ask for payment by ... (date).
We must insist that you settle the invoice within ... (number of days) at the latest.
If we do not receive payment by ... (date) we will have to start legal proceedings.

5 Mr Forbes replies to Carter & Welsh

A few days after Evelyn Allan sends the second reminder to James Forbes at Forbes Office Services (exercise 2, page 91), she receives the letter below.

A Talk in groups. Why has James Forbes taken so long to reply? Why has Forbes Office Services not paid the account? What does James Forbes suggest? Why is it likely that Carter & Welsh will agree to the suggestion? Make notes.

Your invoice of 1 May 20.. and letters of 6 June and 20 June 20..

We are extremely sorry that we have not written to you before about the above-mentioned invoice. We thought we would have been able to settle payment in the meantime but, as one of our major customers has not yet paid his debts to us, we are having temporary cash flow problems.

Because of this, we cannot possibly remit payment of your invoice in full immediately. We hope, therefore, that you will agree to accept payment in three, monthly instalments of £5,000 each.

In view of our long business relationship with Carter & Welsh and our good payment record to date, we hope that you will agree to this suggestion.

We apologize once again for our delay in payment which is due to these difficult circumstances.

Yours sincerely

B Fassen Sie den Inhalt des Briefes kurz auf Deutsch zusammen. KMK

TIP

Replies to reminders

After you have given details of the order number and referred to the reminder letter, continue as follows:

1 apologize;
2 explain the situation – say why you have not paid;
3 make a suggestion – say how you propose to deal with the matter;
4 express hope that your suggestion will be accepted;
5 apologize once more;
6 close politely.

LANGUAGE

Writing replies to reminders

Apology

We are sorry that we have not responded to your letters until now.		
We would like to apologize Please accept our apologies	for the delay in settling	your invoice. our account with you.

Explanation

We have not paid Payment will be late	because … (reason).
Payment has been withheld because	the wrong goods were delivered. we were given the wrong bank account number.

Suggestion

We promise to pay … (amount) by … (date). Please allow us a further … (number of days/weeks) to pay. We would like to pay in … (number) instalments.	
We (sincerely) hope that you will	allow us this extra time. grant us this concession.

Close

Once again, we/I	would like to say that we are / I am sorry about this delay. offer you our/my sincerest apologies.
We hope that, despite this problem, we can continue our successful business relationship. We will make every effort to ensure there are no problems in future.	

6 Writing a reply to a reminder

KMK

Ihre Firma hat eine Mahnung (siehe Seite 95) von Ihrem Lieferanten Patrick Thompson in Edinburgh erhalten. Ihre Vorgesetzte hat Sie gebeten, eine Antwort auf Englisch zu entwerfen.

Schreiben Sie den Brief unter Verwendung ihrer Notizen.

– um Entschuldigung bitten
– Rechner kaputt; kein Zugang (access) zu Daten
– Rechnung wird innerhalb 8 Tagen bezahlt
– Vorfall wird sich nicht wiederholen

Patrick Thompson
27 North Bridge
Edinburgh EH1 1QN

15 July 20..

Dear Sir/Madam

OUR INVOICE NO. PT 76392 OF 28 MAY 20..

We are sure you have overlooked the above-mentioned invoice.

As stated in our Terms and Conditions of Payment, all invoices are payable within 28 days of receipt of goods.

As payment is now more than two weeks overdue, we would be grateful if you could arrange for the outstanding amount to be paid within the next few days.

Yours faithfully
C Todd
Caitlin Todd
Accounts Department

7 A third or final reminder

WEBCODE **OMU1001**

Carter & Welsh have a problem with a new customer. Unlike Mr Forbes, this customer has not replied to any reminders so far. A trainee has drafted another reminder but Evelyn Allan thinks it is too friendly.

Read the draft below and replace the underlined words and phrases with more formal ones from the box.

7 September at the latest • contacted you • disturbed at having to write to you • faithfully • ignored • of 2 and 24 August • settle the account • Sirs • the matter will be placed in the hands of a collection agency • unpaid

Registered mail

Dear <u>Mr Brown</u>

Our invoice no. CW3104; reminders <u>sent last month</u>

We are <u>sorry to have to get in touch with you</u> again about our <u>outstanding</u> invoice. We have <u>written</u> twice but you have <u>not answered</u> our letters.

Please <u>pay the bill</u> by <u>the end of next week</u> otherwise <u>we might have to take further steps</u>.

Yours <u>sincerely</u>

8 Produktion

Sie arbeiten bei der Computerfirma Katz und Maus, Klarastr. 42, 79106 Freiburg. Seit 30. Mai warten Sie vergeblich auf die Bezahlung einer Rechnung für einen Probeauftrag (Rechnung Nr. GG 4873) der Firma Anderson plc, 38 Lothian Road, Edinburgh, EH3 9DD. Am 12. Juni schickten Sie eine erste Mahnung. Heute, am 14. Juli, bittet Ihr Chef Sie, eine zweite Mahnung zu entwerfen.

Schreiben Sie die erste und die zweite Mahnung an die Firma Anderson plc.

9 Produktion

Sie arbeiten bei der Firma Müller in Berlin. Gestern erhielten Sie eine dritte Mahnung von Ihrem Lieferanten aus London. Ihr Chef hat Sie gebeten, eine Antwort zu entwerfen.

Schreiben Sie an Peterson & Patterson, 212 Archway Road, London N6 5AX. Orientieren Sie sich an folgenden Stichpunkten:

- Datum: 4 Juli
- Rechnung-Nr.: 37893
- Äußern Sie Ihr Bedauern, dass Sie bis jetzt nicht auf die vorherige Mahnungen reagiert haben und entschuldigen Sie sich für die Verzögerung der Rechnungsbegleichung.
- Teilen Sie mit, dass Sie mit der Zahlung im Verzug sind, weil einer Ihrer Hauptkunden seine Schulden nicht bezahlt hat.
- Erbitten Sie zwei weitere Wochen für die Zahlung.

10 Rezeption – Leseverstehen

In order to find out about a new customer, a company can write to a bank, a businessperson or a chamber of commerce and industry and ask for background information. Enquirers usually guarantee that any information given to them will be treated confidentially.

Fender and Gibson plc has received an order from a new customer, who has supplied the names and addresses of three companies as sources of reference. Martin Gibson has written to them.

Read Martin Gibson's credit enquiry letter on page 97 and answer these questions.

1. How does he avoid mentioning the name of the firm in the letter?
2. Why do you think he does this?
3. What would he like to know about the firm?
4. What does he offer the addressee in return for his help?

CAN DO

After working through this unit I can ...	Check ...
▪ identify specific details in both a first and a second reminder.	Ex 2, page 90
▪ write a first (hidden) reminder and a second reminder.	Ex 4, page 92 Ex 8, page 96
▪ understand a reply to a reminder; explain contents in German.	Ex 5, page 93
▪ write a reply to a reminder.	Ex 6, page 94 Ex 9, page 96
▪ use appropriate language in a third or final reminder.	Ex 7, page 95

11 A credit enquiry

Dear Sirs

The company named on the enclosed slip has placed a trial order with us for £18,500 and has given your name as a reference.

As we have not done business with this firm before, we would be pleased if you would give us some information regarding their financial standing. We would also like to know if the company enjoys a good reputation.

We assure you that any information given will remain confidential and without any liability on your part.

Please let us know if we can offer you assistance of a similar nature in the future.

Yours faithfully

Read the following three replies carefully. How much is each writer willing to support the new customer? Use examples of vocabulary to support your answers.

Dear Sir

In your letter of 25 March, 20.. you ask us for information about the firm referred to on the enclosed slip of paper.

We are astonished that this firm has given you our name as a reference. We are currently trying to collect payment on two outstanding invoices which have been overdue since the end of last year.

The firm has actually been known to us for several years, and enjoyed a good reputation in the past. However, since the firm's founder retired last year and the running of the company was put into the hands of his three sons, the company no longer appears to be interested in meeting its obligations.

We are sorry to have to give you this information. We would like to remind you that it should be treated confidentially.

Yours faithfully **1**

Dear Mr Gibson

Thank you for your letter of 25 March, 20.. .

We have been doing business with the company you are interested in since it was founded twenty years ago. We have executed hundreds of their orders to date and they have always met their obligations punctually.

All three partners enjoy an excellent reputation in the trade.

We would have no hesitation in recommending them as prospective customers.

Please treat this information in the strictest confidence. It is given without liability on our part.

Yours sincerely **2**

Dear Sir

In your letter of 25 March, 20.. you ask for information about the firm mentioned on the enclosed slip.

We are rather surprised that the firm has given our address as a reference. We executed a small order, totalling £600, at the beginning of the year. Since then, however, no further orders have been placed.

We feel, therefore, that we are in no position to judge the situation of the firm in question.

We regret not being able to assist you.

Yours faithfully **3**

UNIT 11

Attending a trade fair

- making enquiries about trade fairs
- making travel arrangements
- changing travel arrangements

1 Warm-up

A **Which fairs are announced on the website? Which industries are they for?**

B **What other trade fairs do you know? Which of them (if any) have you attended?**

2 Details about a trade fair

Oliver Wilke is doing his work placement in the marketing department of Wind Works, a Scottish company that manufactures wind generators. The head of marketing, Fiona Pirie, has asked Oliver for information on Offshore Wind Power – Boston.

A **Lesen Sie die Webseite auf Seite 99 und notieren Sie folgende Informationen:** KMK

1. Dauer der Messe
2. Zielgruppe der Messe
3. Vorteile für Aussteller
4. Anmeldung und Reservierung der Stände
5. wie man für die eigene Firma bei der Messe Werbung machen kann
6. Kontaktperson für weitere Informationen

Mozilla Firefox

TRADEFAIRSNOW

http://www.tradefairsnow.com/OffshoreWindPower_Boston_html

Google

Facebook | Meistbesuchte… | Erste Schritte | Aktuelle Nachr… | Lesezeichen

Offshore Wind Power – Boston

Venue: Boston Hyatt Regency, Boston, Massachusetts, United States of America
Date: 07 Feb 20.. to 08 Feb 20..

Event profile

Offshore Wind Power – Boston is a two-day exhibition aimed at decision-makers and professionals from the offshore wind industry. This leading event is organized by Green Power Conferences.

Exhibitor profile

Exhibitors include:
- manufacturers of wind turbines, components and equipment;
- engineering companies and consultants;
- power utilities and power dealers;
- research and development organizations. Exhibitor registration

Visitor profile

The fair is of interest to:
- private investors and operating companies;
- wholesale traders;
- banks and insurance companies;
- government representatives;
- educators and the media. Visitor registration

The benefits of exhibiting

By participating in Offshore Wind Power – Boston you bring your company to the attention of leading decision-makers from all over the world.

Registration

Your exhibition stand is a showcase for your company.

Book your exhibition stand

Publicity and promotion

Your company, products and services will be featured in articles in trade publications world-wide.Your company profile will appear online before, during and after the event.

Send your press releases to our PR office

Need more information, for example on quotations, facilities or fixtures and fittings?
Contact Sean.Malone@greenpower.com

B Match the words and phrases from the box to the definitions.

exhibition stand • exhibitor • facilities • fixtures and fittings • press releases • quotations • trade publications

1 magazines and newspapers aimed at professionals in the sector
2 information about a company provided by the company itself
3 the place where products are shown at a trade fair
4 statements saying how much something will cost
5 services, equipment, etc. provided for a particular purpose
6 a firm which presents itself at a fair
7 lighting, electrical sockets, floor coverings, etc.

C Sie arbeiten für eine mittelständische deutsche Firma, die sich mit der Umwelttechnologie beschäftigt. Ein Kollege möchte mehr über die Handelsmesse „Offshore Wind Power – Boston" wissen. Fassen Sie die wichtigsten Details für ihn auf Deutsch zusammen. KMK

3 A well-planned exhibition stand

Oliver looks at the webpage to find some advice about organizing a stand.

A Read the advice and complete the text with words from the box.

display racks • free gifts • information counter • logo • office • presentation board • reception area • seating area

Mozilla Firefox
TRADEFAIRSNOW
http://www.tradefairsnow.com/stand
Facebook   Meistbesuchte…   Erste Schritte   Aktuelle Nachr…   Lesezeichen

Your exhibition stand

Visitors approaching your stand should be immediately aware of who you are and what you are offering, so be sure your company name and … …[1] are in full view.

Place a free-standing … …[2] with pictures showing how clients can benefit by using your services at the back of your stand.

Make sure that people feel welcome on your stand. Have an attractive … …[3] which encourages people to come in. Keep in mind that it's tiring walking around a fair so a comfortable … …[4] where people can relax is always a good idea. Place some company literature in … …[5] nearby and offer coffee or other drinks so that your visitors feel at home. An … …[6], manned by a friendly member of staff, and some attractive … …[7] which people can take away with them will leave a good impression with visitors.

Last but not least, a small … …[8] is always useful. Use it for talks with important visitors or simply as a place where your staff can relax away from the bustle of the fair.

B **Look at the example of an exhibition stand shown on the website. Use words from the box in exercise A to describe the stand.**

C **Work in a group. You work for a company that is going to participate in a trade fair. Brainstorm some ideas about your company (name of company, sector, size of company, etc.) then decide on a trade fair where your company might exhibit. After that, plan your exhibition area and design your company's stand.**

LANGUAGE

Making enquiries about trade fairs and conference facilities

Source of address (if necessary)

We have seen your advertisement	on the … (name of website). in … (name of publication.)

Reason for enquiry

We are looking for	a trade fair an exhibition	where we can	present launch	our	company. products.
	conference facilities	large enough to accommodate with enough room for			20 people.

Request for quotation

Please	quote us prices for let us have your quotation for	… (details). the following: … (details).

General requirements

We would need	an exhibition area a stand/space	measuring … (size). equipped with … (details).	
We would like	an end stand a corner stand	far away from any	competition. competitors.

Facilities, fixtures and fittings

Our requirements	regarding with regard to	facilities are as follows: … (list)
We	require/need would like to have	television(s) / DVD player(s) / telephone(s) photocopier(s) / digital projector(s).

4 Making enquiries about the Boston trade fair

Before the owners of Wind Works make their decision, they would like to know more about the trade fair in Boston. Fiona Pirie asks Oliver to write to Sean Malone for more information.

Use Fiona's notes to write the email.

- *say who we are and what we hope to achieve at the fair*
- *ask for a quotation*

We need:

- *an exhibition area of at least 2,400 square metres*
- *a reception area with 2 sofas and 1 coffee table*
- *a counter with space for 2 computers and two telephones*
- *3 display racks along the wall areas*
- *say that we would like a stand between other stands but not near any direct competition*

5 Booking flights to Boston

Wind Works has now decided to participate at the Offshore Wind Power – Boston trade event. Four employees, including Fiona, are going to attend. Fiona asks Oliver to make the arrangements for the trip. First, he calls BTS Business Travel Solutions to book the flights.

17

A Listen to the phone call and make notes about the flights.

1 What is the date of departure?
2 What time does the flight leave Aberdeen?
3 When does it arrive in Boston?
4 Where is the stop-over?
5 What time does the plane arrive/depart from that airport?
6 What time does the return flight leave Boston?
7 When will the travellers arrive back in Aberdeen?
8 How much is a return ticket?
9 Who is flying to Boston?
10 What is the booking number?

! The word *travel* can be an adjective or a verb: *travel agent*, *travel to the USA*. However, you cannot go on a ~~travel~~. Use *trip* instead: *Enjoy your trip!*

17

B Listen again. Which of these phrases do you hear?

1 a one-way flight
2 return flights
3 economy class
4 local time
5 direct flight
6 available seats
7 a later flight
8 the connecting flight
9 the price for a one-way ticket
10 the cost of a return flight

6 Oliver can go to the fair

Two days before the fair, Fiona Pirie has a skiing accident. Her leg is in plaster and she cannot fly to Boston. She asks Oliver if he would like to take her place at Offshore Wind Power – Boston. Oliver phones Laura to change the reservation.

A Work with a partner. Before you listen to the call, decide together which of these sentences you will hear.

Is it possible to change the reservation? **1**

I'd like to book the flight that departs at 10.00. **2**

Would you like to travel in the morning or in the afternoon? **3**

What changes would you like to make? **4**

I only have one seat available in economy class. **5**

I can offer you an early flight on Monday. **6**

The flight is full. **7**

I'm afraid there's an extra charge for changing a reservation. **8**

18

B Now listen and check.

GRAMMAR

at, on, in with dates, days and times

1 **at** 6 p.m., **at** lunch time
2 **at** night, **at** the weekend/weekends, **at** Christmas/Easter
3 **on** Monday/Mondays, **on** 21 June, **on** my birthday
4 **in** the morning/mornings, **in** summer, **in** January, **in** 1987

- Wir verwenden *at* für die Tageszeit (1) und andere zeitbezogene Ausdrücke (2).
- Wir verwenden *on* für Tage und Termine (3).
- Wir verwenden *in* für längere Zeiträume (4).
- Vor *every, last, next, this* werden *at, on, in* nicht verwendet:
  Wir trafen uns **am letzten** Montag = *We met ~~on~~ **last** Monday*.

7 Practice

Complete the sentences with the correct preposition only where necessary.

1 Fiona was in Boston … 2010.
2 Oliver is happy that he is going to the fair … next week.
3 He has to be at the airport … 4.30 … the morning.
4 Boston can be rather cold … winter.
5 What time does the flight arrive … Boston Airport?
6 The fair ends … 6 p.m. … Sunday evening.

8 Booking a flight and changing a flight reservation

You are going to make two telephone calls between a business customer and a travel agent. In the first call, Partner A is going to book a flight; in the second call, Partner B will change a reservation. Read your role cards carefully and make notes before you start your call.

A **Work with a partner. In this call, Partner A will book a flight.**
Partner A: Look at File 4, page 119
Partner B: Look at File 7, page 120

B **In this call, Partner B is going to change a reservation.**
Partner A: Look at File 5, page 119
Partner B: Look at File 8, page 120

LANGUAGE

Booking hotel accommodation

I/We have seen your home page on the Internet.
The accommodation service at … (name of exhibition) has recommended your hotel.

Request for information

Please let me/us know if your hotel is	near within easy reach of	the airport. the exhibition centre. the city centre.
I/We would like to know if your hotel has	an indoor swimming pool. / a sauna. / a fitness room. / WLAN service. / business service. / 24-hour room service.	

Type of accommodation required / number of nights

I would like to	book reserve	… (number)	single double	room(s) for … night(s).

I/We need/require the rooms from … to … .

Special requests

Please confirm that the rooms are	non-smoking. in a quiet part of the building.

Prices

Please quote your best rates for the above-mentioned accommodation.
Please let us have details of your corporate rates.

Polite ending

Please send us confirmation of this booking	as soon as possible. by … (date) at the latest.

9 Booking accommodation in Boston

KMK

WEBCODE **OMU1101**

Oliver is booking hotel accommodation for himself and his colleagues in the Boston Business Hotel but there is something wrong with the hotel's website. He decides to send a fax.

Write the fax, giving details about dates, times of arrival and names of guests using the information from exercise 5. (Don't forget: Fiona Pirie can't travel to Boston.)

10 Produktion

Sie arbeiten für den Möbelhersteller Jensch in Hamburg. Da Ihre Firma bei der nächsten Ideal Home Exhibition (13.–16. März) in London ausstellen wird, hat Ihre Vorgesetzte Sie gebeten, eine E-Mail Anfrage an info@idealhomes.co.uk zu verfassen.

Verfassen Sie die Anfrage und berücksichtigen Sie die folgenden Punkte:

- Information zur Messe im Internet gefunden
- Information zum eigenen Unternehmen geben
- Grund für Anfrage: Ihre Firma möchte eine Ausstellungsfläche auf der Messe buchen.
- Die Ausstellungsfläche sollte folgende Merkmale aufweisen:
  - Eckposition, mindestens 4.000m^2 mit einem Schalter vorne; Prospekt-Ständer; Anschlüsse für Telefon und Internet
  - die komplette Ausstellungsfläche sollte sehr gut beleuchtet sein.
- Erbitten Sie ein günstiges Angebot.

11 Rezeption – Hörverstehen

19

Tobias Kaufmann arbeitet für eine Firma in Frankfurt. Für die Zeit während der nächsten Handelsmesse in Birmingham möchte er Hotelunterkünfte für sich und seine Kollegen buchen. Sein Versuch, online zu buchen, scheitert, da sämtliche Hotels der Business Class wegen der Messe ausgebucht zu sein scheinen. Deshalb entschließt sich Tobias, es telefonisch bei einer Hotelagentur in Birmingham zu versuchen.

Hören Sie das Telefongespräch an und beantworten Sie folgende Fragen:

1. Für welchen Zeitraum möchte Tobias die Zimmer buchen?
2. Wie viele Zimmer benötigt er?
3. Wie teuer ist ein Einzelzimmer?
4. Wann landet das Flugzeug in Birmingham?
5. Wie lange dauert die Fahrt vom Flughafen zum Hotel ungefähr?
6. Wie lautet die Buchungs-nummer?

CAN DO

After working through this unit I can ...	Check ...
▪ understand details about a trade fair and describe the fair in German to a colleague.	Ex 2, page 98
▪ describe how to organize an exhibition stand.	Ex 3, page 100
▪ write a letter of enquiry about a trade fair.	Ex 4, page 102 Ex 10, page 105
▪ understand details of flight reservations; make and change flight reservations.	Ex 5, page 102 Ex 8, page 104
▪ write a fax booking hotel accommodation.	Ex 9, page 104
▪ understand a short telephone call about a hotel booking.	Ex 11, page 105

12 The Aid and Trade Fair – working for humanitarian relief

The Aid and Trade Fair in Geneva is a unique exhibition that brings together aid agencies and the manufacturers of the products that they need to meet the urgent needs of victims of natural disasters and conflicts.

Read this article then do the tasks below.

AT THIS YEAR'S AID AND TRADE FAIR in Geneva, a videotape shows a group of smiling men quickly and easily assembling a house made of a prefabricated, multi-cellular wall system. It is made of galvanized steel. Tall, hollow, rectangular containers are tied together with strong wire.

Angelo De Iacovo is Project Manager for Hesco, the company that produces the house. He explains the idea behind the invention.

"In disaster areas," he begins, "there are two major problems. One is getting rid of the rubble and clearing the area; the second is building a shelter for people to live in. We thought we could tackle both these problems in one go. The shelter is built from the dirt, sand and rocks of destroyed houses," he goes on. "Builders fill the containers with the rubble and even non-skilled workers can easily erect a house for up to eight people in one or two days."

David Covell works for Mobil Medical International, based in the US state of Vermont. He demonstrates his company's product, a cocoon-shaped tent that operates as a mobile hospital. The tent is equipped with chemical and biological filtering systems.

"In an emergency where speed is important, a couple of people can set up this mobile field hospital in seven minutes," Covell says. "The product was developed for the US military," he explains, "but the company believes it is a versatile product that could be used for humanitarian purposes. That's why it's on display here at Aid and Trade."

Sian Bowen is communications manager for the International Federation of Red Cross and Red Crescent Societies. She says trade fairs that bring together manufacturers and aid professionals are important. "We have to show the latest products and ideas to the people that need them most," she says. "It's important to interact in a proactive way with the commercial sector so that we can find out what they're doing, what their new ideas are, what they may have that can help us in an emergency," she explains. "We need that two-way dialogue."

1 Explain what these numbers from the text refer to.

1 two 2 eight 3 one or two 4 seven

2 Match the statements (1–4) with the people who said them (a–d).

1 "We are not here to market this as a military tool."
2 "Shelter for the homeless is always a priority."
3 "We welcome commercial enterprises that come to Aid and Trade to see how to break into the humanitarian market."
4 "Survivors need a wide variety of aid."

a Angelo De Iacovo
b David Covell
c Sian Bowen
d one of the organizers at Aid and Trade

3 Fassen Sie diesen Artikel kurz auf Deutsch zusammen. Erklären Sie die Ziele der Messe und geben Sie Beispiele dafür aus der aktuellen Ausstellung. KMK

Applying for a job

UNIT 12

- writing a CV
- writing a covering letter
- attending an interview

1: I think your chances depend on how well you fill in the application form. If you don't do that first step correctly, then you will never be considered for an interview.

2: Being able to handle the interview is the most important thing. You should be able to respond to the interview questions and to make positive replies even when you're asked some confusing questions. Try to be positive and confident.

3: Understanding the job advertisement is the most important thing. You need a clear idea of what the job is and what the employer is looking for.

4: Writing a good covering letter is important. It should complement your CV and highlight why you're the right person for the job.

5: I believe that writing a good CV is the most important skill you need. A good CV shows a prospective employer at a glance whether your educational and professional experience matches the needs of the company.

1 Warm-up

An opinion poll was carried out among trainee office management assistants to find out which skills they thought were most important for getting a job in an English-speaking country.

A **Read what some of the trainees said above, then work in groups and put the skills in order of importance.**

B **When you have decided, look at page 117 and compare your list with the trainees who were asked.**

2 A job advertisement

Yvonne Steffens has finished her training as an office management assistant. Since she qualified, Yvonne has been working in a rehabilitation clinic near Bielefeld. She is interested in working abroad and has found the following advertisement on the Internet.

A Study the advertisement below and say …

1. what Yvonne's job would be.
2. what the job requirements are.
3. in which sector the prospective employer is active.
4. what benefits are offered.
5. how Yvonne can apply.
6. what happens if her application is successful.

Mozilla Firefox

M & P Recruitment Agency

www.officematter.com/jobadvertisement

Facebook | Meistbesuchte... | Erste Schritte | Aktuelle Nachr... | Lesezeichen

Date 28 May	Advert #704	Job ref no 20229375

M & P

Recruiter: M & P Recruitment Agency
Job title: Office Management Assistant
Sector: Administration/Reception
Region: London
Salary: £18,000–£19,000 per annum
Job Type: Permanent

We are a leading UK recruitment agency that is looking to recruit an Office Management Assistant on a permanent basis.

Our client is a leading private clinic located in London. The successful candidate will assist the Clinic Manager and work in Reception.

Responsibilities include meeting and greeting international clients, providing secretarial support to the Clinic Manager, appointment management, updating the database and providing general office administration.

What we are looking for:
You will need to be a highly organized individual who is able to work under pressure.
Strong administrative skills are essential.
Office experience necessary; experience of working in reception would be useful.
You will need to be a competent user of standard office software, have good typing skills and an excellent telephone manner.
English and at least one foreign language essential.

What's on offer:
A salary between £18,000 to £19,000 per annum is available.
Luncheon vouchers.
Optional language training classes.
The clinic is located close to train and underground stations.

The position, which is permanent, offers a superb opportunity for a hard-working, enthusiastic person.

If you are interested in applying for this position, please complete our application form.
If your application is successful, you will be asked to send your CV together with a covering letter.

Initial interviews will be conducted by telephone.
Successful candidates will be invited to London for face to face interviews in July.
If you have any questions, see our FAQs or send an email to info@mprecruitment.co.uk

B **Find the English equivalents of these German words in the advertisement.**

1 Bewerber
2 Stelle
3 Verwaltung
4 Bewerbung
5 Lebenslauf
6 Anschreiben

3 Understanding job advertisements

A **Work in groups of three. You are each going to read a job advertisement and answer your partners' questions in German.**

Partner A: Look at File 11 on page 121.
Partner B: Look at File 13 on page 123.
Partner C: Look at File 15 on page 124.

Ask questions in German on ...

1 the type of employer.
2 what the job is.
3 what the requirements are.
4 the salary and benefits.
5 how to apply.
6 what happens if the application is successful.

B **Discuss the job offers in your group. Say which position(s) interests you. Explain why you are (or are not) qualified for the position.**

GRAMMAR

Relative pronouns

1 The person **who/that** wrote the advertisement has a temporary position.
2 He works for a firm **which/that** recruits personnel for other companies.
3 The company, **whose** offices are located in London, is one of the UK's biggest recruitment agencies.
4 This is the candidate (**who/that**) I interviewed last week.

- Relativpronomen (*who, which, that, whose*) leiten Relativsätze ein.
- Ein Relativsatz kann notwendige oder nicht notwendige Information beinhalten. Notwendige Relativsätze sind für das Verständnis des Satzes unbedingt erforderlich (1, 2); nicht notwendige Relativsätze geben lediglich Zusatzinformationen und werden durch Kommas getrennt (3).
- In notwendigen Relativsätzen kann das Relativpronomen wegfallen, wenn es Objekt ist, d.h. wenn im Relativsatz ein Subjekt steht (4).

4 Practice

Translate the following sentences using a suitable relative pronoun where necessary.

1 Die Firma sucht jemanden, der sich im Verwaltungswesen auskennt.
2 Eine Kopie des Bewerbungsformulars, das man im Internet ausgefüllt hat, sollte man behalten.
3 Der Bewerber, der sich auf die Stelle beworben hat, kommt nächste Woche.
4 Der Lebenslauf, den Sie geschrieben haben, ist ausgezeichnet.
5 Das ist die Stelle, auf die ich mich beworben habe.
6 Das Anschreiben, das ich gerade eben gelesen habe, ist hervorragend.

5 Continuing the application process

KMK

Yvonne has been short-listed for the position as Office Management Assistant in the private clinic in London. She has been asked to send her CV. Before she writes her CV, Yvonne checks the "Your Office Matters" website for tips. Unfortunately, there is something wrong with the website and the tips no longer match the elements they refer to.

Work with a partner. Read the tips (1–7) and match them to the headings (a–g).

Mozilla Firefox
Your Office Matters
www.yourofficematters.com/trainee_office_management_assistants_CVs
Google
Facebook Meistbesuchte... Erste Schritte Aktuelle Nachr... Lesezeichen

CVs Your CV is a summary of your abilities, work experience, education and qualifications. There is no set format for a British CV but you should keep it short, using headings to guide the reader. Always keep your CV honest and factual.

Tips

1. Give your name and address, telephone number(s) (home/mobile) and email address.
2. This should be a short message that grabs the attention of the reader and summarizes your skills and experience relevant to the job for which you are applying.
   Use note form and write in the third person throughout. This helps to keep your CV focused and direct, for example: *Motivated office management assistant with experience in foreign trade.*
3. As a general rule, CVs should be in reverse chronological order, listing the most recent position first. For each position held you should provide the dates of the start and end of employment, the employer's name and address, the job title, the main duties and responsibilities and achievements.
4. Give a brief description of qualifications (school, academic and/or professional). Give the names of schools or colleges in reverse chronological order.
5. Here you should write about common skills gained throughout your education and work experience, such as languages, IT skills or a full, clean driving licence. These skills are of interest for any employer. You should also describe your character using words like *good organizing skills, team-orientated, flexible, energetic, ...*
6. This feature is optional, but could help to provide something more personal to discuss at an interview. Be careful about what you write; a dangerous sport or *socializing with friends* may not be what an employer wants to hear!
7. Due to data protection laws, candidates should not provide referees' names, addresses or any other contact details on CVs, but should state that details are available on request. Always ask your referees' permission before you give someone their contact details.

a Education	**b** Hobbies and interests	**c** Personal statement	**d** Personal details
e References	**f** What you are good at; your achievements	**g** Work experience	

TIP

Europass

Europass is a standardized CV and language skills passport, that can be created online or on your own computer. Potential employers throughout Europe can clearly see your skills and qualifications. http://europass.cedefop.europa.eu

6 Preparing your CV

Yvonne has written her CV using tips from the website.

A First, look at Yvonne's details. What differences can you find between her CV and a German CV?

Yvonne Steffens
Am Kattenkamp 236, 33611 Bielefeld, Germany
Phone (+49) 521 394677
Email styvon89@gmx.com

Personal statement
Highly-motivated, team-orientated office management assistant with experience in reception. Seeking experience on the British market using language skills.

Work experience
Since March 20.. Dr Müller Rehabilitation Klinik, Olderdissen
Dealing with administration, contact with health insurance companies, reception

August 20.. – June 20.. Training as Bürokauffrau
certified by the Chamber of Commerce, Bielefeld

Education
August 20.. – July 20.. ABC Berufskolleg, Bielefeld
2 years, part-time vocational school
August 19.. – June 20.. Bielefeld Gymnasium
Abitur (Final exams similar to A-Levels)
Main subjects: English, German, Economics/Social Science

Skills
Excellent IT-Skills (MS Office); data-base management
Good at working under pressure, friendly, flexible
Fluent English (oral and written), good French, conversational Spanish

Hobbies and interests
Travelling, foreign languages

References
Names of referees available on request.

B Use tips from the website to prepare your own CV. Copy the layout of Yvonne's CV and use any words and phrases from that CV that are appropriate.

7 A covering letter

Read Yvonne's covering letter to the London clinic and label the paragraphs (1–5) with explanations from the box.

asking the employer to invite for an interview • reference to details on CV • reference to the position • saying why the applicant is applying for the position • stating why the applicant is the best person for the job

Yvonne Steffens
Am Kattenkamp 236
33611 Bielefeld, Germany
Phone (+49) 521 394677
Email styvon89@gmx.com

Dr Sanjay Patel
Baker Street Clinic
London NW1 2A5
Great Britain

Dear Dr Patel

Office Management Assistant

1 The position of Office Management Assistant advertised on the M & P Recruitment Agency website has caught my interest.

2 I am very interested in the job you are offering as I feel sure it will give me the opportunity to develop both on a personal level and on a career basis. I am particularly keen to work in an English-speaking country where I can apply my knowledge of English on a daily basis. Apart from that, although I am successful in my present position, I feel that it is time for me to look for more of a challenge at work.

3 As you can see from the enclosed CV, I am currently employed in a German rehabilitation clinic as an office management assistant. My duties include dealing with general administration and making contact with health insurance companies. I also work at the reception desk, admitting patients, assisting visitors and dealing with representatives of pharmaceutical companies.

4 Through the experience I have gained in my present position, I believe I can add value to your clinic. My language abilities will also make me an asset to your team. My English is excellent as I studied the language for 8 years for A-levels and 2 years at vocational school. I also have a working knowledge of French and can speak Spanish fluently. My mother-tongue is German.

5 Enclosed is my CV and the names of two referees. I would appreciate it if you consider my application and hope that you will grant me an interview.

I look forward to hearing from you soon.

Yours sincerely
Yvonne Steffens
Encl

TIP

A covering letter

A covering letter is a formal letter with a standard structure. Don't use the same letter for all companies and all jobs but include a different covering letter with your CV for each job you are applying for. Your covering letter should be only one page long and you should try to avoid having too many sentences that begin with "I".

1. Refer to the position for which you are applying; give the source of the employer's address.
2. Give details of your education and training; say what job you are doing at the moment.
3. Say why you are applying for the position.
4. Close politely, referring to enclosures and asking the employer to invite you for an interview.

LANGUAGE

Writing a covering letter

Opening phrases

In reply to With reference to	your advertisement in … (newspaper, etc) of … (date) …

I	see that you are looking for a/an				… (job).
	would like wish	to apply for the above-mentioned	position post	of	

Education/training; present employment

I attended … (school/college) for … (length of time).
I studied … (subjects) at vocational school in … (town/city) from … (date) to … (date).

At present I am working for a/an… (type of company) as a/an… (job).
I will complete my period of training on … (date).

Closing paragraph

I enclose Enclosed is	my CV/résumé. a list of my qualifications and experience.

I hope you will consider my application favourably and …
… (I) look forward to hearing from you in the near future.

8 Writing your covering letter

KMK

WEBCODE OMU1201

Lesen Sie die Stellenanzeigen in Übung 2 (Seite 108) und Übung 4 (Seite 109) noch einmal durch. Wählen Sie eine Stelle aus, die Sie besonders interessiert, und entwerfen Sie dafür ein Bewerbungsschreiben.

Heben Sie Ihren Brief sorgfältig auf, da Sie ihn für Übung 11 brauchen werden.

9 Handling telephone interviews

Yvonne has been informed that she will be interviewed on the telephone one day next week. She checks the Internet for tips.

A Lesen Sie die Webseite unten durch und machen Sie sich Notizen auf Deutsch. Anhand Ihrer Notizen erklären Sie einer Kollegin, wie sie sich am besten auf ein telefonisches Interview vorbereiten sollte. KMK

Mozilla Firefox
Your Office Matters
www.yourofficematters.com/phoneinterviews
Google
Facebook Meistbesuchte... Erste Schritte Aktuelle Nachr... Lesezeichen

Your telephone interview

One short phone call is all it takes to get you to the next level in your job application process – or not. By asking just a few questions, an interviewer can quickly decide if you are a likely candidate for the job.

Don't let your interviewer think that this phone call is not as meaningful to you as if it were a face-to-face interview.

Be prepared!

Have these things ready beside your phone:
- a copy of the job description;
- a copy of your letter of application, your CV and your references;
- a notebook and a couple of pens so that you can take notes during the interview;
- a list of questions you want to ask the interviewer;
- a list of your strengths.

Before the interview, you should also practice all your success stories, whether they are work stories or academic achievements, a good story is much more interesting than a list of job skills.

Remember, if you don't make a good impression on the phone, you won't be invited for the face-to-face meeting.

B Work with a partner and read the questions (1–6) the interviewer asked Yvonne. Reading between the lines, decide together what the interviewer wanted to find out by asking these questions. Choose from the list of suggestions (a–f).

1. Do you have a few minutes to talk with me so that I can get a better idea of what it is you're expecting from the position?
2. What led you to apply for the position?
3. You're currently working as an office management assistant in a German rehabilitation clinic. Why do you want to leave?
4. What would you like to be doing five years from now?
5. I think we've covered everything, but is there anything you'd like to ask me?
6. We'll be interviewing candidates in London next week. Would you be interested in coming in and talking with us?

a) If we were to hire you, would we be investing in the future of the company?
b) Have you done some research on our company?
c) Why do you think you're the right person for the job?
d) What kind of person are you? Should we go further with your application?
e) Are you still interested in the job?
f) Why do you want to change your employer?

10 Preparing for a face-to-face interview

20

Dr Patel, the owner of the London clinic invites Yvonne to London for an interview. First, Yvonne listens to a podcast on the "Your Office Matters" website in which an expert gives tips about face-to-face interviews.

Read the introduction to the podcast and copy the "Five stages of an interview" into your exercise book. After that, listen and make notes.

Mozilla Firefox

Your Office Matters

www.yourofficematters.com/interviews

Facebook | Meistbesuchte... | Erste Schritte | Aktuelle Nachr... | Lesezeichen

Five stages of an interview

In today's podcast, our business coach, Pat Klein, is going to give us some advice about how to prepare for a job interview.

Did you know that an interview is made up of five stages?

Stage 1: Greetings and introductions
Stage 2: Small talk
Stage 3: The main part of the interview
Stage 4: Questions from the candidate
Stage 5: Further arrangements and the end of the interview

Pat is going to describe these stages one by one and offer tips on how to manage each of them.

11 Practising the main part of an interview

In exercise 8, you applied for one of the four jobs which have been advertised in this unit. In this exercise, you are going to develop questions for an interview for that position with a partner and then role-play the interview.

A **Work with a partner who applied for a different job to the one you chose in exercise 8. Develop questions an interviewer might ask during an interview for each of your jobs.**
Compare your questions with the list of common interview questions (and how to answer them) in File 12 on page 122.

B **Work with a partner who applied for same job as you chose. Use the interview questions you developed above (task A) to interview your partner for the job. When you have finished, change roles.**

CAN DO

After working through this unit I can ...	Check ...
▪ understand and talk about job advertisements written in English.	Ex 2, page 108 Ex 3, page 109
▪ prepare my CV and write an application for a job.	Ex 6, page 111 Ex 8, page 113
▪ prepare for and role-play an interview.	Ex 11, page 115
▪ apply for a position advertised in a German newspaper.	Ex 12, page 116
▪ role-play the main part of an interview.	Ex 13, page 116

12 Produktion

Sie sind auf der Suche nach einer festen Anstellung und finden folgendes Stellenangebot im Internet. Sie beschließen, sich auf die Stelle zu bewerben.

Verfassen Sie eine Bewerbung auf Englisch.

Corpus Medical Systems

www.cms.com/jobadvertisement

Corpus Medical Systems

Bürokauffrau/-mann

Wir, Corpus Medical Systems GmbH, sind ein junges Unternehmen mit Sitz in Frankfurt, spezialisiert auf strategische Unternehmensberatung und anspruchsvolles Management im Gesundheitswesen.
Zur Verstärkung unseres Teams suchen wir zur sofortigen Anstellung eine/einen Bürokauffrau/-mann (5-Tage Woche mit flexiblen Arbeitszeiten).

Ihre Aufgaben:
- Allgemeine Büroorganisation
- Korrespondenz und Terminkoordination
- Betreuung und Pflege der Datenbanken
- Ansprechpartner für unsere Geschäftspartner

Ihre Qualifikation:
- Abgeschlossene kaufmännische Ausbildung oder entsprechende berufliche Qualifikation
- IT-Affinität
- Sicherer Umgang mit MS-Office
- Sehr gute Kommunikationsfähigkeiten
- Ausgezeichnete Englischkenntnisse

Interessiert? Dann nutzen Sie Ihre Chance und senden Sie uns Ihre Bewerbungsunterlagen zu (bitte auf Englisch) oder rufen Sie uns an:

Elisabeth Martin
Corpus Medical Systems GmbH
Große Friedberger Straße 22
60313 Frankfurt am Main
Telefon: 069/12212111
E-mail: emartin@cormedsys.de

13 Interaktion

Partner A: Sie erhalten eine Einladung zum Vorstellungsgespräch. Sie wissen, dass das Gespräch auf Englisch stattfinden wird. Zur Vorbereitung haben Sie eine Liste von Fragen zusammengestellt, die auf Sie zukommen könnten.

Schauen Sie File 6 auf Seite 119 an und fertigen Sie als Vorbereitung auf das Vorstellungsgespräch Notizen auf Englisch an. Wie würden Sie die Fragen beantworten?

Partner B: Sie sind Personalleiter/in der Firma, die einen neuen Mitarbeiter sucht. Heute führen Sie ein Vorstellungsgespräch mit einem/einer Bewerber/in. Das Gespräch wird auf Englisch geführt, damit Sie die sprachlichen Fähigkeiten des Bewerbers feststellen können.

Schauen Sie File 16 auf Seite 124 an und fertigen Sie als Vorbereitung auf das Vorstellungsgespräch Notizen auf Englisch an. Welche Themen würden Sie ansprechen und welche Fragen würden Sie dazu stellen? Wenn Sie und Partner A bereit sind, fangen Sie mit dem Vorstellungsgespräch an.

14 Finding a job abroad

A Read the text. Put paragraphs a–e in the correct logical order then explain each paragraph in a single sentence in German.

JOBS ADVICE

TOP TIPS FOR WORKING ABROAD

Working abroad for two or three years can be good for your career. You'll get an insight into another culture and gain experience which could be invaluable later in life. However, getting that job abroad can be quite difficult. Here's a step by step guide about how to do it.

a
The next step is to find that job! Look on the internet at jobsites, check out the jobs pages of newspapers in the country in question.

b
Once you have secured your job offer, work permit and visa it's time to make sure that you have the right health insurance and pension cover to work in the country. The immigration services of the country in question should be able to help you with this.

c
But before deciding that you would like to work in a country, it's important that you visit it first. You can only find out if a particular country is right for you if you spend some time there finding out what the people are like. It's especially important to find out what the cultural differences between your own country and the country you want to live in are.

d
If you are thinking about working in another European Union country, you have the right to enter and live in the country in order to find work. However, countries outside of the EU will generally require you to apply for a visa before entering the country as a resident.

e
Once you've decided that you would like to spend some time working in another country, you should do some research into whether you can realistically expect to secure a job there. The embassy or consulate of the country in question may also be able to provide you with information about your chances of finding employment.

B Work with a partner. What information and advice about working in Germany would you give to someone from another country? Make a list. Compare your information and advice with the rest of the class.

- working hours
- attitudes towards small talk
- smoking in the workplace

For Exercise 1B, page 107

Ranking	Percentage of votes given (2107 trainees voted)
Having a good interview technique	47.4%
Writing a good CV (BE) or résumé (AE)	20.6%
Understanding job advertisements	17.8%
Writing a good covering letter	8.2%
Filling in application forms correctly	6.0%

Source: http://www.bbc.co.uk

1 Unit 1, exercise 7B

Partner B: Dictate these contact details to Partners A and C. Check A and C's answers.

1 Mr Laurence Evanston
Human Resources Manager
Medex Steel Incorporated
57318 Wainwright Circle
Cleveland, OHIO 47820
USA

Telephone +1 21 62 98 54 37

2 the contact details of your firm or your own contact details

2 Unit 2, exercise 1C

Partner A: Dictate these email addresses to Partner B. Then check B's answers.

1 beatrice-kuhn@swiss_pharma.com.ch
2 Hamish.MacPherson@net.uk
3 your own email address
4 the email address of your firm or another email address you write to often

3 Unit 9, exercise 12

Partner B

- Begrüßen Sie Partner A mit "Sales Department" und Ihrem eigenen Namen.
- Hören Sie sich die Beschwerde an und äußern Sie Ihr Bedauern.
- Erklären Sie den vermutlichen Grund des genannten Schadens: Wahrscheinlich war eine neu eingeführte Art der Verpackung die Ursache.
- Wiederholen Sie die Details der Bestellung und die Katalognummer.
- Sagen Sie, dass Sie im Computer nachschauen werden, ob ein Ersatztisch vorrätig ist. Bitten Sie Partner A am Telefon zu bleiben, während Sie das kurz überprüfen.
- Leider sind genau gleiche Tische nicht sofort lieferbar. Sie können jedoch einen ähnlichen Tisch anbieten, Katalognummer GTT 10, mit dickerem Glas. Eigentlich kostet dieser Tisch £50 mehr als GTT 09, doch unter den gegebenen Umständen könnte er ohne Aufpreis geliefert werden.
- Hören Sie der Antwort von Partner A zu.
- Falls Partner A Ihr Angebot annimmt, teilen Sie ihm mit, dass Sie im Lager anrufen werden, damit der Tisch umgehend geliefert wird.
- Beenden Sie das Gespräch mit einer wiederholten Entschuldigung.

4 Unit 11, exercise 8A

Partner A

Business customer booking a flight
You work for a company in Dublin. Your boss, Mary O'Brien, has asked you to book her a return flight to Frankfurt am Main. Use the information below to call the travel agency and book the flights.

17 June: Dublin to Frankfurt, arriving in the early afternoon
19 June: Frankfurt to Dublin, departing in the early evening
Business class if possible

5 Unit 11, exercise 8B

Partner A

Travel agent making changes to a reservation
You work in the corporate customer department of a travel agency. Use the information below to deal with your customer.

Flights to Milan

Day	Departure	Arrival	Seats available	Price including taxes and booking fees
Thursday	09.30	11.00	economy: 12 business: 3	£450 £902
	18.30	20.00	economy: 4 business: 5	£360 £817
Friday	09.30	11.00	economy: 0 business: 7	£550 £1,202
	14.30	16.00	economy: 1 business: 4	£540 £985
Saturday	09.30	11.00	economy: 0 business: 8	£450 £902

6 Unit 12, exercise 13

Partner A

Themen möglicher Fragen:
- Kurze eigene Vorstellung; Stärken und Schwächen
- Verantwortung in bisherigen Stellen
- Sprachkenntnisse – wie gut, wie viel praktische Erfahrung
- Gründe, warum man sich für diese Position bei dieser Firma beworben hat
- Fragen stellen, z.B. nach Fortbildungsmöglichkeiten oder unmittelbaren Vorgesetzten

7 Unit 11, exercise 8A

Partner B

Travel agent taking a booking
You work in the corporate customer department of a travel agency. Use the information below to deal with your customer.

British Airways

From	To	Date	Depar-ture	Arrival	Seats available
Dublin	London Heathrow	17 June	12.00	12.50	economy: 12 business: 3
London Heathrow	Frankfurt/ Main	17 June	13.55	16.30	economy: 4 business: 5
Frankfurt/ Main	London Heathrow	19 June	18.30	18.55	economy: 1 business: 4
London Heathrow	Dublin	19 June	20.15	21.20	economy: 0 business: 8

Lufthansa

From	To	Date	Depar-ture	Arrival	Seats available
Dublin	London Heathrow	17 June	09.30	10.30	economy: 3 business: 2
London Heathrow	Frankfurt/ Main	17 June	11.30	12.55	economy: 4 business: 5
Frankfurt/ Main	London Heathrow	19 June	17.30	18.05	economy: 9 business: 4
London Heathrow	Dublin	19 June	21.15	22.20	economy: 6 business: 8

8 Unit 11, exercise 8B

Partner B

Business customer changing a reservation
At the beginning of the week, you made arrangements to meet a customer at the Milan Fashion Fair. The meeting was planned for Thursday at 2 p.m., so you booked an Economy flight to Milan (Departure: 09.30 / Arrival: 11.00).

This morning, you heard from your business partner that he cannot meet you in Milan on Thursday. He has suggested a meeting on Friday or Saturday.

Phone your travel agent and change your booking.

You would like economy class if possible.

9 Unit 2, exercise 1C

Partner B: Dictate these email addresses to Partner A. Then check A's answers.

1. DavidMcCarthy+list@net.us
2. sergei-nikitin@com.ru
3. your own email address
4. the email address of your firm or another email address you write to often

10 Unit 1, exercise 7B

Partner C: Dictate these contact details to Partners A and B. Check A and B's answers.

1. Mlle Annick Hautefeuille
   SEBARA
   180 rue Drouet-d'Erlon
   5100 Reims
   FRANCE

   Telephone +33 49 29 11 84
2. the contact details of your firm or your own contact details

11 Unit 12, exercise 3A

Partner A

Office management assistant required

We are a major international company producing office equipment.

We have a vacancy in our Berlin office for an office management assistant.

The ideal candidate for the job will be a German native speaker and have a good working knowledge of English. Good telephone manner important.

Qualifications required: Relevant school leaving certificate
Starting salary: €20,000
Training opportunities and possibility of promotion

Please send your application together with your CV to beate.ross@officeone.com.
Telefon: 030/12344321

Successful applicants will be invited to interviews in Berlin on 5 March.

12 Unit 12, exercise 11

Common interview questions	Tips
... about yourself ▪ Tell us about yourself. / How would you describe yourself? ▪ What are your strengths and weaknesses? ▪ What are your hobbies? ▪ Tell us about some mistake you have made in the past and how you handled it. ▪ What question would you not like us to ask you?	▪ Be honest. Show that you are able to use your strengths and indicate that you are working on your "weaknesses". ▪ Always keep in mind that you are applying for a position. ▪ Be positive. Even if a mistake was made, remember to say that you learned from it. ▪ Say that you hope they do not ask you about a particular department/task as you do not yet have much experience in that department/area. / Say that you hope they do not ask you about why you left university (maybe you could no longer afford the fees). Keep it simple and say something positive.
... about your education, work experience and skills ▪ Why did you choose to train at vocational college? ▪ What responsibilities did you have / do you have during the work placement? / at work? ▪ Please tell me about your present job. ▪ What have you learned in your present job that you think would help you in the position you're applying for with us?	▪ Talk about the aspects of your education, work experience and skills that are relevant for the job in question. ▪ Be honest. Don't say you know MS Office if you only learned Word, PowerPoint and Excel. ▪ Tell about a particular project or task which you did successfully.
... about what you know ▪ What languages do you speak? ▪ What computer software are you familiar with?	▪ Answer honestly.
... about your motivation ▪ Why did you apply for this job? ▪ Why do you want to work for this company? ▪ Why do you think you would be a good candidate for this job? ▪ Why do you want to work abroad? ▪ What would you like to achieve in the next five/ten years?	▪ Show that you have researched the company and know what the job is about. ▪ Stress the positive aspects of the company and the job. ▪ Talk about realistic goals and describe how you would like to progress with your career.
... about negative things or gaps in your CV ▪ You started to study rather late in life. Why is that? ▪ Why have you changed your job three times in the last year? ▪ Why did you take a gap year after leaving school?	▪ Explain the situation honestly. ▪ Describe the positive lessons you have learned / the experience you have gained as a result.

►

Questions you can ask the interviewer

- I would like to continue improving my skills. What courses does the company give? What kind of training is given to new employees?
- Who would I report to?
- What are the prospects for promotion?
- What are the next stages of the selection process?
- When do I start?

13 Unit 12, exercise 3A

Partner B

Office management assistant in wholesale and foreign trade

Irish company, dealing mainly with Germany and Eastern Europe, is looking for an office management assistant.

Job responsibilities: goods purchasing and sales customer contact. Frequent contact with German customers both face to face and on the phone

The ideal applicant will have a minimum of GCSE or equivalent and will have successfully completed a period of training in a similar company. At least one foreign language required.

Salary: starting at €20,000 and rising to €25,000 over five years

Opportunities for foreign travel

Please send your CV to: Peter O'Hara, Human Resources, Dublin Wares, 409 Mespil Street, Dublin 2. Quote job reference number W/F 12.

A short list of successful applicants will be contacted by 17 June at the latest and asked to supply references.

14 Unit 8, exercise 8B

Partner A

Describe this line graph to Partner B. Check Partner B's graph when you have finished.

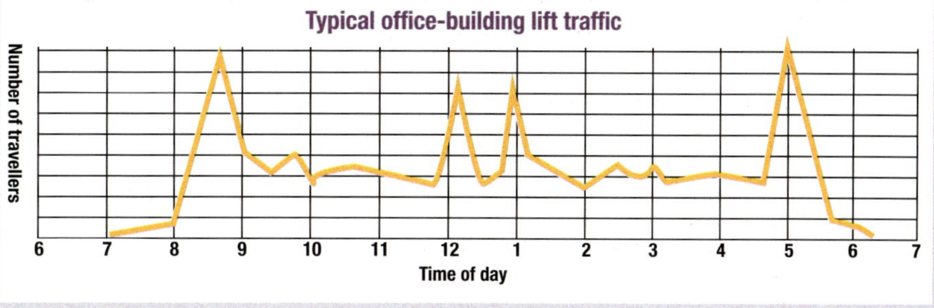

15 Unit 12, exercise 3A

Partner C

Experienced events clerk

This company, in the city of New York, organizes exhibitions, shows and events. As part of a team you will be dealing face to face with the public, giving out information about events and distributing tickets.

You should be a good communicator both orally and in writing. Standard software skills are a must. You should also be used to dealing with people from all walks of life and from overseas. Excellent English required.

Salary: $40,000 p.a. Company apartment available; gym membership

Apply in writing enclosing your résumé to Rebecca Potter, NYNY Events, 76 Broadway, New York.

If your application is successful, you will be invited to take part in a telephone interview.

16 Unit 12, exercise 13

Partner B

Fragen Sie nach:

- Selbstbeschreibung mit eigenen Stärken und Schwächen
- Tätigkeiten und konkrete Verantwortungsbereiche in früheren Stellen
- Bisheriger praktischer Einsatz von Fremdsprachenkenntnissen
- Spezielles Interesse am konkreten Stellenangebot der Firma
- Der Bewerber hat Gelegenheit, Fragen zur Firma zu stellen.

17 Unit 8, exercise 8B

Partner B

Describe this line graph to Partner A. Check Partner A's graph when you have finished.

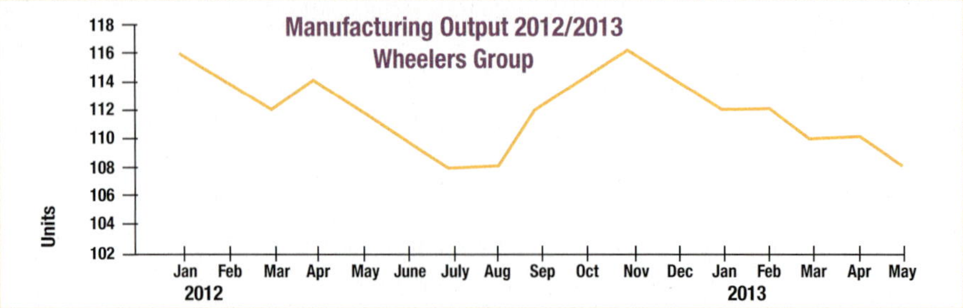

Schriftliche Prüfung

Zeit: **90 Minuten**
Hilfsmittel: **allgemeines zweisprachiges Wörterbuch**
Maximale Punktzahl: **100 Punkte**

Im Rahmen der schriftlichen Prüfung werden die Aufgabenanteile für die drei Kompetenzbereiche wie folgt gewichtet:
- **Rezeption 40 %**
- **Produktion 30 %**
- **Mediation 30 %.**

Im Folgenden werden vier Aufgaben vorgelegt, die Sie bearbeiten sollen. Die erste und die zweite Aufgabe beziehen sich auf Ihre Fähigkeit, englische Texte (gesprochene und geschriebene) zu verstehen = **Rezeption**. Bei der dritten Aufgabe wird von Ihnen erwartet, dass Sie Texte von der deutschen oder englischen in die jeweils andere Sprache übertragen = **Mediation**. In der vierten Aufgabe sollen Sie ein Schriftstück erstellen = **Produktion** eines englischen Textes.

Die Prüfung beginnt mit der Hörverständnisaufgabe. Alle weiteren Aufgaben können in beliebiger Reihenfolge bearbeitet werden.

Rezeption I (Hörverstehen) — 20 Punkte

KMK-Stufe II (B1, Threshold)

Situation: Sie arbeiten bei der Berliner Niederlassung von Caledon, einer internationalen Gesellschaft mit Hauptsitz London. Sie treffen gerade Vorbereitungen für den morgigen Besuch von Jan Novak, einem Kunden aus Osteuropa, als das Telefon klingelt. Es ist Tamsin Young von der Zentrale in London.

21 **Aufgabe:** Hören Sie sich das Gespräch an und beantworten Sie die folgenden Fragen auf Deutsch.

1. Wann wird Herr Novak in Berlin am Flughafen ankommen?
2. Welches der folgenden Angebote sollte unbedingt auf dem Speiseplan fürs Mittagessen stehen?

Eisbein und Sauerkraut • Gemüseauflauf • Fisch mit Pasta

3. Wie sieht das Programm nach dem Essen aus?
4. Welche Dienstleistungen bietet das Berliner Hotel an?
5. Wohin reist Herr Novak am Tag nach seinem Berlinbesuch weiter?

Rezeption II (Leseverstehen)

20 Punkte

KMK-Stufe II (B1, Threshold)

Situation: Für Jan Novaks Besuch ist alles vorbereitet. Ihre Vorgesetzte ist gerade auf einer Konferenz, deshalb haben Sie Zeit, folgenden Zeitschriftenartikel zu lesen.

Aufgabe: Lesen Sie den Artikel und machen Sie sich Notizen, indem Sie die Fragen auf Deutsch beantworten. Danach fassen Sie die genannten Tipps auf Deutsch zusammen.

Success with visitors from abroad

Business today has never been more competitive. Price and quality are two of the important factors for success but the attitude of employees towards customers is perhaps more important. To keep ahead in the race, companies have to give excellent service, especially to their customers from overseas.

It is impossible to cover everything relating to the needs of visitors from all over the world but here is one piece of advice – as soon as you know they are coming, do research into the country and the customs of your overseas clients and use the information to make your foreign customers feel at home.

Here are a few general tips for success:

Courtesy – learn how to meet and greet your visitors, including appropriate body language, degrees of formality and suitable topics of conversation.

Food – do research on dietary restrictions and likes and dislikes regarding drinks.

Entertainment and relaxation – find out what different nationalities expect and also do research on what might be unsuitable.

If your foreign visitors receive a positive first impression, they will feel more relaxed and be happy to do business with you.

1 Warum ist die positive Einstellung von Angestellten gegenüber ausländischen Geschäftspartnern heutzutage so wichtig?
2 Worauf müssen Firmen achten, insbesondere bei ausländischen Geschäftspartnern?
3 Welche Vorbereitungen sind am wichtigsten, wenn Sie wissen, dass ein ausländischer Geschäftspartner zu Besuch kommt?

Fassen Sie die Tipps auf Deutsch zusammen:

- Höflichkeit
- Essgewohnheiten
- Unterhaltung und Entspannung

Mediation

30 Punkte

KMK-Stufe II (B1, Threshold)

Situation: Am späten Nachmittag erhalten Sie eine E-Mail von Jan Novak.

Aufgabe: Fassen Sie die Nachricht auf Deutsch zusammen, damit Sie das weitere Vorgehen mit Ihrer Vorgesetzten, Frau Kaiser, besprechen können.

smartel 100%

Alle (213)

Von: jan.novak@novak.cz Ausblenden

An: jakob.braun@caledon.de

Our meeting 10 July Markieren

Dear Mr Braun
Thank you for making the arrangements for my meeting with Ms Kaiser on 10 July. The itinerary looks very interesting.I am very sorry to have to inform you that, due to a mix up with my calendar, I have to postpone my visit to your company.Would it be possible to have our meeting on 12 July instead? I will be travelling to Berlin by train from Hamburg, arriving at 10.30. I would then get a taxi from the station directly to your office. As I have to fly back to my head office on the same day, I will not need any hotel accommodation. I hope that this new arrangement suits Ms Kaiser. Please give her my apologies.
Yours faithfully
Jan Novak
Sent from my iPhone

Produktion

30 Punkte

KMK-Stufe II (B1, Threshold)

Situation: Ihre Vorgesetzte, Frau Kaiser, fordert Sie auf, eine Antwort an Jan Novak zu schreiben.

Aufgabe: Verfassen Sie die E-Mail auf Englisch. Folgende Punkte sollten enthalten sein:

- Danken Sie Herrn Novak im Namen Ihrer Chefin für seine E-Mail.
- Erklären Sie, dass es Frau Kaiser leidtut, dass das Treffen abgesagt werden musste, aber dass sie Verständnis für die Gründe hat.
- Teilen Sie mit, dass sich das Treffen wie gewünscht verschieben lässt.
- Informieren Sie Herrn Novak, dass am Bahnhof ein Fahrer auf ihn warten wird.
- Äußern Sie Ihre Zuversicht, dass alle anstehenden Punkte zur beidseitigen Zufriedenheit geklärt werden können, obwohl nur wenig Zeit zur Verfügung steht.
- Schreiben Sie, dass Sie sich freuen, Herrn Novak zu treffen, und wünschen Sie eine angenehme Fahrt nach Berlin.

Mündliche Prüfung

Die Prüfung ist eine Gruppenprüfung, bei der Sie Gespräche persönlichen und fachlichen Inhalts in der Fremdsprache führen sollen. Es wird von Ihnen erwartet, dass Sie der vorgegebenen Situation entsprechend sprachlich agieren und reagieren. Es kommt dabei vor allem darauf an, dass Sie sich spontan äußern, dass Sie versuchen, sich verständlich zu machen, und dass Sie gut zuhören.

Die Prüfung besteht aus zwei Teilen und dauert insgesamt ca. 20 Minuten. Zur Vorbereitung haben Sie 20 Minuten Zeit.

Im **ersten Teil** der mündlichen Prüfung werden Sie gebeten, sich zu persönlichen oder beruflichen Themen zu äußern.

Im **zweiten Teil** sollen Sie zusammen mit einem anderen Kandidaten ein Rollenspiel durchführen. Dazu erhalten Sie vom Prüfer Rollenkarten, auf denen eine Situation beschrieben ist, die Sie vorspielen sollen.

Hilfsmittel: allgemeines zweisprachiges Wörterbuch

Mündliche Prüfung Teil II

KMK-Stufe II (B1, Threshold)

Rollenkarten

Kandidat/in A

Situation: Ihre Vorgesetzte, Frau Kaiser, hat Sie aufgefordert, Herrn Novak am Bahnhof abzuholen. Sie warten am Bahnsteig als der Zug aus Hamburg einfährt.

Aufgabe: Führen Sie folgendes Gespräch mit Jan Novak:

- Begrüßung
- Erkundigen Sie sich, wie die Reise war.
- Teilen Sie mit, dass für das Meeting alles vorbereitet ist.
- Bedauern Sie, dass Frau Kaiser heute anderweitig beschäftigt ist.
- Erklären Sie, dass Frau Kaiser von Herrn Michaelis vertreten wird.

Kandidat/in B

Situation: Sie sind Jan Novak. Als Sie am Berliner Hauptbahnhof ankommen, werden Sie von Jakob Braun abgeholt.

Aufgabe: Führen Sie folgendes Gespräch mit ihm:

- Begrüßung
- Ihre Reise war erfolgreich.
- Sie bedauern, dass das Meeting verschoben werden musste.
- Sie hatten sich gefreut, Frau Kaiser wieder zu sehen, und sind enttäuscht, dass sie am Meeting nicht teilnimmt.
- Sie kennen Herrn Michaelis nicht, sind allerdings zuversichtlich, dass das Meeting heute erfolgreich ablaufen wird.

Useful phrases

Making introductions

Unit 1

Greeting people you do not know

Good morning/afternoon/evening. I'm …	*Guten Morgen/Tag/Abend. Ich bin …*
How do you do? My name is …	*Wie geht's? Mein Name ist …*
Nice/Pleased to meet you.	*Es freut mich, Sie kennen zu lernen.*
Nice to meet you, too.	*Ganz meinerseits.*
Excuse me. Are you … ?	*Entschuldigung. Sind Sie … ?*
Yes, I am. / No, I'm not. I'm …	*Ja, das bin ich. / Nein, das bin ich nicht. Ich bin …*
Welcome to …	*Herzlich willkommen bei …*
Thank you. It's nice to be here.	*Dankeschön. Es ist schön, hier zu sein.*

Introducing people

These are my colleagues, John and Mary.	*Das sind meine Kollegen, John und Mary.*
Allow me to / I'd like to introduce … from the … department.	*Darf ich Ihnen … aus der …-abteilung vorstellen?*

Making a phone call

Identifying yourself

Good morning. My name's …	*Guten Morgen. Ich heiße …*
Good afternoon. This is … from (company).	*Guten Tag. Hier spricht … von (Firma).*
Good evening. I work for …	*Guten Abend. Ich arbeite bei …*

Making small talk

How are you?	*Wie geht es Ihnen?*
How's the weather today?	*Wie ist das Wetter bei Ihnen heute?*
Did you have a nice holiday?	*Haben Sie einen schönen Urlaub gehabt?*

Explaining the reason for your call

I was wondering if you could help me …	*Wären Sie so nett, mir bei … zu helfen?*
I'm enquiring about …	*Ich wollte mich nach … erkundigen.*
I'd like some information on …	*Ich hätte gern nähere Informationen zu …*
Could you tell me about … ?	*Könnten Sie mir etwas über … sagen?*

Asking for a person/department

I'd like to speak to Mr/Ms …	*Ich hätte gern (mit) Herrn/Frau … gesprochen.*
Could you put me through to the … department, please?	*Könnten Sie bitte mich zur …-abteilung durchstellen?*

Saying what you want to do

Can I leave a message?	*Kann ich eine Nachricht hinterlassen?*
I'll call again later.	*Ich rufe später noch einmal an.*
There's an urgent matter that I need to discuss with Mr/Ms … .	*Ich muss mit Herrn/Frau … über eine dringende Angelegenheit sprechen.*

Ending the call

Thank you for your help.	*Vielen Dank für Ihre Hilfe.*
You're welcome.	*Gern geschehen. / Bitte sehr.*
Goodbye.	*Auf Wiederhören.*
Have a nice day/evening.	*Einen schönen Tag/Abend noch.*

Writing emails

Unit 2

Salutation

Dear Ms/Mrs/Miss/Mr Smith *(formal)*	*Sehr geehrte Frau / Sehr geehrter Herr Schmidt*
Dear Sirs / Dear Sir or Madam *(formal)*	*Sehr geehrte Damen und Herren*
Dear Paul (and Paula)	*Lieber Paul (, Liebe Paula)*
Good morning, Paul	*Guten Morgen, Paul*
Hi/Hello Paul/Paula	*Hi/Hallo Paul/Paula*

Useful phrases

Complimentary close	
Regards / Best wishes / Yours sincerely *(formal)*	*Mit freundlichen Grüßen*
Cordially *(AE: formal)*	*Mit freundlichen Grüßen*
Yours faithfully *(formal)*	*Hochachtungsvoll*
Regards / Best regards	*Gruß/Grüße*
Best wishes	*Beste/Schöne/Liebe Grüße*
All the best / Take care	*Alles Gute*
Opening sentence	
I'm writing to … *(formal)*	*Ich schreibe Ihnen um zu …*
Just a quick note/message/line to …	*Nur eine kurze Mitteilung/Nachricht …*
Conclusion	
I look forward to your reply. *(formal)*	*Ich freue mich auf Ihre Antwort.*
Many thanks in advance. *(formal)*	*Vielen Dank im Voraus.*
I hope to hear from you soon.	*Ich freue mich darauf, bald von dir zu hören.*

Making arrangements by email

Inviting somebody to a meeting	
Ms Smith would like to invite you to a meeting on (day) at (time).	*Frau Smith möchte Sie zu einem Treffen um (Zeit) Uhr am (Tag) einladen.*
I would like to invite you to lunch/dinner / a working breakfast on (day).	*Ich möchte Sie zum Essen / zum Abendessen / zu einem Arbeitsfrühstück am (Tag) einladen.*
The meeting will take place at my office / our premises in (town/city).	*Das Treffen findet in meinem Büro / in unseren Räumlichkeiten in (Ort/Stadt) statt.*
We have chosen the (name of restaurant) for our breakfast/lunch/dinner.	*Wir haben uns für (Name des Restaurants) für unser Frühstück/Mittagessen/Abendessen entschieden*
Accepting the invitation	
Thank you for your invitation to meet you / to participate in discussions at (place). *(formal)*	*Vielen Dank für Ihre Einladung für das Treffen / zu der Besprechung in (Ort).*
I am pleased / We are delighted to accept your invitation/offer.	*Gern nehme ich / nehmen wir Ihre Einladung / Ihr Angebot an.*
Saying no	
I regret I cannot attend / I cannot come to the meeting/dinner because … *(formal)*	*Ich bedauere sehr, dass ich an dem Treffen/ Abendessen nicht teilnehmen kann, weil …*
I'm sorry, but I can't because (reason) on that date / at that time.	*Es tut mir leid, aber ich kann da nicht, weil ich an diesem Tag / zu dieser Zeit (Grund) …*
Making an alternative suggestion	
I would like to suggest postponing the meeting until (date/time). (formal)	*Ich möchte vorschlagen, den Termin auf (Datum/ Uhrzeit) zu verschieben.*
How about meeting for dinner on (day) at (time) instead?	*Wie wäre es, wenn wir uns stattdessen am (Tag) um (Uhrzeit) zum Abendessen treffen?*
Conclusion	
I look forward to your reply. *(formal)*	*Ich freue mich auf Ihre Antwort.*
I hope to hear from you soon.	*Ich hoffe, von Ihnen bald zu hören.*
Many thanks.	*Besten Dank.*

Writing business letters

Unit 3

Salutation	
Dear Sir or Madam *(BE: to a firm)*	*Sehr geehrte Damen und Herren*
Gentlemen *(AE: to a firm)*	*Sehr geehrte Damen und Herren*
Dear Mr Brown	*Sehr geehrter Herr Brown*
Dear Sharon	*Liebe Sharon*

Useful phrases

Complimentary close

Yours faithfully (*BE: to a firm*)	*Hochachtungsvoll*
Yours very truly / Cordially yours (*AE: to a firm*)	*Hochachtungsvoll*
Yours sincerely (*BE*)	*Mit freundlichen Grüßen*
Sincerely yours / Best personal regards (*AE*)	*mit freundlichen Grüßen / Beste Grüße*

Giving directions

Unit 4

How to get somewhere

Go across the …	*Gehen Sie über …*
Go straight ahead.	*Gehen/Fahren Sie geradeaus.*
Turn left/right.	*Biegen Sie links/rechts ab.*
Take the first right/left.	*Nehmen Sie die erste Straße rechts/links.*
Keep to / Stay on the right/left.	*Halten Sie sich / Bleiben Sie rechts/links.*
It's just after/past/behind the …	*Es ist vor/nach/hinter …*
in the middle of the …	*mitten in … / in der Mitte von …*
in the distance	*in einiger Entfernung/ganz hinten*
on the right-hand side / on the left-hand side	*auf der rechten Seite / auf der linken Seite*

Writing an enquiry

Unit 5

Source of address

We saw your advertisement/brochure/catalogue in …	*Wir haben Ihre Anzeige / Ihren Prospekt/Katalog in … gesehen.*
We have your name from the chamber of commerce / our business partners, (firm), in …	*Ihren Namen haben wir von der Handelskammer / unserem Geschäftspartner, (Firma), in … erhalten.*
We visited your stand/presentation at the trade fair in …	*Wir haben Ihren Stand / Ihre Präsentation auf der Messe in … besucht.*

About your firm

We are a small/medium-sized/well-known firm.	*Wir sind eine kleine/mittelständische/bekannte Firma.*
We are manufacturers/suppliers of … for/to the … trade.	*Wir sind Hersteller/Zulieferer von … für die …-Branche.*
We are interested in your … (products).	*Wir interessieren uns für Ihre … (Produkte).*
We are interested in expanding our range of …	*Wir sind daran interessiert, unser Angebot an … zu erweitern.*

What you require

Please send us samples of your … / your latest catalogue.	*Bitte schicken Sie uns Muster/Proben Ihrer … / Ihren neuesten Katalog.*
Please give/send us a quotation for …	*Bitte schicken Sie uns ein Angebot für …*
Please let us have details of all discounts.	*Bitte informieren Sie uns zu allen Einzelheiten Ihrer Rabatte.*
Full details of your terms of delivery and payment would be appreciated.	*Wir würden uns freuen, genaue Informationen zu Ihren Versand- und Zahlungsbedingungen zu erhalten.*

References

References can be obtained from (name of bank/ company).	*Referenzen können von (Name der Bank/Firma) angefordert werden.*

Polite ending

If your goods/products find our customers' approval, …	*Wenn Ihre Waren/Produkte unseren Kunden zusagen, …*
… we will be able to place / consider placing a sizeable order very soon.	*… werden wir in naher Zukunft eine größere Bestellung in Auftrag geben / in Erwägung ziehen.*
We look forward to hearing from you soon.	*Wir würden uns freuen, bald von Ihnen zu hören.*
We look forward to receiving your reply/offer within the next few days.	*Wir würden uns freuen, Ihre Antwort / Ihr Angebot in den nächsten Tagen zu erhalten.*

Writing offers

Reference to enquiry	
Many thanks for your letter of (date) enquiring about …	*Vielen Dank für Ihren Brief vom (Datum) mit Ihrer Anfrage bzgl. …*
We refer to your enquiry of (date) for …	*Wir beziehen uns auf Ihre Anfrage vom (Datum) für …*
We are pleased to note from your letter of (date) that you are interested in …	*In Ihrem Schreiben vom (Datum) haben Sie Ihr Interesse für … bekundet.*
Reference to information, samples, etc.	
Enclosed please find our latest brochure/catalogue/ leaflet/price list.	*Anbei finden Sie unsere(n) aktuelle(n) Prospekt/ Katalog/Werbeschrift/Preisliste.*
We are sending you a selection of samples.	*Wir übersenden Ihnen eine Auswahl an Mustern/ Proben.*
We would like to draw your attention to our latest special offer / product/range.	*Wir möchten Sie auf unser aktuelles Sonderangebot / Produkt / Sortiment aufmerksam machen.*
Terms	
We would like to point out that our/all prices are quoted (Incoterms® 2010 rule).	*Wir möchten darauf hinweisen, dass sich unsere Preise (Incoterms®-2010-Code) verstehen.*
We draw your attention to the fact that our guarantee / warranty period extends over / is valid for …	*Wir möchten Sie darauf hinweisen, dass unser Garantie-/Haftungszeitraum … beträgt.*
Terms of payment: we offer a 2% cash discount for payment within … days.	*Zahlungsbedingungen: Bei Zahlung binnen … Tagen bieten wir 2% Skonto.*
For orders over … we offer a discount of … %.	*Für Bestellungen über … bieten wir ein Rabatt von … % an.*
We have pleasure in offering you …% discount on/ off the net price for …	*Wir freuen uns, Ihnen ein Rabatt in Höhe von … % vom Nettopreis anbieten zu können.*
Further information	
Our delivery date is approximately … days/weeks after receipt of your order.	*Die Lieferung erfolgt etwa … Tage/Wochen nach Eingang Ihrer Bestellung.*
Delivery time is about … weeks/months.	*Der Lieferzeitraum beträgt etwa … Wochen/Monate.*
We can guarantee immediate delivery.	*Wir können Ihnen die sofortige Lieferung garantieren.*
Polite ending	
We hope that the enclosed samples meet with your approval.	*Wir hoffen, dass die beigefügten Muster/Proben Ihre Zustimmung finden.*
We look forward to receiving your order and assure you that we will give it our prompt and careful attention.	*Wir freuen uns auf Ihre Bestellung und sichern eine zügige und gewissenhafte Abwicklung zu.*

Ordering on the phone

Unit 6

Placing the order	
I'd like to place an order for …	*Ich möchte eine Bestellung über … aufgeben.*
I'm phoning with a repeat order.	*Ich rufe Sie an, um eine Nachbestellung aufzugeben / wegen eines Folgeauftrags.*
Do you have the details of our last order?	*Haben Sie die Daten unserer letzten Bestellung?*
Can you take my order? / supply us from stock?	*Können Sie meine Bestellung entgegennehmen / aus dem Lagerbestand liefern?*
How soon can you deliver? / dispatch the goods?	*Wie schnell können Sie liefern / die Ware ausliefern?*
Shall I repeat that?	*Soll ich das wiederholen?*
Could you read that back to me, please?	*Könnten Sie mir das bitte noch einmal vorlesen?*
Taking the order	
As this is a repeat order, we can give you a discount.	*Da es sich um eine(n) Nachbestellung / Folgeauftrag handelt, können wir Ihnen ein Rabatt anbieten.*
We can dispatch / send out the goods immediately/ tomorrow / next week.	*Wir können die Ware sofort/morgen / nächste Woche ausliefern.*
Can I confirm these details?	*Kann ich diese Einzelheiten/Angaben bestätigen?*
Could you repeat that, please?	*Könnten Sie das bitte wiederholen?*

Placing and acknowledging orders

Placing orders

Thank you for your quotation of … (date).	*Vielen Dank für Ihr Angebot vom … (Datum).*
Many thanks for your quotation.	*Vielen Dank für Ihr Angebot.*
We agree to your terms and are pleased to give you an order for …	*Wir stimmen Ihren Bedingungen zu und freuen uns, Sie mit einer Bestellung über … zu beauftragen.*
We enclose / are enclosing order no. …	*Wir fügen Bestellnr. … bei.*
We understand that all prices are (Incoterms® 2010 rule) / include VAT.	*Wir sind uns bewusst, dass sich alle Preise (Incoterms®-2010-Code) / inklusive Mehrwertsteuer verstehen.*
Payment will be made by (method of payment) on delivery of the goods.	*Die Zahlung erfolgt durch (Zahlungsmethode) bei Lieferung der Ware.*
Payment will be made within … days of receipt of the goods.	*Die Zahlung erfolgt innerhalb von … Tagen nach Lieferung der Ware.*
Please acknowledge this order by return of post.	*Bitte bestätigen Sie diese Bestellung postwendend.*
We look forward to receiving the goods as soon as possible.	*Wir würden uns freuen, die Ware sobald wie möglich zu erhalten.*
We trust you will give this order your prompt/careful attention.	*Wir erwarten eine zügige/gewissenhafte Abwicklung dieser Bestellung.*

Acknowledging orders

Thank you for your order of (date) for (goods).	*Vielen Dank für Ihre Bestellung vom (Datum) für (Ware).*
We were very glad/happy/pleased to receive your order.	*Wir haben Ihre Bestellung dankend erhalten.*
We are pleased/happy to confirm your order.	*Gern bestätigen wir Ihnen den Eingang Ihrer Bestellung.*
We are sure that the items/goods will arrive in good condition.	*Wir sind uns sicher, dass die Ware in bestem Zustand bei Ihnen ankommen wird.*
We will execute your order to your complete/full satisfaction.	*Wir werden Ihre Bestellung zu Ihrer vollsten Zufriedenheit ausführen.*
We look forward to doing business with you again / further orders in the future.	*Wir freuen uns auf die weitere Zusammenarbeit / zukünftige Bestellungen.*

Attending meetings

Unit 7

Invitation to a meeting

The monthly/quarterly/annual meeting of the team/staff/group will be held / will take place on (date) at (time) in (place).	*Das monatliche/vierteljährliche/jährliche Treffen des Teams / der Mitarbeiter/Gruppe findet am (Datum) um (Uhrzeit) in (Ort) statt.*
Please confirm / let us know that you will / are able to attend.	*Bitte den Termin bestätigen / informieren Sie uns über Ihr Kommen.*

Starting a meeting

Thank you all for coming.	*Danke, dass Sie alle gekommen sind.*
I'd like to welcome you all to this meeting.	*Ich möchte Sie alle zu dieser Besprechung willkommen heißen.*
Can we settle down, please?	*Darf ich um Ruhe bitten?*
Who is taking the minutes?	*Wer führt Protokoll?*
(Name of person) sends his/her apologies.	*(Name der Person) lässt sich entschuldigen.*
(Name of person) is going to chair this meeting.	*(Name der Person) wird diese Besprechung leiten/moderieren.*

Introducing people

This is (name of person). He/She is in charge of … (company/department).	*Das ist (Name der Person). Er/Sie leitet die … (Firma/Abteilung).*
(Name of person), this would be a good point for you to tell us about yourself and your position in the firm.	*(Name der Person), dies wäre ein guter Zeitpunkt, uns etwas über sich und Ihre Rolle in der Firma zu berichten.*

Setting the agenda

Our meeting today is to discuss …	*Ziel unserer heutigen Besprechung ist …*
We have a lot to cover today, so I'd like to begin by looking at ...	*Wir haben viel vor heute, also möchte ich mit … anfangen.*
The first / most important item on today's agenda is …	*Der erste/wichtigste Tagesordnungspunkt für heute ist …*
Today, we're going to discuss last month's figures and see where we can make an improvement.	*Heute werden wir die Zahlen des vergangenen Monats besprechen und uns überlegen, wo noch Verbesserungspotenzial besteht.*
Let's get down to business.	*Also an die Arbeit.*

Giving a presentation

Unit 8

Introduction and structure

This morning, I'm going to talk about …	*Heute morgen werde ich über … sprechen.*
Our topic today is …	*Das heutige Thema lautet …*
I've divided the presentation into three main parts, as follows: …	*Ich habe meinen Vortrag / meine Präsentation in drei Hauptthemen unterteilt, und zwar …*
First/Firstly, … ; second/secondly, … ; after that / then	*Erstens, … ; zweitens, … ; anschließend …*
The next topic I'm going to talk about is …	*Das nächste Thema, das ich behandeln möchte, lautet …*
Now I'd like to move on to …	*Jetzt möchte ich zum Thema … übergehen.*

Handouts

I've prepared a few things/handouts for you to take away.	*Ich habe etwas / ein paar Handouts für Sie zum Mitnehmen vorbereitet.*
I hope you'll find these copies of the graphics useful.	*Ich hoffe, dass Sie diese Ausdrucke der Grafiken nützlich finden.*

Graphs

The graph/chart shows/presents …	*Die Grafik / das Diagramm zeigt … / stellt … dar.*
The horizontal/vertical axis has a scale from … to …	*Die waagrechte/senkrechte Achse hat eine Skala von … bis …*
The x axis / The y axis is divided into … units/ sections each representing …	*Die X-Achse / Die Y-Achse unterteilt sich in … Einheiten/Abschnitte, die … darstellen.*

Conclusion

I'm now nearing the end of my talk.	*Ich komme nun zum Ende meines Vortrags.*
Before I finish my presentation, I'd just like to mention …	*Bevor ich meinen Vortrag beende, möchte ich kurz … erwähnen.*
Before I finish, I'd like to remind you of a few important facts and figures.	*Bevor ich meinen Vortrag beende, möchte ich (noch einmal) auf einige Daten und Fakten hinweisen.*
Finally, I'd like to say/stress how important these issues are.	*Abschließend möchte ich sagen/betonen, wie wichtig diese Themen/Fragen sind.*
I'd like to go over the main points/topics again.	*Ich möchte die Hauptpunkte/-themen nochmals kurz darlegen.*
Finally / In conclusion / To conclude / In summary, …	*Zum Schluss / Abschließend / Zusammenfassend …*

Questions

Are there any questions?	*Gibt es / Haben Sie noch Fragen?*
We have time for a few questions / one last question.	*Wir haben noch Zeit für ein paar Fragen / eine letzte Frage.*

Thanking the audience

Well, that's the end of my presentation.	*Damit bin ich am Ende meiner Präsentation angelangt.*
Thank you for your attention / for listening.	*Vielen Dank für Ihre Aufmerksamkeit / fürs Zuhören.*

Making complaints

Situation	
With reference to / We refer to our order number … which arrived / was due on … (date), …	*Mit Bezug auf / Wir beziehen uns auf unsere Bestellnummer …, die am … (Datum) eingetroffen ist / fällig war …*
I'm sorry to have to inform you that …	*Leider müssen wir Ihnen mitteilen, dass …*
When we opened the containers/boxes we discovered/saw that …	*Beim Öffnen der Behälter/Container bemerkten/ sahen wir, dass …*
… some of the items were broken/missing.	*… einige der Artikel kaputt waren / fehlten.*
… the bottles/containers were damaged.	*… die Flaschen/Container beschädigt waren.*
The goods/containers may have been dropped / roughly handled in transit.	*Die Ware/Behälter wurde(n) während des Transports möglicherweise fallen gelassen / unvorsichtig behandelt.*
It seems that the goods were not packed properly / packing was unsuitable.	*Offenbar wurde die Ware nicht ordnungsgemäß verpackt / war die Verpackung ungeeignet.*
Request	
Please investigate the matter as soon as possible.	*Bitte untersuchen Sie diese Angelegenheit so schnell wie möglich.*
Please let us know what can be done to solve this problem.	*Bitte teilen Sie uns mit, welche Maßnahmen getroffen werden können, um dieses Problem zu beheben.*
Could you please explain (why) … ?	*Könnten Sie bitte erklären (warum) … ?*
Reason	
We have a large order from a regular customer, which we have to fill quickly.	*Wir haben eine große Bestellung eines Stammkunden, die wir schnell ausführen müssen.*
We are unable to continue production until we have the equipment.	*Wir können mit der Produktion nicht fortfahren, solange die Geräte nicht da sind.*
If we do not receive the goods within the next … days, we will have to stop production.	*Wenn wir die Ware nicht innerhalb der nächsten … Tagen erhalten, müssen wir die Produktion einstellen.*
Polite ending	
We hope to receive your answer / an explanation immediately / without delay / by … (date).	*Wir hoffen auf Ihre sofortige/unverzügliche Antwort/ Erklärung / bis zum … (Datum).*
We would add that any further business with your company will depend on how this matter is settled.	*Wir möchten hinzufügen, dass zukünftige Geschäfte mit Ihrer Firma davon abhängig sind, wie diese Angelegenheit geklärt wird.*
We must point out that our further business relationship will depend on a satisfactory solution to the problem.	*Wir müssen darauf hinweisen, dass unsere weitere Zusammenarbeit von einer zufriedenstellenden Lösung des Problems abhängt.*

Adjusting complaints

Polite opening	
We are very sorry (to hear) that the goods arrived damaged/broken/late.	*Wir bedauern sehr, dass die Ware bei Ihnen beschädigt/kaputt/verspätet eingetroffen ist.*
We are very sorry (to learn) that you have received faulty/damaged / the wrong goods.	*Es tut uns sehr leid, dass Sie mangelhafte/ schadhafte / die falsche Ware erhalten haben.*
Please accept our sincere apologies.	*Wir bitten vielmals um Entschuldigung.*
We apologize for the inconvenience caused.	*Wir entschuldigen uns vielmals für die entstandenen Unannehmlichkeiten.*
Reason	
Unfortunately, there was a mix-up in our sales department.	*Leider ist es in unserer Vertriebsabteilung zu einer Verwechslung gekommen.*
We are sorry to say that one of our staff was ill and could not complete the order.	*Leider war einer unserer Mitarbeiter krank und konnte daher die Bestellung nicht bearbeiten.*
The damage was caused by bad handling in transit / a problem with the packing.	*Der Schaden ist durch mangelhafte Abfertigung/ Handhabung während des Transports / ein Problem bei Verpackung entstanden.*
We have had some problems with new software but these have now been solved.	*Wir hatten einige Probleme mit der neuen Software, aber diese konnten behoben werden.*

Action taken	
We have sent a replacement consignment by courier / by express delivery which you will receive by … at the latest.	*Wir haben Ihnen per Expresslieferung eine Ersatzlieferung geschickt, die sie spätestens bis … erhalten werden*
We would be greatful if you could return the (incorrect) consignment at our expense.	*Wir wären Ihnen dankbar, wenn Sie die (falsche) Lieferung auf unseren Kosten zurückschicken könnten.*

Polite ending	
We hope that we can continue our successful business relationship, despite this problem.	*Wir hoffen sehr, dass wir trotz dieses Problems unsere erfolgreiche Zusammenarbeit fortsetzen können.*
We assure you that we will make every effort to ensure there are no problems in the future.	*Wir möchten Ihnen versichern, dass wir alles tun werden, um derartige Probleme in Zukunft zu vermeiden.*

Writing reminders

Unit 10

First reminders	
We are writing in connection with the above-mentioned invoice/statement.	*Wir schreiben bezugnehmend auf die oben genannte Rechnung.*
This is to inform you that our invoice for … (sum) is overdue.	*Hiermit möchten wir Ihnen mitteilen, dass unsere Rechnung über … (Summe) überfällig ist.*
We are sure this must be an oversight and have included a copy of the invoice for your convenience.	*Wir sind uns sicher, dass es sich hierbei um einen Irrtum handelt, und fügen zu Ihrer Information eine Kopie der Rechnung bei.*
If your payment of our invoice has crossed with this letter, we kindly ask you to ignore this reminder.	*Falls Sie die Rechnung schon beglichen haben sollten, betrachten dieses Schreiben bitte als gegenstandslos.*

Second reminders	
We refer to our previous letter of … (date) / with regard to the above-mentioned invoice.	*Wir schreiben bezugnehmend auf unser letztes Schreiben vom … (Datum) / auf die oben genannte Rechnung.*
We have not received any reply from you so far.	*Bislang haben wir noch keine Rückmeldung von Ihnen erhalten.*
We must point out that this is our second letter to you.	*Dies ist unser zweites Schreiben an Sie.*
Payment is now … (length of time) overdue.	*Ihre Zahlung ist nun … (Zeitspanne) überfällig.*

Third or final reminders	
Although two previous requests have been made to you for settlement of the overdue account/balance, no remittance has been received.	*Trotz zweimaliger Aufforderung/Bitte, den überfälligen Betrag zu begleichen, haben wir keine Überweisung von Ihnen erhalten.*
We must ask for payment by … (date).	*Wir bitten Sie um Zahlung bis … (Datum).*
We must insist that you settle the invoice within … (number of days) days at the latest.	*Wir möchten Sie dringend bitten, diese Rechnung innerhalb von … (Anzahl Tage) Tagen zu begleichen.*
If we do not receive payment by … (date) we will have to start legal proceedings.	*Wenn wir bis zum … (Datum) keine Zahlung erhalten, werden wir rechtliche Schritte gegen Sie einleiten.*

Writing replies to reminders

Apology	
We are sorry that we have not responded to your letters until now.	*Wir möchten uns entschuldigen, bisher auf Ihre Schreiben nicht reagiert zu haben.*
Please accept our apologies for the delay in settling your invoice / our account with you.	*Bitte verzeihen Sie die Verzögerung beim Begleichen Ihrer Rechnung.*

Explanation	
We have not paid / Payment will be late because … (reason).	*Wir haben bislang noch nicht bezahlt, weil … / Die Zahlung verzögert sich, da … (Grund).*
Payment has been withheld because the wrong goods were delivered / we were given the wrong bank account number.	*Die Zahlung wurde einbehalten, da die falsche Ware geliefert wurde / wir die falsche Kontoverbindung erhalten haben.*

Suggestion	
We promise to pay … (amount) by … (date).	*Wir versichern Ihnen, … (Betrag) bis zum … (Datum) zu überweisen.*
Please allow us a further … (number of days/weeks) to pay.	*Bitte gestatten Sie uns weitere … (Anzahl Tage/Wochen), um den Betrag zu begleichen.*
We would like to pay in … (number) instalments.	*Wir möchten den Betrag in … (Anzahl) Raten zahlen.*
We (sincerely) hope that you will allow us this extra time / grant us this concession.	*Wir hoffen sehr, dass Sie uns diese verlängerte Frist gewähren/einräumen.*
Close	
Once again, we would like to say that we are sorry about this delay / to offer you our sincerest apologies for this delay.	*Wir möchten uns nochmals für die Verzögerung entschuldigen.*
We hope that, despite this problem, we can continue our successful business relationship.	*Wir hoffen, dass wir unsere erfolgreiche Zusammenarbeit trotz dieses Problems fortsetzen können.*
We will make every effort to ensure there are no problems in future.	*Wir werden alles tun, um derartige Probleme in Zukunft zu vermeiden.*

Making enquiries about trade fairs and conference facilities

Reason for enquiry	
We have seen your advertisement on the … (website) / in … (magazine).	*Wir haben Ihre Anzeige auf … (Webseite) / in … (Zeitschrift) gesehen.*
We are looking for a trade fair / an exhibition where we can present/launch our company/products.	*Wir sind auf der Suche nach einer Messe/Ausstellung, wo wir unsere Firma/Produkte präsentieren/vorstellen können.*
We are looking for conference facilities large enough to accommodate / with enough room for 20 people.	*Wir suchen Tagungsräume für 20 Personen.*
Please quote us prices for / let us have your quotation for the following: …	*Bitte teilen Sie uns Ihre Preise für das Folgende mit: …*
General requirements	
We would need an exhibition area / a stand/space measuring … (size) equipped with … (details).	*Wir benötigen eine Ausstellungsfläche / einen Stand/Platz mit den Maßen … (Größe) mit folgender Ausstattung: … (Einzelheiten).*
We would like an end stand / a corner stand far away from any competition/competitors.	*Wir möchten einen Stand am Rand der Ausstellungshalle / Eckstand, der sehr weit von der Konkurrenz / unseren Konkurrenten entfernt ist.*
Facilities, fixtures and fittings	
Our requirements regarding / with regard to facilities are as follows: … (list)	*Unsere Anforderungen bezüglich der Ausstattung sind wie folgt: … (Liste)*
We require/need a television / DVD player / telephone / photocopier / digital projector.	*Wir benötigen/brauchen ein(en) Fernseher / DVD-Spieler / Telefon / Kopierer / Beamer.*

Booking and changing flights

Unit 11

Booking a flight	
I'd like to book … (number) people on a one-way flight / return flights from … to … .	*Ich möchte … (Anzahl) Personen auf Hin- / und Rückflügen von … nach … buchen.*
Please book … (number) seats on the flight leaving … at … (time) and arriving in … at … (time) on the morning of … (date).	*Bitte buchen Sie … (Anzahl) Plätze für den Flug von … um … (Uhrzeit) mit Ankunft in … um … (Uhrzeit) am Morgen des … (Datum).*
Business/first/economy class, please.	*Business Class / Erste Klasse / Economy Class, bitte.*
Is that a direct flight?	*Ist das ein Direktflug?*
Are there any available/free seats on these flights?	*Sind für diese Flüge noch freie Plätze / Plätze verfügbar?*
I'd like an aisle / a window seat, please.	*Ich hätte gern einen Fensterplatz/Gangplatz.*
What about return flights?	*Wie sieht es mit Rückflügen aus?*
Could you send confirmation and tickets, please?	*Könnten Sie mir bitte eine Buchungsbestätigung und die Tickets zukommen lassen?*

Useful phrases

Changing a flight

Is it possible / too late to change/cancel the reservation I made last week?	*Ist es noch möglich / schon zu spät, die Reservierung von letzter Woche zu ändern/stornieren?*
Unfortunately, my boss/colleague can't travel at the moment.	*Leider kann mein Chef/Vorgesetzter/Kollege im Moment nicht reisen.*
Is there an / How much is the extra charge for changing/cancelling a reservation?	*Verlangen Sie für die Reservierungsänderung/-stornierung eine Gebühr?*

Booking hotel accommodation

Request for information

We have seen your home page on the Internet.	*Wir haben Ihre Homepage im Internet gesehen.*
The accommodation service at … (name of exhibition) has recommended your hotel.	*Der Übernachtungsservice bei der … (Name der Messe/Ausstellung) hat uns Ihr Hotel empfohlen.*
Please let me/us know if your hotel is near / within easy reach of the airport / exhibition centre / city centre.	*Bitte teilen Sie mir/uns mit, ob Ihr Hotel in der Nähe des Flughafens / des Messegeländes/Stadtzentrums liegt.*
We would like to know if your hotel has an indoor swimming pool / WLAN service / …	*Wir würden gerne erfahren, ob Ihr Hotel über ein(en) Hallenbad / WLAN-Zugang / … verfügt.*

Type of accommodation required / number of nights

I would like to book/reserve … (number) single/double room(s) for … night(s).	*Ich möchte ein Einzelzimmer/Doppelzimmer für … Nächte buchen/reservieren.*
I/We need/require the rooms from … to … .	*Wir benötigen die Zimmer vom … bis zum … .*
Please confirm that the rooms are non-smoking.	*Bitte bestätigen Sie, dass es sich um Nichtraucherzimmer handelt.*

Prices and confirmation

Please quote your best rates for the above-mentioned accommodation.	*Bitte teilen Sie uns Ihr bestes Preisangebot für die oben genannte Unterkunft mit.*
Please let us have details of your corporate rates.	*Bitte informieren Sie uns zu den Einzelheiten Ihrer Firmenangebote.*
Please send us confirmation of this booking as soon as possible.	*Bitte schicken Sie uns sobald wie möglich eine Bestätigung dieser Buchung.*

Writing a covering letter

Unit 12

Opening phrases

In reply to / With reference to your advertisement in … (newspaper) of … (date), …	*Bezugnehmend auf Ihre Ausschreibung in … (Zeitung) vom … (Datum), …*
I see that you are looking for a/an … (job).	*Wie ich sehe, sind Sie auf der Suche nach einem/einer … (Berufsbezeichnung).*
I would like / wish to apply for the above-mentioned position/post of … (job).	*Hiermit möchte ich mich für die oben genannte Stelle als … (Berufsbezeichnung) bewerben.*

Education/training / present employment

I attended … (school/college) for … (length of time).	*Von … bis … (Jahr) besuchte ich (Schule/Hochschule/Universität).*
I studied … (subjects) at vocational school in … (town/city) from … (date) to … (date).	*An der Berufsfachschule in … (Ort) lernte/belegte ich … (Fächer) von … (Datum) bis … (Datum).*
At present I am working for a/an… (type of company) as a/an… (job).	*Zurzeit arbeite ich für eine / bei einer … (Firmenbezeichnung) als … (Berufsbezeichnung).*
I will complete my period of training on … (date).	*Am … (Datum) werde ich meine Ausbildung abschließen.*

Closing paragraph

I enclose / Enclosed is my CV/résumé / a list of my qualifications and experience.	*Anbei finden Sie meinen Lebenslauf / eine Übersicht/Liste meiner Qualifikationen und Erfahrungen.*
I am available for interview at your earliest convenience.	*Für ein Vorstellungsgespräch stehe ich Ihnen jederzeit gern zur Verfügung.*
I hope you will consider my application favourably and (I) look forward to hearing from you in the near future.	*Ich hoffe, Sie werden meine Bewerbung positiv betrachten und (ich) freue mich darauf, von Ihnen bald zu hören.*

Basic word list

Dieses Liste enthält Grundwörter, die in *Office Matters – 3rd Edition* als bekannt vorausgesetzt werden.

A

able, to be ~ können, in der Lage sein
about über, etwa
above über, oben(stehend), oben genannt
absolutely absolut, völlig
accept annehmen, akzeptieren
across (quer) über
active aktiv(iert)
activity Tätigkeit, Aktivität
add zusammenzählen, hinzufügen
address Adresse; adressieren
advert(isement) Werbung, Anzeige
afraid, I'm ~ leider
after (all) schließlich (doch)
afternoon Nachmittag
again wieder
age Alter
agree zustimmen, vereinbaren
aim Ziel, Absicht
air Luft
airport Flughafen
all alle(s)
allow erlauben, gestatten, (zu)lassen
almost fast, beinahe
alone allein(e)
along entlang
already schon, bereits
also auch, außerdem
although obwohl
altogether insgesamt
always immer
a.m. vormittags, morgens (vor 12 Uhr)
among zwischen, unter
amount Menge, Betrag
angry wütend, verärgert
another noch eine/r/s
answer Antwort, Lösung; (be)antworten
any irgendetwas, -welche, jede
anybody jemand, jede/r
anyone jemand, jede/r
anything etwas, alles
anyway jedenfalls, sowieso
anywhere irgendwo(hin)
apart from abgesehen von, außer
area Gebiet, Bereich
arrange arrangieren, vereinbaren
arrival Ankunft
arrive ankommen
ask fragen, bitten
assistant Assistent/in
away weg, entfernt

B

back Rückseite, Rücken; zurück
bad schlecht, schlimm
badly sehr
bag Tasche, Tüte, Beutel
basic grundsätzlich, einfach
basically grundsätzlich, im Grunde
because weil
become werden
before vor(her)
begin anfangen, beginnen
beginning Anfang
behind hinter, hinten
believe glauben
belong gehören
below unter, unten(stehend)
beneath unter(halb), unten
beside neben
best beste, am besten
better besser
between zwischen
big groß
bit Stück
board Brett, Tafel
body Körper
book Buch; buchen, reservieren
boring langweilig
bored gelangweilt
born geboren
boss Chef/in
both beide
bottle Flasche
bottom Unterseite, Unterteil, Boden, Ende
box Kasten, Kästchen, Kiste, Schachtel
bracket Klammer
breakfast Frühstück
bring bringen, holen
broad breit
broken kaputt
busy beschäftigt, besetzt
button Taste, Knopf
buy kaufen
bye tschüs

C

call Anruf; (an)rufen
caller Anrufer/in
camera Fotoapparat
can dürfen, können
cannot nicht können
car Auto
car park Parkplatz, Parkhaus
care, take ~ of sich kümmern um
careful(ly) vorsichtig, sorgfältig
case Fall
cash Bargeld
chain Kette
chair Stuhl
change (Ver-)Änderung; (aus)wechseln, (sich) ändern
cheap billig, günstig
check überprüfen, kontrollieren
cheque Scheck
choice Wahl, Auswahl
choose (aus)wählen
Christmas Weihnachten
city (Groß-)Stadt
class Klasse
clean sauber; reinigen, säubern
clear klar, deutlich
clever klug, intelligent
clock Uhr
close schließen, zumachen
close (to) nahe (bei)
clothes Kleidung, Kleider
clue Hinweis, Tipp
coffee Kaffee
colour Farbe
come kommen, geliefert werden
comma Komma
common üblich, gemeinsam, verbreitet
commonly häufig, gewöhnlich, üblicherweise
complete vollständig; vervollständigen
completely völlig
contact Kontakt, Verbindung
control Kontrolle; kontrollieren, regeln, steuern, überwachen
copy Exemplar, Kopie; abschreiben, kopieren
corner Ecke
correct richtig, genau; korrigieren
cost Kosten; kosten
could konnte/n, könnte/n
count zählen
country Land, Staat
couple Paar
course Kurs, Lehrgang, Gang
create (er)schaffen, erstellen
creative kreativ, schöpferisch
cross (an)kreuzen
culture Kultur

D

damage Schaden; beschädigen
danger Gefahr
dangerous gefährlich
dark Dunkelheit, dunkel
data Daten
date Datum, Termin
date of birth Geburtsdatum
day Tag
dear liebe/r

death Tod
decide entscheiden, beschließen
definite(ly) (ganz) sicher, bestimmt
delete löschen
describe beschreiben
description Beschreibung, Schilderung
desk (Schreib-)Tisch, Arbeitsplatz
details Einzelheiten, Angaben
dialogue Gespräch, Dialog
diary (Termin-)Kalender
dictionary Wörterbuch
die sterben
difference Unterschied
different unterschiedlich, verschieden
difficult schwer, schwierig
difficulty Schwierigkeit
dinner (Abend-)Essen
direct direkt, gerade
direction Richtung
disadvantage Nachteil, Schaden
dislike nicht mögen
do tun, machen
door Tür
draw zeichnen
drink Getränk; trinken
driver Fahrer/in
during während

E

each jede/r/s
early früh
east (nach) Osten, Ost-
Easter Ostern
easy, easily leicht, einfach
education Erziehung, (Aus-, Schul-)Bildung
educational Bildungs-
either entweder
electricity Elektrizität, Strom
else andere/r/s
empty leer
end Ende, Schluss; (be)enden
ending Ende
energy Energie
enjoy genießen, gefallen, gern tun
enough ausreichend, genug
enter eintreten, betreten, eingeben
entrance Eingang, Einfahrt
equal gleich
especially besonders
even sogar (noch)
evening Abend
ever je(mals)
every jede/r/s
everybody jede/r
everyone jede/r, alle
everything alles
exactly exakt, genau
example Beispiel
excellent hervorragend, ausgezeichnet
excited aufgeregt, begeistert
exciting aufregend, spannend
exercise book (Schul-)Heft
exercise Übung
expensive teuer
experience Erfahrung
expert Fachmann/-frau
express ausdrücken
extra zusätzlich
eye Auge

F

fact Tatsache
factory Fabrik
fairly ziemlich
false falsch
family Familie
far weit (entfernt)
fast schnell
feel (sich) fühlen, meinen, glauben
feeling Gefühl
(a) few ein paar, wenig/e
fight Kampf; (be)kämpfen
file Ordner, Datei
final letzte/r/s
finally schließlich, endlich
financial finanziell
find finden, suchen
find out herausfinden
fine gut, schön
finish (be)enden, abschließen, fertig werden
firm Firma
first(ly) erst; zuerst
fix festlegen, reparieren
flat Wohnung; flach
flight Flug
floor Etage, Stockwerk; (Fuß-)Boden
fly fliegen
follow (be)folgen
(the) following der/die/das Folgende
food Essen, Nahrung
foreign ausländisch, Auslands-, fremd
forget vergessen
form Form, Formular
forward nach vorne
free frei; gratis, kostenlos
friend Freund/in
friendly freund(schaft)lich
front Vorderseite
front, in ~ of vor
full voll
fully völlig
funny komisch, merkwürdig
future Zukunft; (zu)künftig

G

gap Lücke
garage Garage
gate Tor
general allgemein, generell, normal
generally im Allgemeinen, normalerweise
get holen, bekommen, werden
give geben
glad froh
go gehen, fahren
go ahead anfangen, weitermachen
go for sth sich bemühen um, gefallen
go on weitermachen, fortfahren
go out ausgehen
good gut
goodbye auf Wiedersehen
great groß(artig)
greatly in hohem Maße
greet (be)grüßen
greeting Gruß(formel), Begrüßung
ground Boden, Grund
group Gruppe; gruppieren
grow wachsen, werden
guess Annahme; raten, schätzen
guest Gast

H

half Hälfte; halb
hall Diele, Saal, Halle
handle umgehen mit, bearbeiten, erledigen, fertig werden mit
happen passieren, geschehen
happy glücklich, zufrieden
health Gesundheit
hear hören
heart Herz
heavy schwer
height Höhe, Größe
help Hilfe; helfen
helpful hilfreich, nützlich
here hier
high; highly hoch; äußerst
history Geschichte
holiday Ferien, Urlaub, Feiertag
home Zuhause, Heim; nach Hause
hope Hoffnung; hoffen
hopefully hoffentlich
hot heiß
hour Stunde
house Haus
how wie
however doch, jedoch
huge riesig
human menschlich
hurry sich beeilen

I

idea Vorstellung, Idee
identity Identität
if wenn, falls, ob
illness Krankheit
image Bild
important wichtig
impossible unmöglich
individual einzeln, individuell
informal ungezwungen, inoffiziell, informell
inform informieren, unterrichten
information Auskunft, Information(en), Angaben
inside innerhalb, drinnen
instead stattdessen
instead of statt
instruction Anweisung, Anleitung
interest Interesse; interessieren
interested interessiert
interesting interessant
introduce (sich) vorstellen, (miteinander) bekannt machen, einführen
introduction Einleitung, Einführung, Vorstellung

J

job Arbeit(sstelle), Aufgabe
join beitreten, verbinden
just einfach, nur, genau

K

keep (be)halten, weiterhin tun
key Schlüssel, Taste; Haupt-
kind freundlich; Art, Sorte
know kennen, wissen
knowledge Wissen, Kenntnis(se)

L

language Sprache
large groß
last dauern; letzte/r/s
late spät
later später
latest neueste/r/s
lead führen
learn lernen, erfahren
least, at ~ wenigstens
leave lassen, verlassen, ab-/wegfahren
left links; übrig
length Länge
less weniger, abzüglich
let erlauben, (zu)lassen
letter Buchstabe, Brief
level Ebene, Niveau
lie Lüge; lügen
life Leben
lift Fahrstuhl, Aufzug
light Licht, Leuchte; hell, leicht
like mögen; (ähnlich) wie
line Linie, Leitung, Zeile
list Liste; auflisten, notieren
listen zuhören
little klein, wenig
live wohnen, leben
local örtlich, lokal
log in/on einloggen
log off/out ausloggen
long lang
look Blick, Aussehen; (aus)sehen, blicken
look after sich kümmern um
look for suchen nach
look forward to sth sich auf etw freuen
lose verlieren
lots of/a lot of viel, viele
love Liebe; lieben, sehr gern mögen
lovely schön, hübsch, reizend
low niedrig
lunch Mittagessen

M

magazine Zeitschrift
main Haupt-, wichtigste/r/s
make machen
manage leiten, verwalten, regeln, (es) schaffen
manager Manager/in, leitende/r Angestellte
many viele
mark Note
match zuordnen, (zusammen) passen
may dürfen, können, mögen
maybe vielleicht
meal Essen, Mahlzeit
mean bedeuten, meinen, heißen
media Medien
medium mittlere; Medium, Mittel
meet (zusammen)treffen, begegnen
meeting Sitzung, Besprechung, Treffen
memory Gedächtnis, Speicher
message Meldung, Nachricht, Mitteilung, Botschaft
metal Metall
middle Mitte
might könnte(n) (vielleicht)
miss verpassen, vermissen
missing fehlende/r/s
mistake Fehler, Irrtum
mobile (phone) Mobiltelefon, Handy
money Geld
month Monat
monthly monatlich
more mehr
morning Morgen
most der/die/das meiste, die meisten
move (sich) bewegen, umziehen
movement Bewegung
much viel
must müssen

N

name Name; nennen, benennen
national national, staatlich
nationality Staatsangehörigkeit
near in der Nähe von
nearly beinahe, fast
need Bedarf, Bedürfnis; brauchen, benötigen
negative verneinend, negativ
neither … nor weder … noch
never nie(mals)
new neu
news Neuigkeit(en), Nachricht(en)
next nächste/r/s; danach
night Nacht
noon Mittag
normal(ly) normal(erweise)
north (nach) Norden, Nord-
note Notiz, Anmerkung; beachten, notieren
nothing nichts
now nun, jetzt
nowadays heutzutage
number Nummer, Zahl

O

object Gegenstand
of course natürlich, selbstverständlich
offer Angebot; anbieten, bieten
office Büro
often oft, häufig
oil Öl
old alt
once einmal, einst; sobald
only nur, einzig
open öffnen, eröffnen; offen, geöffnet
opposite Gegenteil; gegensätzlich, gegenüber
option Möglichkeit, Option
or oder
order bestellen, ordern
ordinary gewöhnlich, normal
organization Organisation
organize organisieren
original original, ursprünglich; Original(-)
other andere/r/s
ought to sollen
outside außerhalb (von)
over über
own eigene/r/s; besitzen

P

page Seite
pain Schmerz
pair Paar
paper Papier, Zeitung

part Teil, Bauteil
pass (a test) (eine Prüfung) bestehen
passport Pass
pay Lohn, Bezahlung; zahlen, bezahlen
pen Stift
per cent Prozent
perfect vollkommen, perfekt
perfectly völlig
perhaps vielleicht, eventuell
period Zeit(raum)
personal persönlich
phone Telefon; anrufen
photo(graphy) Foto(grafie)
phrase Redewendung, Satz(teil)
picture Bild
piece Stück, Teil
place Stelle, Platz; setzen, stellen
plain einfach
plan Plan; planen
plane Flugzeug
plastic Plastik, Kunststoff
pleasant angenehm, nett
plenty viel, reichlich
p.m. nachmittags, abends (nach 12 Uhr)
point Punkt; Komma
point to zeigen auf
poor arm, schlecht, mangelhaft
popular beliebt, populär
position Stellung, Lage, Position
positive positiv, bejahend
possibility Möglichkeit
possible möglich
possibly möglicherweise
power Kraft, Strom; antreiben
powerful mächtig, stark
practical praktisch
practice Praxis, Training
practise (ein)üben
prefer vorziehen, bevorzugen, lieber mögen
present Gegenwart; Geschenk; vorstellen, präsentieren
press drücken
price Preis
print Druck; drucken, ausdrucken
printer Drucker/in
printout (Computer-)Ausdruck
private privat, persönlich
probably wahrscheinlich
produce produzieren, herstellen
product Produkt, Erzeugnis
program(me) Programm, Sendung
properly richtig
proud stolz
provide liefern, bieten, zur Verfügung stellen
public öffentlich; Öffentlichkeit
push schieben, drücken
put setzen, stellen, legen

Q
quality Eigenschaft, Qualität
(a) quarter past/to Viertel nach/vor
question Frage
quick(ly) schnell
quiet ruhig
quite ziemlich, ganz

R
rarely selten
rather ziemlich, lieber
reach erreichen, greifen
read lesen
reader Leser/in, Lektüre
ready bereit, fertig
real echt, wirklich
really wirklich, eigentlich, tatsächlich
reason Vernunft, Grund
recent aktuell, neu
recently neulich, vor kurzem
record Aufzeichnung, Beleg
regular(ly) regelmäßig
relative Verwandte/r, relativ
relatively relativ, verhältnismäßig
remain (ver)bleiben
remember sich erinnern, daran denken
repair reparieren
repeat wiederholen
reserve reservieren
respect Respekt, Achtung; (be)achten, respektieren
restart neu starten
return zurückkehren, zurückgeben
rich reich
right rechts, richtig
risk Risiko; riskieren
road (Land-)Straße
role Rolle
role play Rollenspiel
room Zimmer, Raum
round Runde; rund
rude unhöflich, unverschämt
rule Regel, Vorschrift
run laufen (lassen); betreiben, leiten

S
sad traurig
safe(ly) sicher
same gleiche/r/s, der-, die-, dasselbe
save retten, sichern, sparen
say sagen
school Schule
screen Bildschirm
search Suche; (durch)suchen
second zweite/r/s, Sekunde
secondary school weiterführende Schule
secondly zweitens
secretary Sekretär/in
see sehen, besuchen, verstehen
seem (er)scheinen
sell (sich) verkaufen
send senden, schicken
sentence Satz
service Dienst, Dienstleistung, Service
set setzen, stellen
several etliche, einige, mehrere
shall sollen, werden
shelf Regal
shop Laden, Geschäft; einkaufen
short kurz, klein, knapp
should solle/n, sollte/n
show zeigen
show sb around jdn herumführen
shut schließen
side Seite
sign Zeichen, Anzeichen, Schild
simple einfach
since da, weil, seit
single einzig, einzeln
sit sitzen, sich hinsetzen
site Website
size Größe
skill Fähigkeit, Fertigkeit
slow langsam
small klein
smile lächeln
so also, damit, deshalb, so
some einige, etwas
someone jemand
something etwas
sometimes manchmal
somewhere irgendwo(hin)
soon bald
sorry traurig; Verzeihung
sound Klang, Geräusch; klingen, sich anhören
south (nach) Süden, Süd-
space Raum, Platz, Abstand
speak sprechen, reden
special besondere/r/s
specially speziell, extra, besonders
speed Geschwindigkeit
spell buchstabieren, schreiben
spelling Rechtschreibung, Schreibweise
spend (Geld) ausgeben, (Zeit) verbringen
stand stehen, aushalten
standard Standard; normal, üblich
start Beginn; anfangen, starten
state (Bundes-)Staat
statement Aussage, Erklärung, Feststellung
stay Aufenthalt; bleiben
step Schritt, Stufe

still still, trotzdem, (immer) noch
stop (an)halten, aufhören (mit)
street Straße
strength Kraft, Stärke
strong stark, heftig
student Student/in, Lernende/r
study lernen, studieren, untersuchen, betrachten
stuff Material, Stoff, Zeug
subject (Schul-)Fach, Thema
success Erfolg
successful erfolgreich
such as wie zum Beispiel
sure sicher
surname Nachname, Familienname
surprise Überraschung; überraschen

T
table Tisch, Tabelle
take nehmen, bringen, dauern
take off ausziehen, abnehmen, abheben
take part teilnehmen, mitmachen
talk Gespräch, Vortrag; sprechen, reden
tall groß, hoch
task Aufgabe
teach unterrichten, lehren
teacher Lehrer/in
team Mannschaft
technology Technik, Technologie
telephone (call) Telefon(anruf)
television Fernsehen, Fernseher
tell sagen, erzählen
test untersuchen, prüfen
than als
thank danken
thank you danke
thanks Dank; danke
then dann
there da, dort(hin)
these diese
thin dünn
thing Sache, Ding, Gegenstand
think denken, meinen, finden, glauben
those jene
though obwohl, allerdings, jedoch
through durch
throughout überall (in), die ganze Zeit hindurch
throw werfen
tick (off) mit einem Häkchen versehen, abhaken
ticket Karte, Fahrschein
tidy aufgeräumt, ordentlich; aufräumen
time Zeit, Mal
timetable Fahrplan, Stundenplan
tip Hinweis, Tipp
today heute
together zusammen
tomorrow morgen
tonight heute Abend/Nacht
too zu, auch
top Spitze, Gipfel; Spitzen-
topic Thema
total (Gesamt-)Summe; gesamte/r/s, Gesamt-
touch anfassen, berühren
town Stadt
toy Spielzeug
traffic Verkehr
train Zug
trainee Auszubildende/r, Praktikant/in
travel Reisen; reisen, fahren
trip Ausflug, Reise, Besuch
trouble Mühe, Umstände, Problem(e), Ärger
true wahr, richtig
try versuchen, probieren
turn (sich) drehen, wenden, werden
twice zweimal
type Art, Sorte, Typ; tippen, Schreibmaschine schreiben
typical typisch

U
unable unfähig, nicht in der Lage
under unter
understand verstehen, begreifen
unfriendly unfreundlich
university Universität
unless es sei denn, außer wenn
unlike anders als, im Gegensatz zu
until bis
use Gebrauch; gebrauchen, benutzen, verwenden
useful nützlich
user Anwender/in, Benutzer/in
usual gewöhnlich, normal, üblich
usually gewöhnlich, normalerweise, meistens

V
vary variieren, schwanken
verb Verb
visit Besuch; besuchen, besichtigen
visitor Besucher/in, Gast

W
wait warten
wall Wand, Mauer
want wollen
wash waschen
watch Armbanduhr
water Wasser
way Weg, Methode, Art (und Weise)
weather Wetter
week Woche
weekend Wochenende
weekly wöchentlich
welcome Willkommen; willkommen heißen
well gesund, gut; also
west (nach) Westen, West-
whatever was auch immer
wheel Rad
when wenn, als, wann
whenever immer wenn
where wo(hin)
whether ob
which welche
while während
who(m) wen, wem
whole ganz
why warum
wide breit, weit
will Wille; werde(n), wollen
window Fenster
wish Wunsch; wünschen
with mit, bei
within innerhalb (von), in
without ohne
woman Frau
wonderful wunderbar
wood Holz
word Wort
work Arbeit; funktionieren, arbeiten
worker Arbeiter/in
world Welt
world-famous weltberühmt
worldwide weltweit
worried besorgt, beunruhigt
worse schlechter, schlimmer
worst schlechteste/r/s, schlimmste/r/s
would würde/n
write schreiben
wrong falsch

Y
year Jahr
yesterday gestern
young jung

Chronological word list

Dieses Wörterverzeichnis enthält alle neuen Wörter aus *Office Matters – New Edition* in der Reihenfolge ihres Erscheinens (Seitenzahlen sind angegeben). Nicht angeführt sind die Wörter aus dem Grundwortschatz (vgl. *Basic word list*). Wörter aus den *Hörverständnisübungen* sind mit einem **T** *(Transkript)* und Wörter aus den *Partner files* mit einem **P** gekennzeichnet. Die Zahl am linken Rand gibt die Seitenzahl an.

Abkürzungen			
	AE = amerikanisches Englisch	*jdm* = jemandem	*pl* = plural noun
	BE = britisches Englisch	*jdn* = jemanden	*sb* = somebody
	etw = etwas	*jds* = jemandes	*sth* = something

UNIT 1

6	**daily** ['deɪli]	täglich
	routine [ru:'ti:n]	(Arbeits-)Ablauf
	office management assistant ['ɒfɪs ˌmænɪdʒmənt əsɪstənt]	Bürokaufmann/-frau
	formal ['fɔ:ml]	formell, förmlich
7	to **excuse** [ɪk'skju:s]	entschuldigen
	colleague ['kɒli:g]	Kollege, Kollegin
	to **consider** [kən'sɪdə]	in Erwägung ziehen, in Betracht ziehen
	career [kə'rɪə]	Laufbahn, Karriere
	to **make up one's mind** [meɪk ˌʌp wʌnz 'maɪnd]	sich entscheiden
	industry ['ɪndəstri]	Gewerbe, Branche, Industrie
	including [ɪn'klu:dɪŋ]	einschließlich
	manufacturing [ˌmænju'fæktʃərɪŋ]	Herstellung, Produktion
	variety [və'raɪəti]	Abwechslung
	support [sə'pɔ:t]	Unterstützung, Hilfe
	staff [stɑ:f]	Personal
	member of staff [ˌmembər əf 'stɑ:f]	Mitarbeiter/in
	workplace ['wɜ:kpleɪs]	Arbeitsplatz
	a good communicator [ə ˌgʊd kə'mju:nɪkeɪtə]	*etwa: jd, der gern auf Menschen zugeht*
	careers officer [kə'rɪəz ɒfɪsə]	Berufsberater/in
	qualification [ˌkwɒlɪfɪ'keɪʃn]	Abschluss, Qualifikation
	job centre ['dʒɒb sentə]	Arbeitsamt
	training ['treɪnɪŋ]	Ausbildung
	to **appear** [ə'pɪə]	erscheinen, auftauchen
	paragraph ['pærəgrɑ:f]	*(Text:)* Absatz
	advice [əd'vaɪs]	Ratschlag, (guter) Rat
8	**incorrect** [ˌɪnkə'rekt]	falsch, unzutreffend
	monotonous [mə'nɒtənəs]	eintönig, monoton, langweilig
	to **employ** [ɪm'plɔɪ]	beschäftigen, einstellen
	to **replace** [rɪ'pleɪs]	ersetzen, austauschen
	to **highlight** ['haɪlaɪt]	hervorheben, markieren
	paperwork ['peɪpəwɜ:k]	Unterlagen, Schriftstücke
	to **make sure** [ˌmeɪk 'ʃʊə]	sicherstellen, sich vergewissern
	envelope ['envələʊp]	Briefumschlag
	stationery ['steɪʃənri]	Schreibwaren, Briefpapier
	data processing [ˌdeɪtə 'prəʊsesɪŋ]	Datenverarbeitung
	to **keep records** [ˌki:p 'rekɔ:dz]	Unterlagen/Akten führen
	office supplies *pl* ['ɒfɪs səplaɪz]	Büromaterial
	spreadsheet ['spredʃi:t]	Tabellenkalkulation (-sdatei/-sprogramm)
	to **work hard** [ˌwɜ:k 'hɑ:d]	fleißig sein, viel arbeiten
	to **be fun** [bi 'fʌn]	Spaß machen
	to **set sth up** [ˌset 'ʌp]	etw einrichten, aufbauen
9	**photocopier** ['fəʊtəʊkɒpiə]	Fotokopierer
	as [əz]	während
	to **cope with sth** ['kəʊp wɪð]	mit etw zurechtkommen
T	**department** [dɪ'pɑ:tmənt]	Abteilung
	college ['kɒlɪdʒ]	Berufsfachschule, Fachhochschule
	administration [əd͵mɪnɪ'streɪʃn]	Verwaltung
	office communication [ˌɒfɪs kəmju:nɪ'keɪʃn]	Bürotätigkeit
	stressed [strest]	gestresst
	to **deal with sth** ['di:l wɪð]	mit etw umgehen
	work placement ['wɜ:k pleɪsmənt]	Praktikum
	open-plan office [ˌəʊpən plæn 'ɒfɪs]	Großraumbüro
	challenge ['tʃælɪndʒ]	Herausforderung, (große) Aufgabe
	book-keeping ['bʊkki:pɪŋ]	Buchhaltung
	word processing ['wɜ:d prəʊsesɪŋ]	Textverarbeitung

T	**office administration** [ˌɒfɪs ədmɪnɪ'streɪʃn]	Bürotätigkeiten
	figure ['fɪgə]	Zahl
	strong point [ˌstrɒŋ 'pɔɪnt]	Stärke
	accurate(ly) ['ækjərət]	genau
10	**country code** ['kʌntri kəʊd]	Ländervorwahl
	digit ['dɪdʒɪt]	Ziffer
	separately ['seprətli]	einzeln
	except for [ɪk'sept fə]	außer
	to **dictate** [dɪk'teɪt]	diktieren
11	**preparation** [ˌprepə'reɪʃn]	Vorbereitung
	to **chat** [tʃæt]	sich unterhalten, plaudern
	specifically [spə'sɪfɪkli]	ausdrücklich, eigens
	first name ['fɜ:st neɪm]	Vorname
	to **identify oneself** [aɪ'dentɪfaɪ]	sich zu erkennen geben
	to **enquire** [ɪn'kwaɪə]	sich erkundigen
	to **put sb through** [ˌpʊt 'θru:]	jdn durchstellen, verbinden
	equivalent [ɪ'kwɪvələnt]	Entsprechung, Übersetzung
	engaged [ɪn'geɪdʒd]	*(Telefon:)* besetzt
	to **be unavailable** [bi ˌʌnə'veɪləbl]	*(Telefon:)* nicht zu sprechen sein
	to **hold the line** [ˌhəʊld ðə 'laɪn]	*(Telefon:)* am Apparat bleiben
	to **connect** [kə'nekt]	verbinden
12	**paper mill** ['peɪpə mɪl]	Papiermühle, Papierfabrik
	business ['bɪznəs]	Geschäft(e), Geschäfts-, Firma, Unternehmen
	to **receive** [rɪ'si:v]	erhalten, empfangen, bekommen
13	**report** [rɪ'pɔ:t]	Bericht T
14	to **translate** [træns'leɪt]	übersetzen
	to **improve** [ɪm'pru:v]	verbessern
	waste of time [ˌweɪst əf 'taɪm]	Zeitverschwendung
	to **get to know sb** [ˌget tə 'nəʊ]	jdn kennen lernen
	to **break the ice** [ˌbreɪk ði 'aɪs]	das Eis brechen
	event [ɪ'vent]	Veranstaltung, Ereignis
	even though ['i:vn ðəʊ]	obwohl
	vocabulary [və'kæbjələri]	Wortschatz
	specific [spə'sɪfɪk]	speziell, bestimmt, Fach-
	unfamiliar (with sth) [ˌʌnfə'mɪliə]	nicht vertraut (mit etw)
	to **slow down** [ˌsləʊ 'daʊn]	langsamer werden
	to **do research** [du: rɪ'sɜ:tʃ]	recherchieren, Nachforschungen anstellen
	to **have sth ready** [həv 'redi]	etw bereithalten
	to **be happy** [bi 'hæpi]	sich freuen
	to **relax** [rɪ'læks]	sich entspannen, sich erholen
	activity [æk'tɪvəti]	Tätigkeit
	to **be likely to do sth** [bi 'laɪkli tə du:]	etw wahrscheinlich tun werden
	current ['kʌrənt]	aktuell
	to **compare** [kəm'peə]	vergleichen
	judgement ['dʒʌdʒmənt]	Urteil, Bewertung
	to **touch on sth** ['tʌtʃ ɒn]	etw berühren
	taboo [tə'bu:]	Tabu
	divorce [dɪ'vɔ:s]	Scheidung
	to **stay away from sth** [ˌsteɪ ə'weɪ frəm]	sich von etw fernhalten, etw meiden
	controversial [ˌkɒntrə'vɜ:ʃl]	strittig, kontrovers, Streit-
	sexual orientation [ˌsekʃuəl ˌɔ:riən'teɪʃn]	sexuelle Orientierung
	religious [rɪ'lɪdʒəs]	religiös
	political [pə'lɪtɪkl]	politisch
	belief [bɪ'li:f]	Überzeugung
	to **convince sb of sth** [kən'vɪns]	jdn von etw überzeugen

UNIT 2

15	**arrangements** *pl* [ə'reɪndʒmənts]	Vorbereitungen, Vereinbarungen
	to **confirm** [kən'fɜ:m]	bestätigen
	capital letter ['kæpɪtl letə]	Großbuchstabe
	dot [dɒt]	Punkt
	hyphen ['haɪfn]	Bindestrich
	underscore [ˌʌndə'skɔ:]	Unterstrich
	etiquette ['etɪket]	Etikette
	subject (line) ['sʌbdʒɪkt]	Betreff(zeile)
	to **include** [ɪn'klu:d]	einbeziehen, einschließen
	to **attach sth** [ə'tætʃ]	*(E-Mail:)* anhängen
	to **report** [rɪ'pɔ:t]	berichten, Bericht erstatten
16	to **participate** [pɑ:'tɪsɪpeɪt]	teilnehmen
	pharmaceutical [ˌfɑ:mə'su:tɪkl]	Pharma-, Arzneimittel-
	fair [feə]	Messe
	reply [rɪ'plaɪ]	Antwort
	to **invite** [ɪn'vaɪt]	einladen
	working breakfast [ˌwɜ:kɪŋ 'brekfəst]	Arbeitsfrühstück
	till [tɪl]	bis

	suitable ['su:təbl]	passend, geeignet
	to **collect sb/sth** [kə'lekt]	jdn/etw abholen
	research [rɪ'sɜ:tʃ]	Forschung
	presentation [,prezn'teɪʃn]	Präsentation
	result [rɪ'zʌlt]	Ergebnis
	to **take place** [,teɪk 'pleɪs]	stattfinden
	to **pick sb up** [,pɪk 'ʌp]	jdn abholen
	plenty of ['plenti əv]	viele
	to **expect** [ɪk'spekt]	erwarten
	postponement [,pə'spəʊnmənt]	Verschiebung, (Termin-)Verlegung
	as far as sth is concerned [əz fɑ:r əz ɪz kən'sɜ:nd]	was etw angeht/betrifft
	to **deal with sth** ['di:l wɪð]	sich mit etw beschäftigen, von etw handeln
	definite ['defɪnət]	endgültig, definitiv
	invitation [,ɪnvɪ'teɪʃn]	Einladung
	in time [ɪn 'taɪm]	rechtzeitig
	participant [pɑ:'tɪsɪpənt]	Teilnehmer/in
	stop-over ['stɒpəʊvə]	Zwischenlandung, -aufenthalt
17	**certain** ['sɜ:tn]	sicher
	flyer ['flaɪə]	Flugblatt, Reklamezettel
	accounts (department) [ə'kaʊnts]	Buchhaltung
	to **move on** [,mu:v 'ɒn]	weitergehen, weiterziehen
	strike [straɪk]	Streik
18	**content** ['kɒntent]	Inhalt
	to **structure** ['strʌktʃə]	strukturieren
	to **get sth across** [,get ə'krɒs]	etw vermitteln, übermitteln
	concise(ly) [kən'saɪs]	knapp, kurz (und bündig)
	on-screen [,ɒn'skri:n]	am Bildschirm
	salutation [,sælju'teɪʃn]	*(Brief:)* Anrede
	complimentary close [,kɒmplɪ,mentri 'kləʊz]	*(Brief:)* Schlussformel
	to **sign off** [,saɪn 'ɒf]	einen Brief beenden
	body ['bɒdi]	*(Brief usw.:)* Hauptteil
	to **separate** ['seprət]	trennen
	exclamation mark [eksklə'meɪʃn mɑ:k]	Ausrufezeichen
	inbox ['ɪnbɒks]	Posteingang
	request [rɪ'kwest]	Bitte, Anfrage
	to **contain** [kən'teɪn]	enthalten
	to **announce** [ə'naʊns]	ankündigen
	covering letter [,kʌvərɪŋ 'letə]	Anschreiben, Begleitschreiben
	to **accompany** [ə'kʌmpəni]	begleiten
	location [ləʊ'keɪʃn]	Veranstaltungsort
	update ['ʌpdeɪt]	Informationen über neueste Entwicklungen
	agenda [ə'dʒendə]	Tagesordnung
19	**inclusive** [ɪn'klu:sɪv]	einschließlich
	application [,æplɪ'keɪʃn]	Antrag
	to **promise** ['prɒmɪs]	versprechen
	to **suggest** [sə'dʒest]	vorschlagen
	Regards [rɪ'gɑ:dz]	Mit freundlichen Grüßen, Viele Grüße
	Best wishes [,best 'wɪʃɪz]	Mit den besten Wünschen
	Yours sincerely [,jɔ:z sɪn'sɪəli]	Mit freundlichen Grüßen
	Cordially *AE* ['kɔ:diəli]	Mit herzlichen Grüßen
	polite [pə'laɪt]	höflich
	relationship [rɪ'leɪʃnʃɪp]	Beziehung, Verhältnis
	to **continue to do sth** [kən'tɪnju:]	etw weiterhin tun
20	**tone** [təʊn]	Ton
	to **assist** [ə'sɪst]	helfen, unterstützen
	in detail [ɪn 'di:teɪl]	genau, im Detail
	prompt [prɒmpt]	prompt, unverzüglich
	to **regret** [rɪ'gret]	bedauern
	to **reply** [rɪ'plaɪ]	antworten
	to **set sth up** [,set 'ʌp]	etw arrangieren
	to **get in touch with sb** [,get ɪn 'tʌtʃ wɪð]	sich mit jdm in Verbindung setzen
	to **check sth out** [,tʃek 'aʊt]	sich etw (genau) ansehen
	exchange [ɪks'tʃeɪndʒ]	Austausch, Wechsel
	to **rewrite** [,ri:'raɪt]	neu schreiben, umformulieren
	accommodation [ə,kɒmə'deɪʃn]	Unterkunft
	notice ['nəʊtɪs]	Hinweis
	reception [rɪ'sepʃn]	Rezeption, Empfang
	in person [ɪn 'pɜ:sn]	persönlich
	at last [ət 'lɑ:st]	endlich
	to **be pleased** [bi 'pli:zd]	sich freuen
21	to **apologize** [ə'pɒlədʒaɪz]	sich entschuldigen
	to **be supposed to do sth** [bi sə'pəʊzd tə du:]	etw (eigentlich) tun sollen
	convenient [kən'vi:niənt]	günstig, praktisch
	to **cancel** ['kænsl]	absagen
	negotiation [nɪ,gəʊʃi'eɪʃn]	Verhandlung
	to **postpone** [pə'spəʊn]	verschieben
	to **suit** [su:t]	passen
	loads of ['ləʊdz əv]	viel(e)
	alternative [ɔ:l'tɜ:nətɪv]	alternativ, Alternativ-

	suggestion [sə'dʒestʃən]	Vorschlag
	to **forward sth** ['fɔːwəd]	etw weiterleiten
	to **get back to sb** [ˌget 'bæk tə]	sich (wieder) bei jdm melden
	neither (of both) ['naɪðə]	keine/r/s (von beiden)
	to **bring sth forward** [ˌbrɪŋ 'fɔːwəd]	etw vorverlegen
	by tomorrow [baɪ tə'mɒrəʊ]	bis morgen
	at the latest [ət ðə 'leɪtɪst]	spätestens
22	**definite** ['defɪnət]	bestimmt
	quarter ['kwɔːtə]	Quartal
	deadline ['dedlaɪn]	Frist
	close of business [ˌkləʊz əv 'bɪznəs]	Geschäftsschluss
	to **borrow sth** ['bɒrəʊ]	sich etw (aus)leihen
	to **attend sth** [ə'tend]	etw besuchen, an etw teilnehmen
	demonstration [ˌdemən'streɪʃn]	Vorführung
	client ['klaɪənt]	Kunde/Kundin
	to **finalize** ['faɪnəlaɪz]	(endgültig) festlegen, abschließen
	contract ['kɒntrækt]	Vertrag
23	**premises** *pl* ['premɪsɪz]	Räumlichkeiten, (Betriebs-)Gelände
	to **accept** [ək'sept]	annehmen, akzeptieren
	to **be delighted** [bi dɪ'laɪtɪd]	sich freuen, sehr erfreut sein
	conclusion [kən'kluːʒn]	Schluss
24	**bank holiday** [ˌbæŋk 'hɒlədeɪ]	gesetzlicher Feiertag
25	**entry** ['entri]	Eintrag
	typical ['tɪpɪkl]	typisch
	to **fire sth off** [ˌfaɪər 'ɒf]	etw loslassen
	to **appreciate** [ə'priːʃieɪt]	schätzen, zu schätzen wissen
	to **pop up** [ˌpɒp 'ʌp]	auftauchen, erscheinen
	downstairs [ˌdaʊn'steəz]	(nach) unten
	efficiency [ɪ'fɪʃnsi]	Effizienz
	to **waste** [weɪst]	vergeuden, verschwenden
	condensed [kən'denst]	gekürzt, Kurz-
	circumstances *pl* ['sɜːkəmstənsɪz]	Umstände, Gegebenheiten
	speed [spiːd]	Geschwindigkeit
	efficient [ɪ'fɪʃnt]	effizient
	acceptable [ək'septəbl]	akzeptabel
	sender ['sendə]	Absender
	time-waster ['taɪm weɪstə]	Zeitfresser
	initials *pl* ['ɪ'nɪʃlz]	Initialen
	abbreviation [əˌbriːvi'eɪʃn]	Abkürzung

UNIT 3

26	**item** ['aɪtəm]	Artikel, Gegenstand
	highlighter ['haɪlaɪtə]	Textmarker
	label ['leɪbl]	Etikett
	notepad ['nəʊtpæd]	Notizblock
	paper clip ['peɪpə klɪp]	Büroklammer
	stapler ['steɪplə]	Klammerhefter
	staple ['steɪpl]	Heftklammer
	heading ['hedɪŋ]	Überschrift
	tool [tuːl]	Werkzeug
27	**business letter** ['bɪznəs letə]	Geschäftsbrief
	reference (ref) ['refərəns]	*(Brief:)* Zeichen
	trade fair ['treɪd feə]	Handelsmesse
	to **note** [nəʊt]	zur Kenntnis nehmen
	responsible [rɪ'spɒnsəbl]	verantwortlich, zuständig
	allocation [ˌælə'keɪʃn]	Zuweisung, Zuteilung
	to **enclose** [ɪn'kləʊz]	*(Brief:)* beifügen
	to **cover** ['kʌvə]	*(Thema)* behandeln
	participation [pɑːˌtɪsɪ'peɪʃn]	Teilnahme
	to **require** [rɪ'kwaɪə]	wünschen, benötigen
	enclosure (enc) [ɪn'kləʊʒə]	*(Brief:)* Anlage(n)
	signature ['sɪgnətʃə]	Unterschrift
28	**jumbled** ['dʒʌmbld]	durcheinander geworfen
	order ['ɔːdə]	Reihenfolge
	Yours faithfully [ˌjɔːz 'feɪθfəli]	Mit freundlichen Grüßen; Hochachtungsvoll
	vocational school [vəʊˌkeɪʃənl 'skuːl]	Berufsschule
	to **be keen to do sth** [bi 'kiːn tə duː]	etw unbedingt/sehr gern tun mögen
	English-speaking ['ɪŋglɪʃspiːkɪŋ]	englischsprachig
	to **apply for sth** [ə'plaɪ fə]	sich für etw bewerben
	unpaid [ˌʌn'peɪd]	unbezahlt
	curriculum vitae (CV) [kəˌrɪkjələm 'viːtaɪ]	Lebenslauf
	certificate [sə'tɪfɪkət]	Zeugnis, Abschluss
	recommendation [ˌrekəmen'deɪʃn]	Empfehlung
29	to **support** [sə'pɔːt]	unterstützen, helfen
	to **conclude** [kən'kluːd]	schließen
	to **summarize** ['sʌməraɪz]	zusammenfassen
	to **draw a conclusion** [ˌdrɔː ə kən'kluːʒn]	einen Schluss ziehen
	to **signal** ['sɪgnəl]	signalisieren
	to **divide** [dɪ'vaɪd]	teilen, unterteilen
	ability [ə'bɪləti]	Fähigkeit
	close(ly) [kləʊs]	genau

	distribution [ˌdɪstrɪˈbjuːʃn]	Vertrieb
	duty [ˈdjuːti]	Pflicht, Aufgabe
	memo [ˈmeməʊ]	Mitteilung, Vermerk, Notiz
	to **pass sth on** [ˌpɑːs ˈɒn]	etw weiterleiten
	interpreter [ɪnˈtɜːprɪtə]	Übersetzer/in
	to **recognize** [ˈrekəgnaɪz]	anerkennen
	particularly [pəˈtɪkjələli]	besonders
	opportunity [ˌɒpəˈtjuːnəti]	Gelegenheit, Chance
	application [ˌæplɪˈkeɪʃn]	Bewerbung
30	to **shorten** [ˈʃɔːtn]	kürzen
	correspondence [ˌkɒrɪˈspɒndəns]	Korrespondenz
	full stop [ˌfʊl ˈstɒp]	Punkt *(Satzzeichen)*
	monolingual [ˌmɒnəˈlɪŋgwəl]	einsprachig
	meaning [ˈmiːnɪŋ]	Bedeutung
	stamped addressed envelope [ˌstæmpt əˌdrest ˈenvələʊp]	Freiumschlag
	enquiry [ɪnˈkwaɪəri]	Anfrage
	employer [ɪmˈplɔɪə]	Arbeitgeber/in, Unternehmer/in
	to **supply** [səˈplaɪ]	zur Verfügung stellen
	reference [ˈrefərəns]	Referenz
31	**announcement** [əˈnaʊnsmənt]	Ankündigung
	advertisment [ədˈvɜːtɪsmənt]	(Werbe-)Anzeige
	to **keep in mind** [ˌkiːp ɪn ˈmaɪnd]	an etw denken
	to **prepare** [prɪˈpeə]	(sich) vorbereiten, erstellen
	framework [ˈfreɪmwɜːk]	Gerüst
	introduction [ˌɪntrəˈdʌkʃn]	Einleitung
	to **sort** [sɔːt]	sortieren, einsortieren
	one by one [ˌwʌn baɪ ˈwʌn]	eins nach dem anderen
	to **build sth up** [ˌbɪld ˈʌp]	etw aufbauen
	to **proof-read** [ˈpruːf riːd]	Korrektur lesen
	to **stick to sth** [ˈstɪk tə]	bei etw bleiben
	complicated [ˈkɒmplɪkeɪtɪd]	kompliziert
	logical [ˈlɒdʒɪkl]	logisch
	necessary [ˈnesəsəri]	nötig, notwendig, erforderlich
32	**substitute** [ˈsʌbstɪtjuːt]	Ersatz
	to **be allowed to do sth** [bi əˈlaʊd tə duː]	etw tun dürfen
	order [ˈɔːdə]	Auftrag, Bestellung

	to **work overtime** [ˌwɜːk ˈəʊvətaɪm]	Überstunden machen
	to **take time off** [teɪk ˌtaɪm ˈɒf]	sich frei nehmen
	further [ˈfɜːðə]	weitere/r/s
	to **concentrate** [ˈkɒnsntreɪt]	sich konzentrieren
	examination [ɪgˌzæmɪˈneɪʃn]	Prüfung
	inhabitant [ɪnˈhæbɪtənt]	Einwohner/in, Bewohner/in
33	to **argue** [ˈɑːgjuː]	argumentieren
T	to **tend** [tend]	dazu neigen
	standard [ˈstændəd]	Anforderung, Norm
	greeting [ˈgriːtɪŋ]	*(Brief:)* Anrede
	sensitive [ˈsensətɪv]	heikel
	destination [ˌdestɪˈneɪʃn]	Bestimmungsort
	security [sɪˈkjʊərəti]	Sicherheit
	legal [ˈliːgl]	rechtlich, gesetzlich, Rechts-
	law [lɔː]	Gesetz
	legally binding [ˌliːgəli ˈbaɪndɪŋ]	rechtsverbindlich
	to **accomplish sth** [əˈkʌmplɪʃ]	etw erreichen
	for a start [fər ə ˈstɑːt]	zunächst, zuallererst
	to **print** [prɪnt]	drucken
	superior-grade [suːˌpɪəriə ˈgreɪd]	hochwertig
	postage [ˈpəʊstɪdʒ]	Porto
	to **come out on top** [ˌkʌm aʊt ɒn ˈtɒp]	vorne liegen, Erste/r werden
	cost advantage [ˈkɒst ədvɑːntɪdʒ]	Kostenvorteil
	expenses *pl* [ɪkˈspensɪz]	Kosten
	extremely [ɪkˈstriːmli]	äußerst
	impact [ˈɪmpækt]	Auswirkung(en), Folge(n)
	to **identify** [aɪˈdentɪfaɪ]	erkennen, benennen
34	**course** [kɔːs]	Ablauf
	buyer [ˈbaɪə]	Käufer/in
	seller [ˈselə]	Verkäufer/in
	flow chart [ˈfləʊ tʃɑːt]	Flussdiagramm
	step [step]	Schritt
	acknowledgement [əkˈnɒlɪdʒmənt]	Auftragsbestätigung
	advice of dispatch [ədˌvaɪs əv dɪˈspætʃ]	Versandanzeige, Versandmitteilung
	complaint [kəmˈpleɪnt]	Reklamation, Beschwerde
	reminder [rɪˈmaɪndə]	Mahnung
	to **request sth** [rɪˈkwest]	etw erbitten, etw anfordern
	payment [ˈpeɪmənt]	Zahlung
	overdue [ˌəʊvəˈdjuː]	fällig, überfällig
	invoice [ˈɪnvɔɪs]	Rechnung

	to **acknowledge** [ək'nɒlɪdʒ]	anerkennen, zugeben
	to **occur** [ə'kɜː]	auftreten, passieren
	goods *pl* [gʊdz]	Ware(n), Güter
	addressee [ˌædre'siː]	Empfänger/in
	customer ['kʌstəmə]	Kunde, Kundin
	store [stɔː]	Lager
	initial contact [ɪˌnɪʃl 'kɒntækt]	Erstkontakt
T	**on offer** [ɒn 'ɒfə]	im Angebot
	to **deliver** [dɪ'lɪvə]	liefern
	on time [ɒn 'taɪm]	pünktlich
	to **advertise** ['ædvətaɪz]	Werbung machen
	latest ['leɪtɪst]	neueste/r/s
	layout ['leɪaʊt]	Anordnung, Lage

UNIT 4

35	to **give directions** [gɪv də'rekʃnz]	den Weg erklären
	sector ['sektə]	Sektor, Bereich
	light industry [ˌlaɪt 'ɪndəstri]	Leichtindustrie
	building industry ['bɪldɪŋ ɪndəstri]	Baugewerbe
	service industry ['sɜːvɪs ɪndəstri]	Dienstleistungsgewerbe
	logistics *pl* [lə'dʒɪstɪks]	Logistik
	financial services *pl* [faɪˌnænʃl 'sɜːvɪsɪz]	Finanzdienstleistungen
	to **operate** ['ɒpəreɪt]	(geschäftlich) tätig sein
	Ltd = Limited Company *BE* [ˌlɪmɪtɪd 'kʌmpəni]	GmbH = Gesellschaft mit beschränkter Haftung
	plc = Public Limited Company *BE* [ˌpʌblɪk ˌlɪmɪtɪd 'kʌmpəni]	AG = Aktiengesellschaft
	shareholder ['ʃeəhəʊldə]	Teilhaber/in, Aktionär/in
	share [ʃeə]	Aktie
	the public [ðə 'pʌblɪk]	die Öffentlichkeit
	Inc = incorporated *AE* [ɪn'kɔːpəreɪtɪd]	(als Gesellschaft) eingetragen
	Corp = Corporation *AE* [ˌkɔːpə'reɪʃn]	Gesellschaft, Körperschaft
	to **register** ['redʒɪstə]	eintragen, registrieren
	legal entity [ˌliːgl 'entəti]	juristische Person, Rechtsträger
	Registrar of Companies [ˌredʒɪstrɑːr əv 'kʌmpəniz]	Handelsregister für Kapitalgesellschaften
36	to **take a risk** [ˌteɪk ə 'rɪsk]	etwas riskieren, ein Risiko eingehen
	steadily ['stedɪli]	kontinuierlich, stetig
	based in/near ['beɪst ɪn/nɪə]	mit Sitz in/bei
	to **supply** [sə'plaɪ]	liefern
	support [sə'pɔːt]	Unterstützung, Kundendienst
	worth [wɜːθ]	wert
	approximately [ə'prɒksɪmətli]	ungefähr, zirka
	to **develop** [dɪ'veləp]	entwickeln, sich entwickeln
	to **manufacture** [ˌmænju'fæktʃə]	herstellen, fertigen
	border ['bɔːdə]	(Landes-)Grenze
	vocational college [vəʊˌkeɪʃənl 'kɒlɪdʒ]	Berufsfachschule
	apprenticeship [ə'prentɪʃɪp]	Lehre, Ausbildung
	to **process sth** ['prəʊses]	etw bearbeiten, verarbeiten
	to **build** [bɪld]	bauen
	factory floor ['fæktəri flɔː]	Produktion(sabteilung)
	to **realize** ['rɪəlaɪz]	erkennen, klar werden, verstehen
	to **graduate** ['grædʒueɪt]	(s)einen Abschluss machen
	to **set up** [ˌset 'ʌp]	gründen
	to **rent** [rent]	mieten
	warehouse ['weəhaʊs]	Lager(halle)
	assembly line [ə'sembli laɪn]	Fließband, Montageband
	on an hourly basis [ɒn ən ˌaʊəli 'beɪsɪs]	auf Stundenbasis
	entrepreneur [ˌɒntrəprə'nɜː]	Unternehmer/in
	prize [praɪz]	Preis, Auszeichnung
	award [ə'wɔːd]	Preis, Auszeichnung
	to **go public** [ˌgəʊ 'pʌblɪk]	an die Börse gehen
	to **expand** [ɪk'spænd]	expandieren, (den Geschäftsbereich) erweitern
	custom-built [ˌkʌstəm 'bɪlt]	eigens (an)gefertigt, maßgefertigt
	industrial estate [ɪnˌdʌstriəl ɪ'steɪt]	Industriegebiet
	to **achieve** [ə'tʃiːv]	erzielen, erreichen
	turnover ['tɜːnəʊvə]	Umsatz
	to **specialize in sth** ['speʃəlaɪz ɪn]	sich auf etw spezialisieren
37	to **require** [rɪ'kwaɪə]	erfordern
	noisy ['nɔɪzi]	laut
	even though ['iːvn ðəʊ]	dennoch, trotzdem
	to **store** [stɔː]	lagern
	edge [edʒ]	Rand
	chart [tʃɑːt]	Diagramm, Grafik
	organization chart [ˌɔːgənaɪ'zeɪʃn tʃɑːt]	Organigramm
	CEO = Chief Executive Officer [ˌtʃiːf ɪg'zekjətɪv ɒfɪsə]	Geschäftsführer/in, Vorstandsvorsitzende/r
	Finance (Department) ['faɪnæns]	Rechnungswesen

	Human Resources (HR) [ˌhju:mən rɪ'sɔ:sɪz]	Personal(abteilung)
	Legal Department [ˌli:gl dɪ'pɑ:tmənt]	Rechtswesen
	Market Research [ˌmɑ:kɪt rɪ'sɜ:tʃ]	Marktforschung-(sabteilung)
	production [prə'dʌkʃn]	Produktion, Herstellung, Fertigung
	Purchasing (Department) ['pɜ:tʃəsɪŋ]	Einkauf(sabteilung)
	Research and Development (Department, R&D) [rɪˌsɜ:tʃ ən dɪ'veləpmənt]	Forschung(s-) und Entwicklung-(sabteilung)
	Sales (Department) [seɪlz]	Verkauf(sabteilung), Vertrieb
	accounts *pl* [ə'kaʊnts]	(Geschäfts-)Bücher, Buchführung
	revenue ['revənju:]	Einnahmen, Einkünfte
	raw material [ˌrɔ: mə'tɪəriəl]	Rohstoff, Rohmaterial
	agreement [ə'gri:mənt]	Vereinbarung
	to **design** [dɪ'zaɪn]	entwerfen, gestalten
	possibility [ˌpɒsə'bɪləti]	Möglichkeit
	job title ['dʒɒb taɪtl]	Berufsbezeichnung
	accountant [ə'kaʊntənt]	Buchhalter/in
	managing director [ˌmænɪdʒɪŋ də'rektə]	Geschäftsführer/in
	customer relations manager [ˌkʌstəmə rɪ'leɪʃnz mænɪdʒə]	Kundenbetreuer/in
	receptionist [rɪ'sepʃənɪst]	Empfangsmitarbeiter/in
	employee [ɪm'plɔɪi:]	Arbeitnehmer/in, Beschäftigte/r
	sales representative ['seɪlz reprɪzentətɪv]	Handelsvertreter/in
	head [hed]	Leiter/in, Chef/in
	in charge of sth [ɪn 'tʃɑ:dʒ əv]	für etw zuständig
	to **report to sb** [rɪ'pɔ:t tə]	jdm unterstellt sein
	to **take care of sth** [ˌteɪk 'keər əv]	sich um etw kümmern
38	**yet** [jet]	schon
	not yet [nɒt 'jet]	noch nicht
	bill [bɪl]	Rechnung
	electronics [ˌɪlek'trɒnɪks]	Elektronik
	to **meet a deadline** [ˌmi:t ə 'dedlaɪn]	eine Frist einhalten
	native speaker [ˌneɪtɪv 'spi:kə]	Muttersprachler/in
	edition [ɪ'dɪʃn]	Ausgabe
39 T	**Pleased/Nice to meet you.** [ˌpli:zd/ˌnaɪs tə 'mi:t ju]	Schön, Sie/dich/euch kennen zu lernen.
	delay [dɪ'leɪ]	Verspätung, Verzögerung
	That's a pity. [ˌðæts ə 'pɪti]	Das ist schade.
	to **show sb around** [ˌʃəʊ ə'raʊnd]	jdn herumführen
	upstairs [ˌʌp'steəz]	oben
	section ['sekʃn]	Abteilung, Abschnitt
	by the way [baɪ ðə 'weɪ]	übrigens
	restroom *AE* ['rest ru:m]	Toilette
T	**corridor** ['kɒrɪdɔ:]	Flur, Gang
	over there [ˌəʊvə 'ðeə]	dort (drüben)
	next door to [ˌnekst 'dɔ: tə]	neben
	to **go on** [ˌgəʊ 'ɒn]	passieren, geschehen, vor sich gehen
	past sth [pɑ:st]	an etw vorbei
	stairs *pl* [steəz]	Treppe
	at the bottom of sth [ət ðə 'bɒtəm əv]	am Ende von etw
	handy ['hændi]	praktisch
40	**ground floor** [ˌgraʊnd 'flɔ:]	Erdgeschoss
	top floor [ˌtɒp 'flɔ:]	oberstes Stockwerk
	basement ['beɪsmənt]	Keller, Souterrain
	building ['bɪldɪŋ]	Gebäude
	sheet (of paper) [ʃi:t]	Blatt (Papier)
	to **swap** [swɒp]	tauschen
	appointment [ə'pɔɪntmənt]	Termin
	to **see sb** [si:]	sich mit jdm treffen
T	to **turn left/right** [tɜ:n 'left, tɜ:n 'raɪt]	links/rechts abbiegen
	left-/right-hand side [ˌleft/ˌraɪt hænd 'saɪd]	linke/rechte Seite
	crossroads ['krɒsrəʊdz]	Kreuzung
	roundabout ['raʊndəbaʊt]	Kreisverkehr
	to **pass sth** [pɑ:s]	an etw vorbeigehen, etw passieren
	straight ahead [ˌstreɪt ə'hed]	geradeaus
	railway track ['reɪlweɪ træk]	Bahngleis
	railway crossing ['reɪlweɪ krɒsɪŋ]	Bahnübergang
	traffic lights *pl* ['træfɪk laɪts]	Ampel
	huge [hju:dʒ]	groß
	t-junction ['ti: dʒʌŋkʃn]	Einmündung
	entrance ['entrəns]	Eingang, Einfahrt
	security office [sɪ'kjʊərəti ɒfɪs]	Büro des Wachdienstes
	pedestrian crossing [pəˌdestriən 'krɒsɪŋ]	Zebrastreifen
41	**in the middle of** [ɪn ðə 'mɪdl əv]	mitten in/auf, in der Mitte von
	in the distance [ɪn ðə 'dɪstəns]	weit hinten

	to take turns [ˌteɪk ˈtɜːnz]	sich abwechseln
42	**heading towards** [ˈhədɪŋ təwɔːdz]	in Richtung
	to get off (a bus, a car etc.) [ˌget ˈɒf]	*(aus einem Bus, Auto, usw.)* aussteigen
	towards [təˈwɔːdz]	in Richtung, auf … zu
	to continue [kənˈtɪnjuː]	weitergehen
	along [əˈlɒŋ]	entlang
	half-way [ˌhɑːf ˈweɪ]	auf halbem Wege
43	**retailer** [ˈriːteɪlə]	Einzelhändler/in
	development [dɪˈveləpmənt]	Entwicklung
	three times [ˈθriː taɪmz]	dreimal, drei Mal
	rival [ˈraɪvl]	Rivale/Rivalin, Konkurrent/in
	to launch sth [lɔːntʃ]	etw starten, etw einführen, etw auf den Markt bringen
	to dream sth up [driːm]	sich etw ausdenken
	bookstore [ˈbʊkstɔː]	Buchhandlung
	drive [draɪv]	Fahrt
	attention [əˈtenʃn]	Aufmerksamkeit
	to come to sb's attention [ˌkʌm tə əˈtenʃn]	auf etw aufmerksam werden
	businessman [ˈbɪznəsmən]	Geschäftsmann, Unternehmer
	member [ˈmembə]	Mitglied
	board (of directors) [bɔːd]	Geschäftsführung, Vorstand
	high-powered [ˌhaɪ ˈpaʊəd]	Spitzen-, führende/r/s
	to invest [ɪnˈvest]	investieren
	review [rɪˈvjuː]	Rezension, Besprechung
	to feel involved [ˌfiːl ɪnˈvɒlvd]	sich einbezogen/ beteiligt fühlen
	community [kəˈmjuːnəti]	Gemeinde, Gemeinschaft
	to generate [ˈdʒenəreɪt]	erwirtschaften, generieren
	domestic appliance [dəˌmestɪk əˈplaɪəns]	Haushaltsgerät
	to register [ˈredʒɪstə]	verbuchen
	sales *pl* [seɪlz]	Verkäufe, Umsatz
	to lay sb off [ˌleɪ ˈɒf]	jdn entlassen
	determined [dɪˈtɜːmɪnd]	entschlossen
	to save sb/sth [seɪv]	jdn/etw retten
	chronological [ˌkrɒnəˈlɒdʒɪkl]	chronologisch
	time-line [ˈtaɪmlaɪn]	Zeitleiste, Zeitstrahl

UNIT 5

44	**supplier** [səˈplaɪə]	Lieferant
	potential [pəˈtenʃl]	potentiell
	wooden [ˈwʊdn]	Holz-, aus Holz
	furniture [ˈfɜːnɪtʃə]	Möbel
	familiar [fəˈmɪliə]	vertraut
	creditworthiness [ˈkredɪt wɜːðinəs]	Kreditwürdigkeit
45	**trade magazine** [ˌtreɪd mægəˈziːn]	Branchenzeitschrift, Fachblatt
	leading [ˈliːdɪŋ]	führend
	importer [ɪmˈpɔːtə]	Importeur
	household [ˈhaʊshəʊld]	Haushalt, Haushalts-
	to extend [ɪkˈstend]	ausweiten, erweitern
	range [reɪndʒ]	Angebot(spalette), Auswahl
	grateful [ˈgreɪtfl]	dankbar
	catalogue [ˈkætəlɒg]	Katalog
	line of products [ˌlaɪn əv ˈprɒdʌkts]	Produktlinie, -angebot
	terms *pl* [tɜːmz]	Bedingungen, Konditionen
	delivery [dɪˈlɪvəri]	Lieferung
	terms of delivery *pl* [ˌtɜːmz əv dɪˈlɪvəri]	Lieferbedingungen
	terms of payment *pl* [ˌtɜːmz əv ˈpeɪmənt]	Zahlungsbedingungen
	requirement [rɪˈkwaɪəmənt]	Anforderung
	to meet a requirement [ˌmiːt ə rɪˈkwaɪəmənt]	eine Anforderung erfüllen
	to be prepared to do sth [bi prɪˈpeəd tə]	bereit sein, etw zu tun
	to place an order [ˌpleɪs ən ˈɔːdə]	einen Auftrag erteilen
46	**in bulk** [ɪn ˈbʌlk]	en gros
	discount [ˈdɪskaʊnt]	Rabatt, Nachlass
	creditworthy [ˈkredɪtwɜːði]	kreditwürdig
	account [əˈkaʊnt]	Konto, Kreditkonto
	to settle [ˈsetl]	begleichen, bezahlen
	by the (+ date) [baɪ ðə]	zum (+ Datum)
	to place [pleɪs]	platzieren
	by Friday [baɪ ˈfraɪdeɪ]	bis Freitag
	satisfactory [ˌsætɪsˈfæktəri]	zufriedenstellend
	confirmation [ˌkɒnfəˈmeɪʃn]	Bestätigung
	to cancel [ˈkænsl]	stornieren
	to fax [fæks]	faxen
	to transfer [ˈtrænsfɜː]	*(Geld)* überweisen
	to reduce [rɪˈdjuːs]	reduzieren
	to increase [ˈɪŋkriːs]	erhöhen
	quantity [ˈkwɒntəti]	Menge
	sample [ˈsɑːmpl]	Muster
	to sign [saɪn]	unterschreiben, unterzeichnen
	stock [stɒk]	Ware(n), (Lager-) Bestand
47	**close** [kləʊz]	*(Brief:)* Schluss

	source [sɔːs]	Quelle
	leaflet ['liːflət]	Informationsblatt, Faltblatt
	brochure ['brəʊʃə]	Prospekt
	chamber of commerce [ˌtʃeɪmbər əv 'kɒmɜːs]	Handelskammer
	small-sized company [ˌsmɔːl saɪzd 'kʌmpəni]	Kleinunternehmen
	middle-sized company [ˌmɪdl saɪzd 'kʌmpəni]	mittelständisches Unternehmen
	distributor [dɪ'strɪbjətə]	Vertragshändler, Vertriebspartner
	wholesaler ['həʊlseɪlə]	Großhändler
	quotation [kwəʊ'teɪʃn]	Kostenvoranschlag, Angebot
	to **obtain** [əb'teɪn]	erhalten
	approval [ə'pruːvl]	Zustimmung, Genehmigung
	sizeable ['saɪzəbl]	beträchtlich, (ziemlich) groß
48	**outlet** ['aʊtlet]	Verkaufsstelle, Geschäft
	with reference to [wɪð 'refrəns tə]	bezüglich, mit Bezug auf
	in stock [ɪn 'stɒk]	am/auf Lager, vorrätig, lieferbar
	to **draw sb's attention to sth** [ˌdrɔː sʌmbədiz ə'tenʃn tə]	jdn auf etw aufmerksam machen
	addition [ə'dɪʃn]	Ergänzung
	executive [ɪg'zekjətɪv]	Manager/in, leitende/r Angestellte/r
	to **quote** [kwəʊt]	*(Preis)* angeben, nennen
	EXW = Ex Works [eks 'wɜːks]	ab Werk
	cash discount ['kæʃ dɪskaʊnt]	Skonto, Barzahlungsrabatt
	to **pack** [pæk]	verpacken
	individually [ˌɪndɪ'vɪdʒuəli]	einzeln
	cardboard box ['kɑːdbɔːd bɒks]	Pappkarton
	to **deal with sth** ['diːl wɪð]	etw bearbeiten, erledigen
	immediately [ɪ'miːdiətli]	unmittelbar, sofort
	reliable [rɪ'laɪəbl]	zuverlässig
	trial order [ˌtraɪəl 'ɔːdə]	Probeauftrag
49	**insurance** [ɪn'ʃʊərəns]	Versicherung
	customs duties *pl* ['kʌstəmz djuːtiːz]	Zollgebühren
	rule [ruːl]	Regel, Vorschrift
	property ['prɒpəti]	Eigentum
	trade [treɪd]	Handel
	exporter [ɪk'spɔːtə]	Exporteur
	to **rely on sth** [rɪ'laɪ ɒn]	sich auf etw verlassen
	environmentally-friendly [ɪnˌvaɪrənˌmentəli 'frendli]	umweltfreundlich
	packaging ['pækɪdʒɪŋ]	Verpackung
50	**order number** ['ɔːdə nʌmbə]	Bestellnummer
	to **refer to sth** [rɪ'fɜː tə]	sich auf etw beziehen
	valid ['vælɪd]	gültig
	to **focus on sth** ['fəʊkəs ɒn]	sich auf etw konzentrieren
	reliability [rɪˌlaɪə'bɪləti]	Zuverlässigkeit
	to **assure** [ə'ʃʊə]	zusichern, versichern
	reference ['refərəns]	Erwähnung, Bezug
	specific [spə'sɪfɪk]	konkret
	selection [sɪ'lekʃn]	Auswahl
	special offer [ˌspeʃl 'ɒfə]	Sonderangebot
	guarantee [ˌgærən'tiː]	Garantie
	to **extend** [ɪk'stend]	sich erstrecken
	warranty period ['wɒrənti pɪəriəd]	Gewährleistungsdauer
	pleasure ['pleʒə]	Vergnügen
	net [net]	netto
	receipt [rɪ'siːt]	Erhalt, (Waren-)Eingang
	to **guarantee** [ˌgærən'tiː]	garantieren
	immediate [ɪ'miːdiət]	sofortig
51	to **meet sb's approval** [ˌmiːt ə'pruːvl]	jds Zustimmung finden
	method ['meθəd]	Verfahren, Weise
	commercial correspondence [kəˌmɜːʃl ˌkɒrə'spɒndəns]	Geschäftskorrespondenz
	guided ['gaɪdɪd]	*hier:* nach Vorlage
52	**set** [set]	Menge
	definition [ˌdefɪ'nɪʃn]	Definition
	publish ['pʌblɪʃ]	veröffentlichen
	to **update** [ˌʌp'deɪt]	aktualisieren, auf den neuesten Stand bringen
	trader ['treɪdə]	Händler/in
	to **conduct business** [kənˌdʌkt 'bɪznəs]	Geschäfte machen/abschließen
	voluntary ['vɒləntri]	freiwillig, willkürlich
	to **take precedence over sth** [teɪk 'presɪdəns əʊvə]	vor etw Vorrang haben
	mandatory law [ˌmændətəri 'lɔː]	zwingende gesetzliche Bestimmungen
	certainty ['sɜːtnti]	Sicherheit, Gewissheit
	to **base sth upon sth** ['beɪs əpɒn]	etw auf etw gründen
	to **apply for sb/sth** [ə'plaɪ fə]	für jdn/etw gelten
	party ['pɑːti]	(Vertrags-)Partei

	method of payment [ˌmeθəd əv ˈpeɪmənt]	Zahlungsweise
	transfer [ˈtrænsfɜː]	Übertragung
	ownership [ˈəʊnəʃɪp]	Eigentum(srecht)
	breach of contract [ˌbriːtʃ əv ˈkɒntrækt]	Vertragsbruch
	product liability [ˈprɒdʌkt laɪəbɪləti]	Produkthaftung
	issue [ˈɪʃuː]	Frage, Problem, (Streit-)Punkt
	to **consider** [kənˈsɪdə]	berücksichtigen
	contract of sale [ˌkɒntrækt əv ˈseɪl]	Kaufvertrag
	to **represent** [ˌreprɪˈzent]	darstellen
	obligation [ˌɒblɪˈgeɪʃn]	Verpflichtung
	point of sale [ˌpɔɪnt əf ˈseɪl]	Verkaufsort, -stelle
	carrier [ˈkæriə]	Frachtführer, Spedition

UNIT 6

53	to **acknowledge an order** [əkˌnɒlɪdʒ ən ˈɔːdə]	einen Auftrag bestätigen
	equipment [ɪˈkwɪpmənt]	Ausstattung, Ausrüstung, Geräte
	order form [ˈɔːdə fɔːm]	Bestellformular
	bank transfer [ˈbæŋk trænsfɜː]	Überweisung
	cheque [tʃek]	Scheck
T	**stainless steel** [ˌsteɪnləs ˈstiːl]	rostfreier Stahl
	to **interrupt** [ˌɪntəˈrʌpt]	(jdn) unterbrechen
	basic [ˈbeɪsɪk]	einfach
	to **call sth up** [ˌkɔːl ˈʌp]	etw aufrufen
	moveable [ˈmuːvəbl]	beweglich
	pack [pæk]	Packung
	cash on delivery (COD) [ˌkæʃ ɒn dɪˈlɪvəri]	zahlbar bei Lieferung, per Nachnahme
	postcode [ˈpəʊstkəʊd]	Postleitzahl
54	**unlined** [ˌʌnˈlaɪnd]	unliniert
	square [skweə]	quadratisch
	cork [kɔːk]	Kork
	rectangular [rekˈtæŋgjələ]	rechteckig
	multi-coloured [ˌmʌltiˈkʌləd]	vielfarbig, bunt
	pin [pɪn]	Nadel
	electronic [ˌɪlekˈtrɒnɪk]	elektronisch
	white board [ˈwaɪt bɔːd]	weiße Tafel, Weißwandtafel
	built-in [ˌbɪltˈɪn]	eingebaut
	pointer [ˈpɔɪntə]	Zeiger
	stable [ˈsteɪbl]	stabil
	case [keɪs]	Koffer
	integrated [ˈɪntɪgreɪtɪd]	integriert
	wall bracket [ˈwɔːl brækɪt]	Wandhalter
	width [wɪdθ]	Breite
	length [leŋθ]	Länge
	weight [weɪt]	Gewicht
55	**up-to-date** [ˌʌp tə ˈdeɪt]	auf dem neuesten Stand der Technik
	machine [məˈʃiːn]	Gerät, Maschine
	fan [fæn]	Ventilator
	to **handle sth** [ˈhændl]	mit etw umgehen, etw handhaben
	strange [streɪndʒ]	seltsam
	display [dɪˈspleɪ]	Anzeige, Bildschirm
56	**repeat order** [rɪˌpiːt ˈɔːdə]	Folgeauftrag
	to **dispatch** [dɪˈspætʃ]	versenden, absenden
	dimension [dɪˈmenʃn]	Abmessung
	cash in advance [ˌkæʃ ɪn ədˈvɑːns]	Vorauszahlung/ Vorkasse
	documentary letter of credit [dɒkjuˌmentri ˌletər əv ˈkredɪt]	Dokumentenakkreditiv
	documents against acceptance [ˌdɒkjumənts əgenst əkˈseptəns]	Dokumente gegen Akzept
	documents against payment [ˌdɒkjumənts əgenst ˈpeɪmənt]	Dokumente gegen Zahlung
	open account [ˌəʊpən əˈkaʊnt]	Forderung
57	to **ship** [ʃɪp]	versenden
	due [djuː]	fällig
	to **release** [rɪˈliːs]	freigeben
	bill of exchange [ˌbɪl əv ɪksˈtʃeɪndʒ]	Wechsel
	value [ˈvæljuː]	Wert
	to **present sth** [prɪˈzent]	etw vorlegen
	shipping documents *pl* [ˈʃɪpɪŋ dɒkjumənts]	Versandpapiere
	attractive [əˈtræktɪv]	attraktiv, reizvoll
	pine [paɪn]	Kiefer, Kiefernholz
	FOB = free on board [ˌfriː ɒn ˈbɔːd]	frei an Bord
58	**i.e.** [ˌaɪ ˈiː]	d.h.
	VAT = value added tax [ˌviː eɪ ˈtiː / ˌvæljuː ˈædɪd tæks]	MwSt = Mehrwertsteuer
	by return of post [baɪ rɪˌtɜːn əf ˈpəʊst]	per Antwortschreiben, postwendend
	to **trust** [trʌst]	(darauf) vertrauen
	condition [kənˈdɪʃn]	Zustand
	to **execute** [ˈeksɪkjuːt]	ausführen
	satisfaction [ˌsætɪsˈfækʃn]	Zufriedenheit
59	**cherry wood** [ˈtʃeri wʊd]	Kirschbaumholz

	depth [depθ]	Tiefe
	inexpensive [ˌɪnɪk'spensɪv]	preiswert, preisgünstig
	craftsman ['krɑ:ftsmən]	Handwerker
	pull-out ['pʊl aʊt]	ausziehbar
	solid ['sɒlɪd]	massiv
	oak [əʊk]	Eiche
	shape [ʃeɪp]	Form
	to **fit** [fɪt]	passen
	walnut ['wɔ:lnʌt]	Walnuss
	comfortable ['kʌmftəbl]	bequem
	leather ['leðə]	Leder
	value for money [ˌvælju: fə 'mʌni]	Preis-Leistungs-Verhältnis
	storage cabinet ['stɔ:rɪdʒ kæbɪnət]	Aktenschrank
	steel [sti:l]	Stahl
	lock [lɒk]	Schloss
	container [kən'teɪnə]	Behälter
	available [ə'veɪləbl]	erhältlich, verfügbar
60	**environmental** [ɪnˌvaɪrən'mentl]	Umwelt-
	to **make up** [ˌmeɪk 'ʌp]	ausmachen
	solid ['sɒlɪd]	fest
	waste [weɪst]	Müll
	toxic ['tɒksɪk]	giftig, toxisch
	material [mə'tɪəriəl]	Stoff, Material
	to **sink into the ground** [ˌsɪŋk ɪntə ðə 'graʊnd]	in den Boden sickern
	to **contaminate** [kən'tæmɪneɪt]	kontaminieren
	eventually [ɪ'ventʃuəli]	schließlich, letztendlich
	to **spread** [spred]	sich verbreiten
	component [kəm'pəʊnənt]	Bauteil
	battery ['bætəri]	Akku, Batterie
	various ['veəriəs]	verschiedene/r/s
	scheme [ski:m]	Programm, Plan
	trade-in ['treɪd ɪn]	Eintausch-, Austausch-
	to **dismantle** [dɪs'mæntl]	auseinanderbauen, demontieren
	to **function** ['fʌŋkʃn]	funktionieren
	to **donate** [dəʊ'neɪt]	spenden
	non-profit [ˌnɒn'prɒfɪt]	gemeinnützig
	cartridge ['kɑ:trɪdʒ]	Patrone
	case [keɪs]	Behälter
	crack [kræk]	Riss
	to **charge sb** [tʃɑ:dʒ]	von jdm Gebühren verlangen
	ribbon ['rɪbən]	Band
	check-out ['tʃekaʊt]	Kasse
	to **dispose of sth** [dɪ'spəʊz əv]	etw entsorgen
	incinerator [ɪn'sɪnəreɪtə]	Verbrennungsanlage, -ofen
	to **burn sth** [bɜ:n]	etw verbrennen
	to **cause** [kɔ:z]	verursachen, dazu bringen
	to **explode** [ɪk'spləʊd]	explodieren
	healthy ['helθi]	gesund

UNIT 7

61	**airy** ['eəri]	geräumig, luftig
	minutes *pl* ['mɪnɪts]	Protokoll
	to **share** [ʃeə]	teilen, mitteilen
	essential [ɪ'senʃl]	wesentlich
	ingredient [ɪn'gri:diənt]	Bestandteil; Zutat
62	**internal** [ɪn'tɜ:nl]	intern
	external [ɪk'stɜ:nl]	extern
	to **relate to sth** [rɪ'leɪt tə]	mit etw in Zusammenhang stehen, sich auf etw beziehen
	any other business (AOB) [ˌeni ˌʌðə 'bɪznəs]	Verschiedenes
	to **mention** ['menʃn]	erwähnen, nennen
	chairperson ['tʃeəpɜ:sn]	Leiter/in
	to **announce** [ə'naʊns]	ankündigen, verkünden
	item ['aɪtəm]	(Tagesordnungs-)Punkt
	apology [ə'pɒlədʒi]	Entschuldigung
	absence ['æbsəns]	Abwesenheit
	previous ['pri:viəs]	vorherige/r/s
63	to **dislike** [dɪs'laɪk]	nicht mögen, nicht gern haben
	head office [ˌhed 'ɒfɪs]	Zentrale
	monthly ['mʌnθli]	monatlich
	progress report ['prəʊgres rɪpɔ:t]	Zwischenbericht
	agent ['eɪdʒənt]	Vertragshändler/in
	consumer [kən'sju:mə]	Verbraucher/in
	preference ['prefrəns]	Vorliebe
	action plan ['ækʃn plæn]	Maßnahmenkatalog
	entry ['entri]	Eintritt
64	**there's no point in doing sth** [ðeəz ˌnəʊ ˌpɔɪnt ɪn 'duɪŋ]	es hat keinen Sinn, etw zu tun
	to **chair** [tʃeə]	leiten
	distribution agent [ˌdɪstrɪ'bju:ʃn eɪdʒənt]	Vertragshändler, Vertriebspartner
	object ['ɒbdʒɪkt]	Zweck, Gegenstand
	to **act** [ækt]	handeln, fungieren
	tour [tʊə]	Rundgang
65	**quarterly** ['kwɔ:təli]	vierteljährlich
	annual ['ænjuəl]	jährlich
	to **dress** [dres]	sich kleiden
	intercultural [ˌɪntə'kʌltʃərəl]	interkulturell

	competence ['kɒmpɪtəns]	Kompetenz
	to **make sense** [ˌmeɪk 'sens]	sinnvoll sein
	to **take the chair** [ˌteɪk ðə 'tʃeə]	die Sitzung leiten
T	to **send one's apologies** [ˌsend wʌnz ə'pɒlədʒiz]	sich entschuldigen lassen
	established [ɪ'stæblɪʃt]	etabliert, bekannt
	to **persuade** [pə'sweɪd]	überzeugen
	confident ['kɒnfɪdənt]	zuversichtlich, überzeugt
	to **aim** [eɪm]	beabsichtigen, vorhaben, wollen
66	**attendee** [əˌten'diː]	Teilnehmer/in
	aim [eɪm]	Ziel, Zweck
	to **settle down** [ˌsetl 'daʊn]	zur Ruhe kommen
	advertising agency ['ædvətaɪzɪŋ eɪdʒənsi]	Werbeagentur
	artwork ['ɑːtwɜːk]	Grafik, Illustrationen
	indirect [ˌɪndə'rekt]	indirekt
	respectful [rɪ'spektfl]	respektvoll
68	**record** ['rekɔːd]	Aufzeichnung, Protokoll
	to **approve** [ə'pruːv]	genehmigen, annehmen
	brief [briːf]	kurz, knapp
	seating position ['siːtɪŋ pəzɪʃn]	Sitzplatz, -position
	to **write up** [ˌraɪt 'ʌp]	ausarbeiten, erstellen
	review [rɪ'vjuː]	Überblick
	vote (on sth) [vəʊt]	Abstimmung (über etw)
	outline ['aʊtlaɪn]	Übersicht
	blank [blæŋk]	frei, leer
	underneath [ˌʌndə'niːθ]	unten, unterhalb
	action ['ækʃn]	Handlung, Aktion

UNIT 8

69	**graph** [grɑːf]	Diagramm, Grafik
	to **read out** [ˌriːd 'aʊt]	vorlesen
	slide [slaɪd]	Dia
	visuals *pl* ['vɪʒuəlz]	visuelle Hilfsmittel
	handout ['hændaʊt]	Handreichung; ausgeteilte Unterlage
	explanation [ˌeksplə'neɪʃn]	Erläuterung, Erklärung
	microphone ['maɪkrəfəʊn]	Mikrofon
	marker pen ['mɑːkə pen]	Marker
70	**graphics** *pl* ['græfɪks]	Grafik(en)
	session ['seʃn]	Sitzung
	audience ['ɔːdiəns]	Publikum, Zuhörerschaft
	coach [kəʊtʃ]	Trainer/in
	memorable ['memərəbl]	einprägsam
	takeaway ['teɪkəweɪ]	etw zum Mitnehmen
	understandable [ˌʌndə'stændəbl]	verständlich
	guidance ['gaɪdəns]	Führung
	simplicity [sɪm'plɪsəti]	Einfachheit
	to **guide** [gaɪd]	führen
	argument ['ɑːgjumənt]	Argumentation
	signal ['sɪgnəl]	Zeichen
	to **illustrate** ['ɪləstreɪt]	illustrieren, veranschaulichen
	to **support** [sə'pɔːt]	untermauern
	to **talk down** [ˌtɔːk 'daʊn]	von oben herab reden
71	to **train sb** [treɪn]	jdn schulen
	to **deliver** [dɪ'lɪvə]	vortragen, *(Rede usw.)* halten
	to **awaken** [ə'weɪkən]	wecken
	visual ['vɪʒuəl]	visuell
	surprising [sə'praɪzɪŋ]	überraschend
	to **grab sb's attention** [ˌgræb ə'tenʃn]	jds Aufmerksamkeit fesseln
	to **get sb involved** [ˌget ɪn'vɒlvd]	jdn einbeziehen
	thought-provoking ['θɔːt prəvəʊkɪŋ]	zum Nachdenken anregend
	opener ['əʊpnə]	Eröffnung(ssatz)
	appropriate(ly) [ə'prəʊpriət]	angemessen, passend
	patronising ['pætrənaɪzɪŋ]	herablassend, oberlehrerhaft
	vital ['vaɪtl]	unerlässlich
	listener ['lɪsnə]	Zuhörer/in
	to **pass sth out** [ˌpɑːs 'aʊt]	etw verteilen
	aware [ə'weə]	bewusst
	to **put sth to good use** [ˌpʊt tə ˌgʊd 'juːs]	etw sinnvoll einsetzen
72	**stage** [steɪdʒ]	Phase, Etappe
T	**as follows** [əz 'fɒləʊz]	wie folgt, folgendermaßen
	body language ['bɒdi læŋgwɪdʒ]	Körpersprache
	voice [vɔɪs]	Stimme
	tone of voice [ˌtəʊn əv 'vɔɪs]	Tonfall
T	**to begin with** [tə bɪ'gɪn wɪð]	zunächst
	confident ['kɒnfɪdənt]	sicher, selbstbewusst
	to **shake** [ʃeɪk]	zittern
	stiff [stɪf]	starr, steif
	tense [tens]	angespannt
	posture ['pɒstʃə]	Körperhaltung
	lack [læk]	Mangel
	confidence ['kɒnfɪdəns]	Selbstvertrauen

	to take a deep breath [teɪk ə ˌdiːp 'breθ]	tief einatmen
	to vary ['veəri]	variieren
	intonation [ˌɪntə'neɪʃn]	Sprachmelodie
	to break sth up [ˌbreɪk 'ʌp]	etw auflockern
	to wonder ['wʌndə]	sich fragen
	(in a certain) fashion ['fæʃn]	(auf eine bestimmte) Art und Weise
	afterwards ['ɑːftəwədz]	hinterher
	to get at sth ['get ət]	auf etw hinaus wollen
	to award sth [ə'wɔːd]	etw zuerkennen, *(Punkte usw.)* geben
73	**growth** [grəʊθ]	Wachstum, Zunahme
	precision [prɪ'sɪʒn]	(Detail-)Genauigkeit
	pie chart ['paɪ tʃɑːt]	Tortendiagramm
	bar chart ['bɑː tʃɑːt]	Säulendiagramm
	line chart ['laɪn tʃɑːt]	Liniendiagramm
74	**currency** ['kʌrənsi]	Währung
	exchange rate [ɪks'tʃeɪndʒ reɪt]	Wechselkurs
	average ['ævərɪdʒ]	durchschnittlich, Durchschnitts-
	income ['ɪnkʌm]	Einkommen
	contribution [ˌkɒntrɪ'bjuːʃn]	Beitrag, Anteil
	to shoot up [ˌʃuːt 'ʌp]	in die Höhe schießen
	to shoot down [ˌʃuːt 'daʊn]	abstürzen
	to increase [ɪn'kriːs]	steigen, zunehmen
	increase ['ɪŋkriːs]	Steigerung, Zunahme
	to hit sth [hɪt]	etw erreichen
	to flatten out [ˌflætn 'aʊt]	(sich) abflachen
	to level off [ˌlevl 'ɒf]	sich einpendeln
	to decrease [dɪ'kriːs]	abnehmen, sinken
	decrease ['diːkriːs]	Abnahme
	to drop [drɒp]	fallen
	drop [drɒp]	Abnahme
	to rise [raɪz]	steigen, ansteigen
	rise [raɪz]	Anstieg, Zunahme
	to fluctuate ['flʌktʃueɪt]	schwanken
	fluctuation [ˌflʌktʃu'eɪʃn]	Schwankung, Schwanken
	to climb [klaɪm]	klettern, ansteigen
	climb [klaɪm]	Anstieg, Zunahme
	to recover [rɪ'kʌvə]	sich erholen
	recovery [rɪ'kʌvəri]	Erholung
	to peak [piːk]	einen Spitzenwert erreichen
	peak [piːk]	Spitzenwert
	to plunge [plʌndʒ]	abstürzen
	plunge [plʌndʒ]	Absturz, Sturz
	axis ['æksɪs]	Achse
	unit ['juːnɪt]	Einheit
	scale [skeɪl]	Skala
T	**financial year** [faɪˌnænʃl 'jɪə]	Geschäftsjahr
	rapid(ly) ['ræpɪd]	schnell
	drastic(ally) ['dræstɪk]	drastisch
	volume of sales [ˌvɒljuːm əf 'seɪlz]	Umsatzvolumen
	at a glance [ət ə 'glɑːns]	auf einen Blick
75	**key issues** *pl* [ˌkiː 'ɪʃuːz]	Hauptpunkte, wichtigste Fragen
	to remind sb of sth [rɪ'maɪnd əv]	jdn an etw erinnern, jdn auf etw hinweisen
	to near [nɪə]	sich nähern
	to gain [geɪn]	gewinnen, bekommen
76	**lunch break** ['lʌntʃ breɪk]	Mittagspause
77	**impression** [ɪm'preʃn]	Eindruck
	opinion [ə'pɪniən]	Meinung, Ansicht
	appearance [ə'pɪərəns]	Aussehen, Erscheinungsbild
	authority [ɔː'θɒrəti]	Autorität
	nervousness ['nɜːvəsnəs]	Nervosität
	nervous ['nɜːvəs]	nervös
	stranger ['streɪndʒə]	Fremde/r, Unbekannte/r
	rapport [ræ'pɔː]	gutes Verhältnis, Kontakt
	to establish sth [ɪ'stæblɪʃ]	etw aufbauen
	in turn [ɪn 'tɜːn]	der Reihe nach
	edge [edʒ]	Kante
	slightly ['slaɪtli]	etwas, ein wenig
	to wave sth about [ˌweɪv ə'baʊt]	mit etw herumfuchteln
	to influence ['ɪnfluəns]	beeinflussen
	to speed up [ˌspiːd 'ʌp]	schneller werden
	to pause [pɔːz]	innehalten
	volume ['vɒljuːm]	Lautstärke
	to fall asleep [ˌfɔːl ə'sliːp]	einschlafen

UNIT 9

78	**to complain** [kəm'pleɪn]	sich beschweren, reklamieren, sich beklagen
	to adjust a complaint [əˌdʒʌst ə kəm'pleɪnt]	eine Reklamation bearbeiten/regulieren
	to report [rɪ'pɔːt]	melden
	to ensure [ɪn'ʃʊə]	sicherstellen, gewährleisten
	to look into sth [ˌlʊk 'ɪntə]	einer Sache nachgehen
	to cross [krɒs]	*hier:* sich überschneiden
79	**to recondition** [ˌriːkən'dɪʃn]	generalüberholen

	medical equipment [ˌmedɪkl ɪˈkwɪpmənt]	medizinische Geräte
	dental clinic [ˌdentl ˈklɪnɪk]	Zahnklinik
	attention [əˈtenʃn]	*(Brief:)* zu Händen
	regarding [rɪˈɡɑːdɪŋ]	bezüglich, betreffend
	x-ray [ˈeksreɪ]	Röntgenstrahlen, Röntgen-
	to **date** [tə deɪt]	bis heute, bisher
	handling [ˈhændlɪŋ]	Umgang, Behandlung
	to **determine** [dɪˈtɜːmɪn]	bestimmen, entscheiden
	practice [ˈpræktɪs]	(Arzt-)Praxis
80	**consignment** [kənˈsaɪnmənt]	Sendung
	to **fulfil** [fʊlˈfɪl]	erfüllen, abwickeln
	cause [kɔːz]	Anlass, Grund
	up to now [ʌp tə ˈnaʊ]	bis jetzt, bislang
	summary [ˈsʌməri]	Zusammenfassung
81	**underway** [ˌʌndəˈweɪ]	unterwegs
	to **found** [faʊnd]	gründen
	letter of apology [ˌletər əv əˈpɒlədʒi]	Entschuldigungsschreiben
82	to **discover** [dɪˈskʌvə]	entdecken, feststellen
	cask [kɑːsk]	Fass
	damaged [ˈdæmɪdʒd]	beschädigt
	leaking [ˈliːkɪŋ]	undicht
	to **drop sth** [drɒp]	etw fallen lassen
	to **handle sth roughly** [ˌhændl ˈrʌfli]	etw grob behandeln
	in transit [ɪn ˈtrænzɪt]	während des Transports
	apparent [əˈpærənt]	klar, offensichtlich
	to **be up to standard** [bi ˌʌp tə ˈstændəd]	der Norm/den Anforderungen genügen
	to **investigate** [ɪnˈvestɪɡeɪt]	untersuchen
	solution (to sth) [səˈluːʃn]	Lösung (für etw)
	to **solve** [sɒlv]	lösen
	to **fill an order** [ˌfɪl ən ˈɔːdə]	einen Auftrag erledigen
	to **point out** [ˌpɔɪnt ˈaʊt]	darauf hinweisen
	to **settle** [ˈsetl]	klären, regeln
83	**overdue** [ˌəʊvəˈdjuː]	überfällig, ausstehend
	straight away [ˌstreɪt əˈweɪ]	sofort, unverzüglich
	nearby [ˈnɪəbaɪ]	in der Nähe
	state [steɪt]	Status
	by rail [baɪ ˈreɪl]	mit der Bahn, auf der Schiene
	once again [ˌwʌns əˈɡen]	noch einmal
84	to **take action** [ˌteɪk ˈækʃn]	Maßnahmen ergreifen
	to **sort sth out** [ˌsɔːt ˈaʊt]	etw in Ordnung bringen
	to **dock** [dɒk]	anlegen
	to **divert** [daɪˈvɜːt]	umleiten
85	**faulty** [ˈfɔːlti]	defekt, schadhaft
	sincere [sɪnˈsɪə]	aufrichtig
	inconvenience [ˌɪnkənˈviːniəns]	Unannehmlichkeiten
	unfortunately [ʌnˈfɔːtʃənətli]	leider
	mix-up [ˈmɪks ʌp]	Missverständnis, Verwechslung
	extreme [ɪkˈstriːm]	extrem
	condition [kənˈdɪʃn]	Bedingung
	accident [ˈæksɪdənt]	Unfall
	replacement [rɪˈpleɪsmənt]	Ersatz
	courier [ˈkʊriə]	Kurier
	despite [dɪˈspaɪt]	trotz
	to **make an effort** [ˌmeɪk ən ˈefət]	sich bemühen, sich Mühe geben
T	**scratched** [skrætʃt]	verkratzt
	dented [ˈdentɪd]	verbeult, eingebeult
	casing [ˈkeɪsɪŋ]	Gehäuse
	disappointed [ˌdɪsəˈpɔɪntɪd]	enttäuscht
	superior [suːˈpɪəriə]	Vorgesetzte/r, Chef/in
86	**purpose** [ˈpɜːpəs]	Zweck
	pre-printed [ˌpriːˈprɪntɪd]	vorgedruckt
	satisfied [ˈsætɪsfaɪd]	zufrieden
88	to **be proactive** [bi ˌprəʊˈæktɪv]	eigenständig agieren, die Initiative ergreifen
	to **anticipate** [ænˈtɪsɪpeɪt]	rechnen mit, erwarten, vorhersehen
	sympathetic [ˌsɪmpəˈθetɪk]	einfühlsam

UNIT 10

89	**credit enquiry** [ˈkredɪt ɪnkwaɪəri]	Bonitätsauskunft
	to **settle (a bill)** [ˈsetl]	(eine Rechnung) begleichen, bezahlen
	stage [steɪdʒ]	Stufe
	final demand [ˌfaɪnl dɪˈmɑːnd]	letzte Mahnung
	registered mail/post [ˌredʒɪstəd ˈmeɪl/ˈpəʊst]	Einschreiben
90	**calendar** [ˈkælɪndə]	Kalender
	to **settle an account** [ˌsetl ən əˈkaʊnt]	ein Konto ausgleichen, eine Rechnung bezahlen
	non-payment [ˌnɒnˈpeɪmənt]	Nicht(be)zahlung
	to **carry sth out** [ˌkæri ˈaʊt]	etw ausführen
	according to [əˈkɔːdɪŋ tə]	gemäß, laut, nach
	advice of payment [ədˌvaɪs əf ˈpeɪmənt]	Zahlungsanzeige

	to mislay [ˌmɪs'leɪ]	verlegen
	for your convenience [fə jɔː kən'viːniəns]	*etwa:* als Service-leistung *(wird nicht übersetzt!)*
	in the meantime [ɪn ðə 'miːntaɪm]	in der Zwischenzeit
	to ignore [ɪg'nɔː]	nicht beachten
91	**outstanding** [aʊt'stændɪŋ]	ausstehend
	balance ['bæləns]	Saldo
	to assume [ə'sjuːm]	davon ausgehen, annehmen
	to be due to sth [bi 'djuː tə]	auf etw zurückzuführen sein
	error ['erə]	Irrtum, Fehler
	otherwise ['ʌðəwaɪz]	sonst, ansonsten
	to arrange for sth [ə'reɪndʒ fə]	für etw sorgen, etw veranlassen
92	**hidden** ['hɪdn]	verborgen
	less [les]	abzüglich
	thereafter [ˌðeər'ɑːftə]	danach
	to insist on sth [ɪn'sɪst ɒn]	auf etw bestehen
	in case [ɪn 'keɪs]	für den Fall, dass
	to be referred to as sth [bi rɪ'fɜːd tə əz]	als etw bezeichnet werden
	excuse [ɪk'skjuːs]	Vorwand
	to take legal action [teɪk ˌliːgl 'ækʃn]	rechtliche Schritte einleiten, gerichtlich gegen jdn vorgehen
93	**in connection with** [ɪn kə'nekʃn wɪð]	in Verbindung mit
	statement ['steɪtmənt]	Beleg, (Konto-)Auszug
	sum [sʌm]	Betrag, Summe
	oversight ['əʊvəsaɪt]	Versehen
	remittance [rɪ'mɪtns]	Zahlung, Überweisung
	to start legal proceedings [stɑːt ˌliːgl prə'siːdɪŋz]	gerichtlich gegen jdn vorgehen, Klage erheben
	major ['meɪdʒə]	Groß-, Haupt-, bedeutend
	debts *pl* [dets]	Schulden
	temporary ['temprəri]	vorübergehend
	cash flow problems *pl* [ˌkæʃ fləʊ 'prɒbləmz]	Liquiditätsprobleme
	to remit [rɪ'mɪt]	überweisen
	in full [ɪn 'fʊl]	in voller Höhe
	therefore ['ðeəfɔː]	daher
	instalment [ɪn'stɔːlmənt]	Rate
	record ['rekɔːd]	Historie
94	**to propose** [prə'pəʊz]	vorschlagen
	to withhold [wɪð'həʊld]	vorenthalten
	to grant sth [grɑːnt]	etw einräumen, zugestehen, gewähren
	concession [kən'seʃn]	Zugeständnis
95	**to access sth** ['ækses]	auf etw zugreifen
	to overlook [ˌəʊvə'lʊk]	übersehen
	payable ['peɪəbl]	zahlbar
	to draft [drɑːft]	entwerfen, aufsetzen
	disturbed [dɪ'stɜːbd]	beunruhigt
	collection agency [kə'lekʃn eɪdʒənsi]	Inkasso-Agentur
96	**slip** [slɪp]	Zettel
	financial standing [faɪˌnænʃl 'stændɪŋ]	Bonität, Kreditwürdigkeit
	reputation [ˌrepju'teɪʃn]	Ruf
	confidential [ˌkɒnfɪ'denʃl]	vertraulich
	liability [ˌlaɪə'bɪləti]	Haftung
	similar ['sɪmələ]	ähnlich
97	**enquirer** [ɪn'kwaɪərə]	Angragende/r, Interessent/in
	in return [ɪn rɪ'tɜːn]	als Gegenleistung
	willing ['wɪlɪŋ]	bereit, willens
	astonished [ə'stɒnɪʃt]	erstaunt
	to collect payment [kəˌlekt 'peɪmənt]	(einen Kunden) zur Zahlung veranlassen, Inkasso vornehmen
	founder ['faʊndə]	Gründer/in
	to retire [rɪ'taɪə]	sich zur Ruhe setzen
	to meet one's obligations [ˌmiːt wʌnz ˌɒblɪ'geɪʃnz]	seine Verpflichtungen erfüllen
	punctual(ly) ['pʌŋktʃuəl]	pünktlich
	trade [treɪd]	Branche
	to recommend [ˌrekə'mend]	empfehlen
	strict [strɪkt]	streng
	to total ['təʊtl]	(insgesamt) betragen
	to judge [dʒʌdʒ]	beurteilen

UNIT 11

98	**directory** [də'rektəri]	Verzeichnis
	exhibition [ˌeksɪ'bɪʃn]	Ausstellung, Messe
	featuring ['fiːtʃərɪŋ]	mit
	automotive [ˌɔːtə'məʊtɪv]	Automobil-
	offshore [ˌɒf'ʃɔː]	vor der Küste, Hochsee-
	wind power ['wɪnd paʊə]	Windkraft, Windenergie
	to target sb ['tɑːgɪt]	jdn als Zielgruppe haben
	to register ['redʒɪstə]	(sich) anmelden
99	**profile** ['prəʊfaɪl]	Profil, Porträt
	aimed at sb ['eɪmd ət]	an jdn gerichtet
	decision-maker [dɪ'sɪʒn meɪkə]	Entscheidungsträger/in
	exhibitor [ɪg'zɪbɪtə]	Aussteller/in
	engineering [ˌendʒɪ'nɪərɪŋ]	Maschinenbau
	consultant [kən'sʌltənt]	Berater/in

	power utilities *pl* ['paʊə ju:tɪlətiz]	Stromversorger
	registration [ˌredʒɪ'streɪʃn]	Anmeldung, Registrierung
	operating company [ˌɒpəreɪtɪŋ 'kʌmpəni]	Betreiberfirma, Trägergesellschaft
	wholesale trader ['həʊlseɪl treɪdə]	Großhändler
	government ['gʌvənmənt]	Regierung
	representative [ˌreprɪ'zentətɪv]	Vertreter/in
	educator ['edʒukeɪtə]	Pädagoge/-in
	benefit ['benɪfɪt]	Nutzen, Vorteil
	to **exhibit** [ɪg'zɪbɪt]	ausstellen
	showcase ['ʃəʊ keɪs]	Schaufenster
	publicity [pʌb'lɪsəti]	Werbung, Publicity
	promotion [prə'məʊʃn]	Werbung
	to **feature** ['fi:tʃə]	vorkommen, eine Rolle spielen
	publication [ˌpʌblɪ'keɪʃn]	Veröffentlichung
	press release ['pres rɪli:s]	Pressemitteilung
	facilities *pl* [fə'sɪlətiz]	Einrichtungen
	fixtures and fittings *pl* [ˌfɪkstʃəz ənd 'fɪtɪŋz]	Ausstattung und Installationen
100	**lighting** ['laɪtɪŋ]	Beleuchtung, Licht
	(electric) socket ['sɒkɪt]	Steckdose
	floor covering ['flɔ: kʌvərɪŋ]	Bodenbelag
	target group ['tɑ:gɪt gru:p]	Zielgruppe
	display rack [dɪ'spleɪ ræk]	Ausstellungsregal
	gift [gɪft]	Geschenk
	counter ['kaʊntə]	Tresen, Schalter
	reception area [rɪ'sepʃn eəriə]	Empfangsbereich
	seating area ['si:tɪŋ eəriə]	bestuhlter Bereich
	to **approach** [ə'prəʊtʃ]	sich nähern, herantreten
	in full view [ɪn ˌfʊl 'vju:]	gut sichtbar
	to **encourage** [ɪn'kʌrɪdʒ]	ermuntern
	tiring ['taɪərɪŋ]	ermüdend
	to **man** [mæn]	besetzen, betreuen
	bustle [bʌsl]	(geschäftiges) Treiben
101	to **accommodate** [ə'kɒmədeɪt]	unterbringen, Platz bieten für
	to **measure** ['meʒə]	messen
	to **equip** [ɪ'kwɪp]	ausstatten, ausrüsten
	corner ['kɔ:nə]	Ecke
	competition [ˌkɒmpə'tɪʃn]	Konkurrenz
	competitor [kəm'petɪtə]	Konkurrent/in, Konkurrenz, Wettbewerber/in
102	**decision** [dɪ'sɪʒn]	Entscheidung
	square metre ['skweə mi:tə]	Quadratmeter
	departure [dɪ'pɑ:tʃə]	Abreise, Abfahrt, Abflug
	to **depart** [dɪ'pɑ:t]	abfliegen, abfahren
	return flight [rɪˌtɜ:n 'flaɪt]	Hin- und Rückflug
	traveller ['trævələ]	Reisende/r
T	**tax** [tæks]	Steuer
	fee [fi:]	Gebühr
	passenger ['pæsɪndʒə]	Passagier
	one-way flight [ˌwʌn weɪ 'flaɪt]	einfacher Flug
	seat [si:t]	Sitz, Sitzplatz
	connecting flight [kəˌnektɪŋ 'flaɪt]	Anschlussflug
103	**plaster** ['plɑ:stə]	Gips
	reservation [ˌrezə'veɪʃn]	Reservierung, Buchung
	extra charge [ˌekstrə 'tʃɑ:dʒ]	Aufpreis
104	**corporate** ['kɔ:pərət]	Unternehmens- P
	within easy reach [wɪðɪn ˌi:zi 'ri:tʃ]	gut erreichbar
	indoor swimming pool [ˌɪndɔ: 'swɪmɪŋ pu:l]	Hallenbad
	non-smoking [ˌnɒn'sməʊkɪŋ]	Nichtraucher-
	rate [reɪt]	Preis, Satz
105 T	**fully booked** [ˌfʊli 'bʊkt]	ausgebucht
	vacant ['veɪkənt]	frei
	to **get caught up in sth** [get ˌkɔ:t 'ʌp ɪn]	in etw geraten
	to **take ages** [ˌteɪk 'eɪdʒɪz]	ewig dauern
106	**aid** [eɪd]	Hilfe
	humanitarian [hju:ˌmænɪ'teəriən]	humanitär
	relief [rɪ'li:f]	Hilfe
	unique [ju'ni:k]	einzigartig
	to **meet sb's needs** [ˌmi:t 'ni:dz]	jds Bedürfnis erfüllen
	victim ['vɪktɪm]	Opfer
	natural disaster [ˌnætʃrəl dɪ'zɑ:stə]	Naturkatastrophe
	conflict ['kɒnflɪkt]	Konflikt, kriegerische Auseinandersetzung
	to **assemble** [ə'sembl]	montieren, zusammenbauen
	prefabricated [ˌpri:'fæbrɪkeɪtɪd]	vorgefertigt
	multi-cellular [ˌmʌlti 'seljʊlə]	in Zellbauweise

galvanized ['gælvənaɪzd]	verzinkt
hollow ['hɒləʊ]	hohl
to **tie** [taɪ]	binden
wire [waɪə]	Draht
invention [ɪn'venʃn]	Erfindung
disaster area [dɪˌzɑːstə 'eəriə]	Katastrophengebiet
to **get rid of sth** [ˌget 'rɪd əv]	etw loswerden
rubble ['rʌbl]	Schutt
to **clear** [klɪə]	räumen
shelter ['ʃeltə]	Unterkunft
to **tackle** ['tækl]	*(Problem usw.)* angehen
dirt [dɜːt]	Schmutz, Dreck
rock [rɒk]	Stein
to **destroy** [dɪ'strɔɪ]	zerstören
builder ['bɪldə]	Bauarbeiter/in
non-skilled [ˌnɒn 'skɪld]	ungelernt
to **erect** [ɪ'rekt]	errichten
to **demonstrate** ['demənstreɪt]	vorführen
cocoon-shaped [kə'kuːn ʃeɪpt]	kokonförmig
tent [tent]	Zelt
to **operate** ['ɒpəreɪt]	fungieren, dienen
chemical ['kemɪkl]	chemisch
biological [ˌbaɪə'lɒdʒɪkl]	biologisch
filtering system ['fɪltərɪŋ sɪstəm]	Filtersystem
emergency [ɪ'mɜːdʒənsi]	Notfall
field hospital ['fiːld hɒspɪtl]	Feldlazarett
military ['mɪlətri]	Militär
versatile ['vɜːsətaɪl]	vielseitig
to **be on display** [bi ɒn dɪ'spleɪ]	ausgestellt werden
federation [ˌfedə'reɪʃn]	Vereinigung, Verband
to **interact** [ˌɪntər'ækt]	miteinander umgehen
two-way [ˌtuː 'weɪ]	gegenseitig, in beide Richtungen
to **be a priority** [bi ə praɪ'ɒrəti]	(hohe) Priorität haben
enterprise ['entəpraɪz]	Unternehmen
to **break into the market** [ˌbreɪk ɪntə ðə 'mɑːkɪt]	auf den Markt vordringen
survivor [sə'vaɪvə]	Überlebende/r
variety [və'raɪəti]	Vielfalt

UNIT 12

107	**interview** ['ɪntəvjuː]	Vorstellungsgespräch
	confusing [kən'fjuːzɪŋ]	verwirrend
	to **complement** ['kɒmplɪmənt]	ergänzen
	prospective [prə'spektɪv]	potentiell
	opinion poll [ə'pɪniən pəʊl]	Meinungsumfrage
	importance [ɪm'pɔːtns]	Bedeutung, Wichtigkeit
P	**percentage** [pə'sentɪdʒ]	Anteil, Prozentsatz
	vote [vəʊt]	Stimme
	technique [tek'niːk]	Technik
	résumé *AE* ['rezjumeɪ]	Lebenslauf
108	to **qualify** ['kwɒlɪfaɪ]	seinen/ihren Abschluss machen
	benefits *pl* ['benɪfɪts]	Zusatzleistungen, Sozialleistungen
	recruiter [rɪ'kruːtə]	Personalvermittler/in
	recruiting agency [rɪ'kruːtɪŋ eɪdʒənsi]	Personalvermittlung, Personalagentur
	per annum [pər 'ænəm]	im Jahr
	permanent ['pɜːmənənt]	dauerhaft, *hier:* unbefristet
	to **recruit** [rɪ'kruːt]	(Personal) werben, einstellen
	to **be located in ...** [bi ləʊ'keɪtɪd ɪn]	in ... sein/liegen
	candidate ['kændɪdət]	Kandidat/in, Bewerber/in
	responsibility [rɪˌspɒnsə'bɪləti]	Aufgabe(nbereich), Verantwortlichkeit
	pressure ['preʃə]	Druck
	manner ['mænə]	Art, Weise
	salary ['sæləri]	Gehalt
	luncheon voucher ['lʌntʃən vaʊtʃə]	Essensgutschein
	superb [suː'pɜːb]	ausgezeichnet
	hard-working [ˌhɑːd 'wɜːkɪŋ]	fleißig
	enthusiastic [ɪnˌθjuːzi'æstɪk]	begeisterungsfähig
	initial [ɪ'nɪʃl]	anfängliche/r/s
	to **conduct sth** [kən'dʌkt]	etw durchführen, (Gespräch, usw) führen
	face to face [ˌfeɪs tə 'feɪs]	persönlich
109	**vacancy** ['veɪkənsi]	freie/offene Stelle
P	**school leaving certificate** [ˌskuːl liːvɪŋ sə'tɪfɪkət]	Schulabgangszeugnis, Schulabschluss
	promotion [prə'məʊʃn]	Beförderung
	applicant ['æplɪkənt]	Bewerber/in
	foreign trade [ˌfɒrən 'treɪd]	Außenhandel
	mainly ['meɪnli]	hauptsächlich
	frequent ['friːkwənt]	häufig
	GCSE [ˌdʒiː siː es 'iː]	*Abschlussprüfung für die Sekundarstufe I in Großbritannien*
	equivalent [ɪ'kwɪvələnt]	entsprechende/r/s
	temporary ['temprəri]	befristet

	to **interview sb** ['ɪntəvju:]	mit jdm ein Vorstellungsgespräch führen
110	**process** ['prəʊses]	Verfahren
	to **be short-listed** [bi ˌʃɔ:t 'lɪstɪd]	in die engere Auswahl kommen
	set [set]	vorgeschrieben, fest(gesetzt)
	honest ['ɒnɪst]	ehrlich
	factual ['fæktʃuəl]	sachlich (korrekt)
	throughout [θru:'aʊt]	durchgehend
	focused ['fəʊkəst]	konzentriert, zielgerichtet
	reverse [rɪ'vɜ:s]	umgekehrt
	achievement [ə'tʃi:vmənt]	Leistung, Erfolg
	driving licence ['draɪvɪŋlaɪsns]	Führerschein
	energetic [ˌenə'dʒetɪk]	aktiv
	feature ['fi:tʃə]	Merkmal
	to **socialize with sb** ['səʊʃəlaɪz wɪð]	sich mit jdm treffen, mit jdm ausgehen
	data protection ['deɪtə prətekʃn]	Datenschutz
	referee [ˌrefə'ri:]	Referenz
	on request [ɒn rɪ'kwest]	auf Wunsch
	permission [pə'mɪʃn]	Erlaubnis
111	to **seek** [si:k]	suchen
	health insurance ['helθ ɪnʃʊərəns]	Krankenversicherung
	to **certify** ['sɜ:tɪfaɪ]	bescheinigen, anerkenne
	A levels ['eɪ levlz]	*höchster Schulabschluss in England, Wales und Nordirland*
	economics [ˌi:kə'nɒmɪks]	Wirtschaftswissenschaften
	fluent ['flu:ənt]	*(Sprachkenntnisse:)* fließend
	oral ['ɔ:rəl]	mündlich
	conversational [ˌkɒnvə'seɪʃənl]	Umgangs-
112	to **label** ['leɪbl]	beschriften, etikettieren
	to **advertise (a job)** ['ædvətaɪz]	(eine Stelle) ausschreiben
	level ['levl]	Ebene
	to **apply sth** [ə'plaɪ]	etw anwenden
	apart from that [ə'pɑ:t frəm ðət]	außerdem
	present ['preznt]	aktuell, gegenwärtig
	to **admit sb** [əd'mɪt]	jdn aufnehmen
	to **add value to sth** [ˌæd 'vælju: tə]	aufwerten, einen Mehrwert verleihen, hier *etwa: gut ergänzen*
	to **be an asset to sb/sth** [bi ən 'æset tə]	für jdn/etw von Wert sein
	mother-tongue ['mʌðə tʌŋ]	Muttersprache
113	**post** [pəʊst]	Stelle, Posten
	favourably ['feɪvərəbli]	positiv, günstig
114	**meaningful** ['mi:nɪŋfl]	wichtig, bedeutsam
	to **hire sb** ['haɪə]	jdn einstellen
115	to **calm down** [ˌkɑ:m 'daʊn]	sich beruhigen
T	**smart** [smɑ:t]	*(Kleidung:)* schick, elegant
	to **shake hands with sb** [ˌʃeɪk 'hændz wɪð]	jdm die Hand geben
	shy [ʃaɪ]	schüchtern
	to **get into the habit of sth** [ˌget ɪntə ðə 'hæbɪt əv]	sich etw zur Gewohnheit machen
	weakness ['wi:knəs]	Schwäche
	to **clarify** ['klærəfaɪ]	erklären, erläutern
	prospects *pl* ['prɒspekts]	Aussichten
	to **occur** [ə'kɜ:]	auftreten, vorkommen
	concerning [kən'sɜ:nɪŋ]	bezüglich, hinsichtlich
	evaluation [ɪˌvælju'eɪʃn]	Bewertung, Beurteilung
	handshake ['hændʃeɪk]	Händedruck
P	to **afford sth** [ə'fɔ:d]	sich etw leisten können
	to **stress** [stres]	betonen, hervorheben
	goal [gəʊl]	Ziel
	to **progress** [prə'gres]	vorankommen
117	**insight** ['ɪnsaɪt]	Einblick
	invaluable [ɪn'væljuəbl]	unschätzbar
	to **secure sth** [sɪ'kjʊə]	sich etw sichern
	work permit ['wɜ:k pɜ:mɪt]	Arbeitserlaubnis
	visa ['vi:zə]	Visum
	pension cover ['penʃn kʌvə]	Altersvorsorge
	to **enter (a country)** ['entə]	(in ein Land) einreisen
	resident ['rezɪdənt]	Bewohner/in, Einwohner/in
	embassy ['embəsi]	Botschaft
	consulate ['kɒnsjələt]	Konsulat
	in question [ɪn 'kwestʃən]	fraglich, betreffend
	attitude towards sth ['ætɪtju:d təwɔ:dz]	Einstellung zu etw

Alphabetical word list

Dieses Wörterverzeichnis enthält alle neuen Wörter aus *Office Matters – 3rd Edition* in alphabetischer Reihenfolge. Nicht angeführt sind Wörter, die zum Grundwortschatz (*Basic word list*) gehören. Die Zahl nach dem Stichwort bezieht sich auf die Seite, auf der das Wort zum ersten Mal erscheint. Wörter aus den Hörverständnisübungen sind zusätzlich mit einem **T** (Transkript) und Wörter aus den *Partner files* mit einem **P** gekennzeichnet.

A

abbreviation *25* Abkürzung
ability *29* Fähigkeit
absence *62* Abwesenheit
to **accept** *23* annehmen, akzeptieren
acceptable *25* akzeptabel
acceptance, documents against ~ *56* Dokumente gegen Akzept
to **access sth** *95* auf etw zugreifen
accident *85* Unfall
to **accommodate** *101* unterbringen, Platz bieten für
accommodation *20* Unterkunft
to **accompany** *18* begleiten
according to *90* gemäß, laut, nach
account *46* Konto, Kreditkonto
account, open ~ *56* Forderung
account, to **settle an ~** *90* ein Konto ausgleichen, eine Rechnung bezahlen
accounts *37* (Geschäfts-)Bücher, Buchführung
accounts department *17* Buchhaltung
accountant *37* Buchhalter/in
accurate(ly) *9T* genau
to **achieve** *36* erzielen, erreichen
achievement *110* Leistung, Erfolg
to **acknowledge** *34* anerkennen, zugeben
to **acknowledge an order** *53* einen Auftrag bestätigen
acknowledgement *34* Auftragsbestätigung
across, to **get sth ~** *18* etw vermitteln, übermitteln
to **act** *64* handeln, fungieren
action *68* Handlung, Aktion
action plan *63* Maßnahmenkatalog
action, to **take ~** *84* Maßnahmen ergreifen
action, to **take legal ~** *92* rechtliche Schritte einleiten, gerichtlich gegen jdn vorgehen
activity *14* Tätigkeit
to **add value to sth** *112* aufwerten, einen Mehrwert verleihen, *hier etwa:* gut ergänzen
addition *48* Ergänzung
addressee *34* Empfänger/in
to **adjust a complaint** *78* eine Reklamation bearbeiten/regulieren
administration *9T* Verwaltung
to **admit sb** *112* jdn aufnehmen
to **advertise** *34T* Werbung machen
to **advertise (a job)** *112* (eine Stelle) ausschreiben
advertising agency *66* Werbeagentur
advice *7* Ratschlag, (guter) Rat
advice of dispatch *34* Versandanzeige, Versandmitteilung
advice of payment *90* Zahlungsanzeige
to **afford sth** *115P* sich etw leisten können
afterwards *72T* hinterher
age, to **take ~s** *105T* ewig dauern
agenda *18* Tagesordnung
agent *63* Vertragshändler/in
agreement *37* Vereinbarung
aid *106* Hilfe
aim *66* Ziel, Zweck
to **aim** *65T* beabsichtigen, vorhaben, wollen
aimed at sb *99* an jdn gerichtet
airy *61* geräumig, luftig
A levels *111 höchster Schulabschluss in England, Wales und Nordirland*
allocation *27* Zuweisung, Zuteilung
allowed, to **be ~ to do sth** *32* etw tun dürfen
along *42* entlang
alternative *21* alternativ, Alternativ-
to **announce** *18* ankündigen; *62* verkünden
announcement *31* Ankündigung
annual *65* jährlich
annum, per ~ *108* im Jahr
to **anticipate** *88* rechnen mit, erwarten, vorhersehen
any other business (AOB) *62* Verschiedenes
apart from that *112* außerdem
to **apologize** *21* sich entschuldigen
apology *62* Entschuldigung
apology, letter of ~ *81* Entschuldigungsschreiben
apology, to **send one's apologies** *65T* sich entschuldigen lassen
apparent *82* klar, offensichtlich
to **appear** *7* erscheinen, auftauchen
appearance *77* Aussehen, Erscheinungsbild
appliance, domestic ~ *43* Haushaltsgerät
applicant *109P* Bewerber/in
application *19* Antrag; *29* Bewerbung
to **apply sth** *112* etw anwenden
to **apply for sb/sth** *52* für jdn/etw gelten
to **apply for sth** *28* sich für etw bewerben
appointment *40* Termin
to **appreciate** *25* schätzen, zu schätzen wissen
apprenticeship *36* Lehre, Ausbildung
to **approach** *100* sich nähern, herantreten
appropriate(ly) *71* angemessen, passend
approval *47* Zustimmung, Genehmigung
approval, to **meet sb's ~** *50* jds Zustimmung finden
to **approve** *68* genehmigen, annehmen
approximately *36* ungefähr, zirka
to **argue** *33T* argumentieren
argument *70* Argumentation
to **arrange for sth** *91* für etw sorgen, etw veranlassen
arrangements pl *15* Vorbereitungen, Vereinbarungen
artwork *66* Grafik, Illustrationen
as *9* während
as far as sth is concerned *16* was etw angeht/betrifft
as follows *72T* wie folgt, folgendermaßen
asleep, to **fall ~** *77* einschlafen
to **assemble** *106* montieren, zusammenbauen
assembly line *36* Fließband, Montageband
asset, to **be an ~ to sb/sth** *112* für jdn/etw von Wert sein
to **assist** *20* helfen, unterstützen
to **assume** *91* davon ausgehen, annehmen
to **assure** *50* zusichern, versichern
astonished *97* erstaunt

Alphabetical word list

at a glance *74T* auf einen Blick
at last *20* endlich
at the latest *21* spätestens
to **attach sth** *15* *(E-Mail:)* anhängen
to **attend sth** *22* etw besuchen, an etw teilnehmen
attendee *66* Teilnehmer/in
attention *43* Aufmerksamkeit; *79* *(Brief:)* zu Händen
attention, to **come to sb's ~** *43* auf etw aufmerksam werden
attention, to **draw sb's ~ to sth** *48* jdn auf etw aufmerksam machen
attention, to **grab sb's ~** *71* jds Aufmerksamkeit fesseln
attitude towards sth *117* Einstellung zu etw
attractive *57* attraktiv, reizvoll
audience *70* Publikum, Zuhörerschaft
authority *77* Autorität
automotive *98* Automobil-
available *59* erhältlich, verfügbar
average *74* durchschnittlich, Durchschnitts-
to **awaken** *71* wecken
award *36* Preis, Auszeichnung
to **award sth** *72* etw zuerkennen, *(Punkte usw.)* geben
aware *71* bewusst
axis *74* Achse

B

balance *91* Saldo
bank holiday *24* gesetzlicher Feiertag
bank transfer *53* Überweisung
bar chart *73* Säulendiagramm
to **base sth upon sth** *52* etw auf etw gründen
based in/near *36* mit Sitz in/bei
basement *40* Keller, Souterrain
basic *53T* einfach
battery *60* Akku, Batterie
begin, to **~ with** *72T* zunächst
belief *14* Überzeugung
benefit *99* Nutzen, Vorteil
benefits pl *108* Zusatzleistungen, Sozialleistungen
Best wishes *19* Mit den besten Wünschen
bill *38* Rechnung
bill of exchange *57* Wechsel
binding, legally ~ *33T* rechtsverbindlich
biological *106* biologisch
blank *68* frei, leer
board (of directors) *43* Geschäftsführung, Vorstand
body *18* *(Brief usw.:)* Hauptteil
body language *72* Körpersprache
book-keeping *9T* Buchhaltung
bookstore *43* Buchhandlung
border *36* (Landes-)Grenze
to **borrow sth** *22* sich etw (aus) leihen
bottom, at the ~ of sth *39T* am Ende von etw
breach of contract *52* Vertragsbruch
to **break into the market** *106* auf den Markt vordringen
to **break sth up** *72T* etw auflockern
to **break the ice** *14* das Eis brechen
breath, to **take a deep ~** *72T* tief einatmen
brief *68* kurz, knapp
to **bring sth forward** *21* etw vorverlegen
brochure *47* Prospekt
to **build** *36* bauen
to **build sth up** *31* etw aufbauen
builder *106* Bauarbeiter/in
building *40* Gebäude
building industry *35* Baugewerbe
built-in *54* eingebaut
bulk, in ~ *46* en gros
to **burn sth** *60* etw verbrennen
business *12* Geschäft(e), Geschäfts-, Firma, Unternehmen
business, any other ~ (AOB) *62* Verschiedenes
business, close of ~ *22* Geschäftsschluss
business letter *27* Geschäftsbrief
business, to **conduct ~** *52* Geschäfte machen/abschließen
businessman *43* Geschäftsmann, Unternehmer
bustle *100* (geschäftiges) Treiben
buyer *34* Käufer/in
by (tomorrow) *21* bis (morgen)
by rail *83* mit der Bahn, auf der Schiene
by return of post *58* per Antwortschreiben, postwendend
by the (+ date) *46* zum (+ Datum)
by the way *39T* übrigens

C

cabinet, storage ~ *59* Aktenschrank
calendar *90* Kalender
to **call sth up** *53T* etw aufrufen
to **calm down** *115T* sich beruhigen
to **cancel** *21* absagen; *46* stornieren
candidate *108* Kandidat/in, Bewerber/in
capital letter *15* Großbuchstabe
care, to **take ~ of sth** *37* sich um etw kümmern
cardboard box *48* Pappkarton
career *7* Laufbahn, Karriere
careers officer *7* Berufsberater/in
carrier *52* Frachtführer, Spedition
to **carry sth out** *90* etw ausführen
cartridge *60* Patrone
case *54* Koffer; *60* Behälter
case, in ~ *92* für den Fall, dass
cash discount *48* Skonto, Barzahlungsrabatt
cash flow problems *pl* *93* Liquiditätsprobleme
cash in advance *56* Vorauszahlung/Vorkasse
cash on delivery (COD) *53T* zahlbar bei Lieferung, per Nachnahme
casing *85T* Gehäuse
cask *82* Fass
catalogue *45* Katalog
caught up , to **get ~ in sth** *105T* in etw geraten
cause *80* Anlass, Grund
to **cause** *60* verursachen, dazu bringen
CEO = Chief Executive Officer *37* Geschäftsführer/in, Vorstandsvorsitzende/r
certain *17* sicher
certainty *52* Sicherheit, Gewissheit
certificate *28* Zeugnis, Abschluss
to **certify** *111* bescheinigen, anerkenne
chair, to **take the ~** *65* die Sitzung leiten
to **chair** *64* leiten
chairperson *62* Leiter/in
challenge *9T* Herausforderung, (große) Aufgabe
chamber of commerce *47* Handelskammer
charge, extra ~ *103* Aufpreis
charge, in ~ of sth *37* für etw zuständig
to **charge sb** *60* von jdm Gebühren verlangen
chart *37* Diagramm, Grafik
chart, bar ~ *73* Säulendiagramm
chart, line ~ *73* Liniendiagramm
chart, pie ~ *73* Tortendiagramm
to **chat** *11* sich unterhalten, plaudern
to **check sth out** *20* sich etw (genau) ansehen
check-out *60* Kasse
chemical *106* chemisch
cheque *53* Scheck
cherry wood *59* Kirschbaumholz
chronological *43* chronologisch

circumstances pl *25* Umstände, Gegebenheiten
to **clarify** *115T* erklären, erläutern
to **clear** *106* räumen
client *22* Kunde/Kundin
climb *74* Anstieg, Zunahme
to **climb** *74* klettern, ansteigen
close *47* *(Brief:)* Schluss
close of business *22* Geschäftsschluss
close(ly) *29* genau
coach *70* Trainer/in
cocoon-shaped *106* kokonförmig
colleague *7* Kollege, Kollegin
to **collect payment** *97* (einen Kunden) zur Zahlung veranlassen, Inkasso vornehmen
to **collect sb/sth** *16* jdn/etw abholen
collection agency *95* Inkasso-Agentur
college *9T* Berufsfachschule, Fachhochschule
to **come out on top** *33T* vorne liegen, Erste/r werden
comfortable *59* bequem
commercial correspondence *51* Geschäftskorrespondenz
communicator, a good ~ *7* *etwa: jd, der gern auf Menschen zugeht*
community *43* Gemeinde, Gemeinschaft
company, middle-sized ~ *47* mittelständisches Unternehmen
to **compare** *14* vergleichen
competence *65* Kompetenz
competition *101* Konkurrenz
competitor *101* Konkurrent/in, Konkurrenz, Wettbewerber/in
to **complain** *78* sich beschweren, reklamieren, sich beklagen
complaint *34* Reklamation, Beschwerde
complaint, to **adjust a ~** *78* eine Reklamation bearbeiten/ regulieren
to **complement** *107* ergänzen
complicated *31* kompliziert
complimentary close *18* *(Brief:)* Schlussformel
component *60* Bauteil
to **concentrate** *32* sich konzentrieren
concerned, as far as sth is ~ *16* was etw angeht/betrifft
concerning *115T* bezüglich, hinsichtlich
concession *94* Zugeständnis
concise(ly) *18* knapp, kurz (und bündig)
to **conclude** *29* schließen
conclusion *23* Schluss
conclusion, to **draw a ~** *29* einen Schluss ziehen
condensed *25* gekürzt, Kurz-
condition *58* Zustand; *85* Bedingung
to **conduct business** *52* Geschäfte machen/abschließen
to **conduct sth** *108* etw durchführen, *(Gespräch, usw)* führen
confidence *72T* Selbstvertrauen
confident *65T* zuversichtlich, überzeugt; *72T* sicher, selbstbewusst
confidential *96* vertraulich
to **confirm** *15* bestätigen
confirmation *46* Bestätigung
conflict *106* Konflikt, kriegerische Auseinandersetzung
confusing *107* verwirrend
to **connect** *11* verbinden
connecting flight *102* Anschlussflug
connection, in ~ with *93* in Verbindung mit
to **consider** *7* in Erwägung ziehen, in Betracht ziehen; *52* berücksichtigen
consignment *80* Sendung
consulate *117* Konsulat
consultant *99* Berater/in
consumer *63* Verbraucher/in
to **contain** *18* enthalten
container *59* Behälter
to **contaminate** *60* kontaminieren
content *18* Inhalt
to **continue** *42* weitergehen
to **continue to do sth** *19* etw weiterhin tun
contract *22* Vertrag
contract of sale *52* Kaufvertrag
contribution *74* Beitrag, Anteil
controversial *14* strittig, kontrovers, Streit-
convenience, for your ~ *90* *etwa:* als Serviceleistung *(wird nicht übersetzt!)*
convenient *21* günstig, praktisch
conversational *111* Umgangs-
to **convince sb of sth** *14* jdn von etw überzeugen
to **cope with sth** *9* mit etw zurechtkommen
Cordially AE *19* Mit herzlichen Grüßen
cork *54* Kork
corner *101* Ecke
corporate *104P* Unternehmens-
corporation *35* Gesellschaft, Körperschaft
correspondence *30* Korrespondenz
corridor *39T* Flur, Gang
cost advantage *33T* Kostenvorteil
counter *100* Tresen, Schalter
country code *10* Ländervorwahl
courier *85* Kurier
course *34* Ablauf
to **cover** *27* *(Thema)* behandeln
covering letter *18* Anschreiben, Begleitschreiben
crack *60* Riss
craftsman *59* Handwerker
credit, documentary letter of ~ *56* Dokumentenakkreditiv
credit enquiry *89* Bonitätsauskunft
creditworthiness *44* Kreditwürdigkeit
creditworthy *46* kreditwürdig
to **cross** *78* *hier:* sich überschneiden
crossroads *40T* Kreuzung
currency *74* Währung
current *14* aktuell
curriculum vitae (CV) *28* Lebenslauf
custom-built *36* eigens (an) gefertigt, maßgefertigt
customer *34* Kunde, Kundin
customer relations manager *37* Kundenbetreuer/in
customs duties pl *49* Zollgebühren

D

daily *6* täglich
damaged *82* beschädigt
data processing *8* Datenverarbeitung
data protection *110* Datenschutz
date, to ~ *79* bis heute, bisher
deadline *22* Frist
deadline, to **meet a ~** *38* eine Frist einhalten
to **deal with sth** *9T* mit etw umgehen; *16* sich mit etw beschäftigen, von etw handeln; *48* etw bearbeiten, erledigen
debts *pl* *93* Schulden
decision *102* Entscheidung
decision-maker *99* Entscheidungsträger/in
decrease *74* Abnahme
to **decrease** *74* abnehmen, sinken
definite *16* endgültig, definitiv; *22* bestimmt
definition *52* Definition
delay *39T* Verspätung, Verzögerung
delighted, to **be ~** *23* sich freuen, sehr erfreut sein
to **deliver** *34T* liefern; *71* vortragen, *(Rede usw.)* halten

to **explode** 60 explodieren
exporter 49 Exporteur
external 62 extern
to **extend** 45 ausweiten, erweitern; 50 sich erstrecken
extra charge 103 Aufpreis
extreme 85 extrem
extremely 33T äußerst
EXW = Ex Works 48 ab Werk

F

face to face 108 persönlich
facilities pl 99 Einrichtungen
factory floor 36 Produktion(sabteilung)
factual 110 sachlich (korrekt)
fair 16 Messe
to **fall asleep** 77 einschlafen
familiar 44 vertraut
fan 55 Ventilator
fashion, in a certain ~ 72T auf eine bestimmte Art und Weise
faulty 85 defekt, schadhaft
favourably 113 positiv, günstig
to **fax** 46 faxen
feature 110 Merkmal
to **feature** 99 vorkommen, eine Rolle spielen
featuring 98 mit
federation 106 Vereinigung, Verband
fee 102T Gebühr
field hospital 106 Feldlazarett
figure 9T Zahl
to **fill an order** 82 einen Auftrag erledigen
filtering system 106 Filtersystem
final demand 89 letzte Mahnung
to **finalize** 22 (endgültig) festlegen, abschließen
Finance (Department) 37 Rechnungswesen
financial services pl 35 Finanzdienstleistungen
financial standing 96 Bonität, Kreditwürdigkeit
financial year 74T Geschäftsjahr
to **fire sth off** 25 etw loslassen
first name 11 Vorname
to **fit** 59 passen
fixtures and fittings pl 99 Ausstattung und Installationen
to **flatten out** 74 (sich) abflachen
floor covering 100 Bodenbelag
flow chart 34 Flussdiagramm
to **fluctuate** 74 schwanken
fluctuation 74 Schwankung, Schwanken
fluent 111 *(Sprachkenntnisse:)* fließend
flyer 17 Flugblatt, Reklamezettel
FOB = Free On Board 57 frei an Bord
to **focus on sth** 50 sich auf etw konzentrieren
focused 110 konzentriert, zielgerichtet
follow, as ~s 72T wie folgt, folgendermaßen
for a start 33T zunächst, zuallererst
for your convenience 90 *etwa:* als Serviceleistung *(wird nicht übersetzt!)*
foreign trade 109P Außenhandel
formal 6 formell, förmlich
to **forward sth** 21 etw weiterleiten
to **found** 81 gründen
founder 97 Gründer/in
framework 31 Gerüst
frequent 109P häufig
to **fulfil** 80 erfüllen, abwickeln
full, in ~ 93 in voller Höhe
full stop 30 Punkt *(Satzzeichen)*
fully booked 105T ausgebucht
fun, to **be ~** 8 Spaß machen
to **function** 60 funktionieren
furniture 44 Möbel
further 32 weitere/r/s

G

to **gain** 75 gewinnen, bekommen
galvanized 106 verzinkt
GCSE 109P *Abschlussprüfung für die Sekundarstufe I in Großbritannien*
to **generate** 43 erwirtschaften, generieren
to **get at sth** 72T auf etw hinaus wollen
to **get back to sb** 21 sich (wieder) bei jdm melden
to **get off** (a bus, a car etc.) 42 *(aus einem Bus, Auto, usw.)* aussteigen
to **get rid of sth** 106 etw loswerden
to **get sth across** 18 etw vermitteln, übermitteln
to **get to know sb** 14 jdn kennen lernen
gift 100 Geschenk
to **give directions** 35 den Weg erklären
glance, at a ~ 74T auf einen Blick
to **go on** 39T passieren, geschehen, vor sich gehen
to **go public** 36 an die Börse gehen
goal 115P Ziel
goods pl 34 Ware(n), Güter
government 99 Regierung
to **grab sb's attention** 71 jds Aufmerksamkeit fesseln
to **graduate** 36 (s)einen Abschluss machen
to **grant sth** 94 etw einräumen, zugestehen, gewähren
graph 69 Diagramm, Grafik
graphics pl 70 Grafik(en)
grateful 45 dankbar
greeting 33T *(Brief:)* Anrede
ground floor 40 Erdgeschoss
growth 73 Wachstum, Zunahme
guarantee 50 Garantie
to **guarantee** 50 garantieren
guidance 70 Führung
to **guide** 70 führen
guided 51 *hier:* nach Vorlage

H

habit, to **get into the ~ of sth** 115T sich etw zur Gewohnheit machen
half-way 42 auf halbem Wege
hand, left-/right-~ side 40T linke/rechte Seite
to **handle sth** 55 mit etw umgehen, etw handhaben
handling 79 Umgang, Behandlung
handout 69 Handreichung; ausgeteilte Unterlage
handshake 115T Händedruck
handy 39T praktisch
happy, to **be ~** 14 sich freuen
hard-working 108 fleißig
head 37 Leiter/in, Chef/in
head office 63 Zentrale
heading 26 Überschrift
heading towards 42 in Richtung
health insurance 111 Krankenversicherung
healthy 60 gesund
hidden 92 verborgen
to **highlight** 8 hervorheben, markieren
highlighter 26 Textmarker
high-powered 43 Spitzen-, führende/r/s
to **hire sb** 114 jdn einstellen
to **hit sth** 74 etw erreichen
to **hold the line** 11 *(Telefon:)* am Apparat bleiben
hollow 106 hohl
honest 110 ehrlich
hourly, on an ~ basis 36 auf Stundenbasis
household 45 Haushalt, Haushalts-
huge 40T groß
Human Resources (HR) 37 Personal(abteilung)
humanitarian 106 humanitär
hyphen 15 Bindestrich

I

ice, to **break the ~** 14 das Eis brechen

to **identify** *33* erkennen, benennen
to **identify oneself** *11* sich zu erkennen geben
i.e. *58* d.h.
to **ignore** *90* nicht beachten
to **illustrate** *70* illustrieren, veranschaulichen
immediate *50* sofortig
immediately *48* unmittelbar, sofort
impact *33T* Auswirkung(en), Folge(n)
importance *107* Bedeutung, Wichtigkeit
importer *45* Importeur
impression *77* Eindruck
to **improve** *14* verbessern
inbox *18* Posteingang
incinerator *60* Verbrennungsanlage, -ofen
to **include** *15* einbeziehen, einschließen
including einschließlich
inclusive *19* einschließlich
income *74* Einkommen
inconvenience *85* Unannehmlichkeiten
incorporated *35* (als Gesellschaft) eingetragen
incorrect *8* falsch, unzutreffend
increase *74* Steigerung, Zunahme
to **increase** *46* erhöhen; *74* steigen, zunehmen
indirect *66* indirekt
individually *48* einzeln
indoor swimming pool *104* Hallenbad
industrial estate *36* Industriegebiet
industry *7* Gewerbe, Branche, Industrie
inexpensive *59* preiswert, preisgünstig
to **influence** *77* beeinflussen
ingredient *61* Bestandteil; Zutat
inhabitant *32* Einwohner/in, Bewohner/in
initial *108* anfängliche/r/s
initial contact *34* Erstkontakt
initials pl *25* Initialen
insight *117* Einblick
to **insist on sth** *92* auf etw bestehen
instalment *93* Rate
insurance *49* Versicherung
integrated *54* integriert
to **interact** *106* miteinander umgehen
intercultural *65* interkulturell
internal *62* intern
interpreter *29* Übersetzer/in
to **interrupt** *53T* (jdn) unterbrechen
interview *107* Vorstellungsgespräch
to **interview sb** *109* mit jdm ein Vorstellungsgespräch führen
intonation *72T* Sprachmelodie
introduction *31* Einleitung
invaluable *117* unschätzbar
invention *106* Erfindung
to **invest** *43* investieren
to **investigate** *82* untersuchen
invitation *16* Einladung
to **invite** *16* einladen
invoice *34* Rechnung
involved, to **feel ~** *43* sich einbezogen/beteiligt fühlen
involved, to **get sb ~** *71* jdn einbeziehen
issue *52* Frage, Problem, (Streit-)Punkt
item *26* Artikel, Gegenstand; *62* (Tagesordnungs-)Punkt

J

job centre *7* Arbeitsamt
job title *37* Berufsbezeichnung
to **judge** *97* beurteilen
judgement *14* Urteil, Bewertung
jumbled *28* durcheinander geworfen

K

keen, to **be ~ to do sth** *28* etw unbedingt/sehr gern tun mögen
to **keep in mind** *31* an etw denken
to **keep records** *8* Unterlagen/Akten führen
key issues pl *75* Hauptpunkte, wichtigste Fragen
know, to **get to ~ sb** *14* jdn kennen lernen

L

label *26* Etikett
to **label** *112* beschriften, etikettieren
lack *72T* Mangel
last, at ~ *20* endlich
latest *34T* neueste/r/s
latest, at the ~ *21* spätestens
to **launch sth** *43* etw starten, etw einführen, etw auf den Markt bringen
law *33T* Gesetz
to **lay sb off** *43* jdn entlassen
layout *35* Anordnung, Lage
leading *45* führend
leaflet *47* Informationsblatt, Faltblatt
leaking *82* undicht
leather *59* Leder
left-/right-hand side *40T* linke/rechte Seite
legal *33T* rechtlich, gesetzlich, Rechts-
Legal Department *37* Rechtswesen
legal entity *35* juristische Person, Rechtsträger
legally binding *33T* rechtsverbindlich
length *54* Länge
less *92* abzüglich
letter of apology *81* Entschuldigungsschreiben
level *112* Ebene
to **level off** *74* sich einpendeln
liability *96* Haftung
light industry *35* Leichtindustrie
lighting *100* Beleuchtung, Licht
likely, to **be ~ to do sth** *14* etw wahrscheinlich tun werden
line chart *73* Liniendiagramm
line of products *45* Produktlinie, -angebot
listener *71* Zuhörer/in
loads of *21* viel(e)
located, to **be ~ in ...** *108* in ... sein/liegen
location *18* Veranstaltungsort
lock *59* Schloss
logical *31* logisch
logistics pl *35* Logistik
to **look into sth** *78* einer Sache nachgehen
Ltd = Limited Company *35* GmbH = Gesellschaft mit beschränkter Haftung
lunch break *76* Mittagspause
luncheon voucher *108* Essensgutschein

M

machine *55* Gerät, Maschine
mainly *109P* hauptsächlich
major *93* Groß-, Haupt-, bedeutend
to **make sense** *65* sinnvoll sein
to **make sure** *8* sicherstellen, sich vergewissern
to **make up** *60* ausmachen
to **make up one's mind** *7* sich entscheiden
to **man** *100* besetzen, betreuen
managing director *37* Geschäftsführer/in
mandatory law *52* zwingende gesetzliche Bestimmungen
manner *108* Art, Weise
to **manufacture** *36* herstellen, fertigen
manufacturing *7* Herstellung, Produktion
marker pen *69* Marker

Market Research *37* Marktforschung(sabteilung)
material *60* Stoff, Material
meaning *30* Bedeutung
meaningful *114* wichtig, bedeutsam
meantime, in the ~ *90* in der Zwischenzeit
to **measure** *101* messen
medical equipment *79* medizinische Geräte
to **meet a deadline** *38* eine Frist einhalten
to **meet a requirement** *45* eine Anforderung erfüllen
to **meet one's obligations** *97* seine Verpflichtungen erfüllen
to **meet sb's approval** *50* jds Zustimmung finden
to **meet sb's needs** *106* jds Bedürfnis erfüllen
meet, Pleased/Nice to ~ you. *39T* Schön, Sie/dich/euch kennen zu lernen.
member *43* Mitglied
member of staff *7* Mitarbeiter/in
memo *29* Mitteilung, Vermerk, Notiz
memorable *70* einprägsam
to **mention** *62* erwähnen, nennen
method *51* Verfahren, Weise
method of payment *52* Zahlungsweise
microphone *69* Mikrofon
middle, in the ~ of *41* mitten in/auf, in der Mitte von
middle-sized company *47* mittelständisches Unternehmen
military *106* Militär
mind, to **keep in ~** *31* an etw denken
mind, to **make up one's ~** *7* sich entscheiden
minutes pl *61* Protokoll
to **mislay** *90* verlegen
mix-up *85* Missverständnis, Verwechslung
monolingual *30* einsprachig
monotonous *8* eintönig, monoton, langweilig
monthly *63* monatlich
mother-tongue *112* Muttersprache
to **move on** *17* weitergehen, weiterziehen
moveable *53T* beweglich
multi-cellular *106* in Zellbauweise
multi-coloured *54* vielfarbig, bunt

N

native speaker *39* Muttersprachler/in
natural disaster *106* Naturkatastrophe
to **near** *75* sich nähern
nearby *83* in der Nähe
necessary *31* nötig, notwendig, erforderlich
need, to **meet sb's ~s** *106* jds Bedürfnis erfüllen
negotiation *21* Verhandlung
neither (of both) *21* keine/r/s (von beiden)
nervous *77* nervös
nervousness *77* Nervosität
net *50* netto
next door to *39T* neben
noisy *37* laut
non-payment *90* Nicht(be)zahlung
non-profit *60* gemeinnützig
non-skilled *106* ungelernt
non-smoking *104* Nichtraucher-
not yet *38* noch nicht
to **note** *27* zur Kenntnis nehmen
notepad *26* Notizblock
notice *20* Hinweis

O

oak *59* Eiche
object *64* Zweck, Gegenstand
obligation *52* Verpflichtung
obligation, to **meet one's ~s** *97* seine Verpflichtungen erfüllen
to **obtain** *47* erhalten
to **occur** *34* auftreten, passieren; *115T* vorkommen
offer, on ~ *34T* im Angebot
office administration *9T* Bürotätigkeiten
office communication *9T* Bürotätigkeit
office management assistant *6* Bürokaufmann/-frau
office supplies pl *8* Büromaterial
offshore *98* vor der Küste, Hochsee-
once again *83* noch einmal
one by one *31* eins nach dem anderen
one-way flight *102* einfacher Flug
open account *56* Forderung
opener *71* Eröffnung(ssatz)
open-plan office *9T* Großraumbüro
to **operate** *35* (geschäftlich) tätig sein; *106* fungieren, dienen
operating company *99* Betreiberfirma, Trägergesellschaft
opinion *77* Meinung, Ansicht
opinion poll *107* Meinungsumfrage
opportunity *29* Gelegenheit, Chance
oral *111* mündlich
order *28* Reihenfolge; *32* Auftrag, Bestellung
order form *53* Bestellformular
order number *50* Bestellnummer
order, repeat ~ *56* Folgeauftrag
order, to **fill an ~** *82* einen Auftrag erledigen
order, to **place an ~** *45* einen Auftrag erteilen
order, trial ~ *48* Probeauftrag
organization chart *37* Organigramm
otherwise *91* sonst, ansonsten
outlet *48* Verkaufsstelle, Geschäft
outline *68* Übersicht
outstanding *91* ausstehend
over there *39T* dort (drüben)
overdue *34* fällig, überfällig; *83* ausstehend
to **overlook** *95* übersehen
overtime, to **work ~** *32* Überstunden machen
oversight *93* Versehen
ownership *52* Eigentum(srecht)

P

pack *53T* Packung
to **pack** *48* verpacken
packaging *49* Verpackung
paper clip *26* Büroklammer
paper mill *12* Papiermühle, Papierfabrik
paperwork *8* Unterlagen, Schriftstücke
paragraph *7* *(Text:)* Absatz
participant *16* Teilnehmer/in
to **participate** *16* teilnehmen
participation *27* Teilnahme
particularly *29* besonders
party *52* (Vertrags-)Partei
to **pass sth** *40T* an etw vorbeigehen, etw passieren
to **pass sth on** *29* etw weiterleiten
to **pass sth out** *71* etw verteilen
passenger *102T* Passagier
past sth *39T* an etw vorbei
patronising *71* herablassend, oberlehrerhaft
to **pause** *77* innehalten
payable *95* zahlbar
payment *34* Zahlung
payment, advice of ~ *90* Zahlungsanzeige
payment, documents against ~ *56* Dokumente gegen Zahlung
payment, to **collect ~** *97* (einen Kunden) zur Zahlung veranlassen, Inkasso vornehmen
peak *74* Spitzenwert
to **peak** *74* einen Spitzenwert erreichen

Alphabetical word list

pedestrian crossing *40T* Zebrastreifen
pension cover *117* Altersvorsorge
per annum *108* im Jahr
percentage *107P* Anteil, Prozentsatz
permanent *108* dauerhaft, *hier:* unbefristet
permission *110* Erlaubnis
permit, work ~ *117* Arbeitserlaubnis
person, in ~ *20* persönlich
to **persuade** *65T* überzeugen
pharmaceutical *16* Pharma-, Arzneimittel-
photocopier *9* Fotokopierer
to **pick sb up** *16* jdn abholen
pie chart *73* Tortendiagramm
pin *54* Nadel
pine *57* Kiefer, Kiefernholz
pity, That's a ~. *39T* Das ist schade.
place, to **take ~** *16* stattfinden
to **place** *46* platzieren
to **place an order** *45* einen Auftrag erteilen
placement, work ~ *9T* Praktikum
plaster *103* Gips
plc = Public Limited Company *35* AG = Aktiengesellschaft
pleased, to **be ~** *20* sich freuen
pleasure *50* Vergnügen
plenty of *16* viele
plunge *74* Absturz, Sturz
to **plunge** *74* abstürzen
point, there's no ~ in doing sth *64* es hat keinen Sinn, etw zu tun
point of sale *52* Verkaufsort, -stelle
to **point out** *82* darauf hinweisen
pointer *54* Zeiger
polite *19* höflich
political *14* politisch
poll, opinion ~ *107* Meinungsumfrage
to **pop up** *25* auftauchen, erscheinen
possibility *37* Möglichkeit
post *113* Stelle, Posten
postage *33T* Porto
postcode *53T* Postleitzahl
to **postpone** *21* verschieben
postponement *16* Verschiebung, (Termin-)Verlegung
posture *72T* Körperhaltung
potential *44* potentiell
power, green ~ *99* Ökostrom
power utilities *pl* *99* Stromversorger
practice *79* (Arzt-)Praxis
precedence, to **take ~ over sth** *52* vor etw Vorrang haben
precision *73* (Detail-)Genauigkeit
prefabricated *106* vorgefertigt
preference *63* Vorliebe
premises pl *23* Räumlichkeiten, (Betriebs-)Gelände
preparation *11* Vorbereitung
to **prepare** *31* (sich) vorbereiten, erstellen
prepared, to **be ~ to do sth** *45* bereit sein, etw zu tun
pre-printed *86* vorgedruckt
present *112* aktuell, gegenwärtig
to **present sth** *57* etw vorlegen
presentation *16* Präsentation
press release *99* Pressemitteilung
pressure *108* Druck
previous *62* vorherige/r/s
to **print** *33T* drucken
priority, to **be a ~** *106* (hohe) Priorität haben
prize *36* Preis, Auszeichnung
proactive, to **be ~** *88* eigenständig agieren, die Initiative ergreifen
proceedings, to **start legal ~** *93* gerichtlich gegen jdn vorgehen, Klage erheben
process *110* Verfahren
to **process sth** *36* etw bearbeiten, verarbeiten
product liability *52* Produkthaftung
production *37* Produktion, Herstellung, Fertigung
profile *99* Profil, Porträt
to **progress** *115P* vorankommen
progress report *63* Zwischenbericht
to **promise** *19* versprechen
promotion *99* Werbung; *109P* Beförderung
prompt *20* prompt, unverzüglich
to **proof-read** *31* Korrektur lesen
property *49* Eigentum
to **propose** *94* vorschlagen
prospective *107* potentiell
prospects pl *115T* Aussichten
public, the ~ *35* die Öffentlichkeit
public, to **go ~** *36* an die Börse gehen
publication *99* Veröffentlichung
publicity *99* Werbung, Publicity
publish *52* veröffentlichen
pull-out *59* ausziehbar
punctual(ly) *97* pünktlich
Purchasing (Department) *37* Einkauf(sabteilung)
purpose *86* Zweck
to **put sb through** *11* jdn durchstellen, verbinden

Q

qualification *7* Abschluss, Qualifikation
to **qualify** *108* seinen/ihren Abschluss machen
quantity *46* Menge
quarter *22* Quartal
quarterly *65* vierteljährlich
question, in ~ *117* fraglich, betreffend
quotation *47* Kostenvoranschlag, Angebot
to **quote** *48* *(Preis)* angeben, nennen

R

rail, by ~ *83* mit der Bahn, auf der Schiene
railway crossing *40T* Bahnübergang
railway track *40T* Bahngleis
range *45* Angebot(spalette), Auswahl
rapid(ly) *74T* schnell
rapport *77* gutes Verhältnis, Kontakt
rate *104* Preis, Satz
raw material *37* Rohstoff, Rohmaterial
reach, within easy ~ *104* gut erreichbar
to **read out** *69* vorlesen
ready, to **have sth ~** *14* etw bereithalten
to **realize** *36* erkennen, klar werden, verstehen
receipt *50* Erhalt, (Waren-) Eingang
to **receive** *12* erhalten, empfangen, bekommen
reception *20* Rezeption, Empfang
reception area *100* Empfangsbereich
receptionist *37* Empfangsmitarbeiter/in
to **recognize** *29* anerkennen
to **recommend** *97* empfehlen
recommendation *28* Empfehlung
to **recondition** *79* generalüberholen
record *68* Aufzeichnung, Protokoll; *93* Historie
record, to **keep ~s** *8* Unterlagen/ Akten führen
to **recover** *74* sich erholen
recovery *74* Erholung
to **recruit** *108* *(Personal)* werben, einstellen
recruiter *108* Personalvermittler/in
recruiting agency *108* Personalvermittlung, Personalagentur
rectangular *54* rechteckig

to **reduce** *46* reduzieren
to **refer to sth** *50* sich auf etw beziehen
referee *110* Referenz
reference *30* Referenz; *50* Erwähnung, Bezug
reference (ref) *27 (Brief:)* Zeichen
reference, with ~ to *48* bezüglich, mit Bezug auf
referred, to **be ~ to as sth** *92* als etw bezeichnet werden
regarding *79* bezüglich, betreffend
Regards *19* Mit freundlichen Grüßen, Viele Grüße
to **register** *35* eintragen, registrieren; *43* verbuchen; *98* (sich) anmelden
registered mail/post *89* Einschreiben
Registrar of Companies *35* Handelsregister für Kapitalgesellschaften
registration *99* Anmeldung, Registrierung
to **regret** *20* bedauern
to **relate to sth** *62* mit etw in Zusammenhang stehen, sich auf etw beziehen
relationship *19* Beziehung, Verhältnis
to **relax** *14* sich entspannen, sich erholen
to **release** *57* freigeben
reliability *50* Zuverlässigkeit
reliable *48* zuverlässig
relief *106* Hilfe
religious *14* religiös
to **rely on sth** *49* sich auf etw verlassen
to **remind sb of sth** *75* jdn an etw erinnern, jdn auf etw hinweisen
reminder *34* Mahnung
to **remit** *93* überweisen
remittance *93* Zahlung, Überweisung
to **rent** *36* mieten
repeat order *56* Folgeauftrag
to **replace** *8* ersetzen, austauschen
replacement *85* Ersatz
reply *16* Antwort
to **reply** *20* antworten
report *13T* Bericht
to **report** *15* berichten, Bericht erstatten; *78* melden
to **report to sb** *37* jdm unterstellt sein
to **represent** *52* darstellen
representative *99* Vertreter/in
reputation *96* Ruf
request *18* Bitte, Anfrage
request, on ~ *110* auf Wunsch
to **request sth** *34* etw erbitten, etw anfordern
to **require** *27* wünschen, benötigen; *37* erfordern
requirement *45* Anforderung
requirement, to **meet a ~** *45* eine Anforderung erfüllen
research *16* Forschung
Research and Development (Department, R&D) *37* Forschung(s-) und Entwicklung(sabteilung)
research, to **do ~** *14* recherchieren, Nachforschungen anstellen
reservation *103* Reservierung, Buchung
resident *117* Bewohner/in, Einwohner/in
respectful *66* respektvoll
responsibility *108* Verantwortlichkeit, Aufgabe(nbereich)
responsible *27* verantwortlich, zuständig
restroom AE *39* Toilette
result *16* Ergebnis
résumé AE *107P* Lebenslauf
retailer *43* Einzelhändler/in
to **retire** *97* sich zur Ruhe setzen
return, by ~ of post *58* per Antwortschreiben, postwendend
return flight *102* Hin- und Rückflug
return, in ~ *97* als Gegenleistung
revenue *37* Einnahmen, Einkünfte
reverse *110* umgekehrt
review *43* Rezension, Besprechung; *68* Überblick
to **rewrite** *20* neu schreiben, umformulieren
ribbon *60* Band
rid, to **get ~ of sth** *106* etw loswerden
rise *74* Anstieg, Zunahme
to **rise** *74* steigen, ansteigen
risk, to **take a ~** *36* etwas riskieren, ein Risiko eingehen
rival *43* Rivale/Rivalin, Konkurrent/in
rock *106* Stein
roughly, to **handle sth ~** *82* etw grob behandeln
roundabout *40T* Kreisverkehr
routine *6* (Arbeits-)Ablauf
rubble *106* Schutt
rule *49* Regel, Vorschrift

S

salary *108* Gehalt
sale, contract of ~ *52* Kaufvertrag
sale, point of ~ *52* Verkaufsort, -stelle
sales *pl 43* Verkäufe, Umsatz
Sales (Department) *37* Verkauf(sabteilung), Vertrieb
sales representative *37* Handelsvertreter/in
sales, volume of ~ *74T* Umsatzvolumen
salutation *18 (Brief:)* Anrede
sample *46* Muster
satisfaction *58* Zufriedenheit
satisfactory *46* zufriedenstellend
satisfied *86* zufrieden
to **save sb/sth** *43* jdn/etw retten
scale *74* Skala
scheme *60* Programm, Plan
school leaving certificate *109P* Schulabgangszeugnis, Schulabschluss
scratched *85T* verkratzt
screen, on-~ *18* am Bildschirm
seat *102* Sitz, Sitzplatz
seating area *100* bestuhlter Bereich
seating position *68* Sitzplatz, -position
section *39T* Abteilung, Abschnitt
sector *35* Sektor, Bereich
to **secure sth** *117* sich etw sichern
security *33T* Sicherheit
security office *40T* Büro des Wachdienstes
to **see sb** *40* sich mit jdm treffen
to **seek** *111* suchen
selection *50* Auswahl
seller *34* Verkäufer/in
to **send one's apologies** *65T* sich entschuldigen lassen
sender *25* Absender
sense, to **make ~** *65* sinnvoll sein
sensitive *33T* heikel
to **separate** *18* trennen
separately *10* einzeln
service industry *35* Dienstleistungsgewerbe
session *70* Sitzung
set *52* Menge; *110* fest(gesetzt), vorgeschrieben
to **set sth up** *8* etw einrichten, aufbauen; *20* etw arrangieren; *36* etw gründen
to **settle** *46* begleichen, bezahlen; *82* klären, regeln
to **settle (a bill)** *89* (eine Rechnung) begleichen, bezahlen
to **settle an account** *90* ein Konto ausgleichen, eine Rechnung bezahlen
to **settle down** *66* zur Ruhe kommen
sexual orientation *14* sexuelle Orientierung
to **shake** *72T* zittern

to **shake hands with sb** *115T* jdm die Hand geben
shape *59* Form
to **share** *61* teilen, mitteilen
share *35* Aktie
shareholder *35* Teilhaber/in, Aktionär/in
sheet (of paper) *40* Blatt (Papier)
shelter *106* Unterkunft
to **ship** *57* versenden
shipping documents pl *57* Versandpapiere
to **shoot down** *74* abstürzen
to **shoot up** *74* in die Höhe schießen
to **shorten** *30* kürzen
short-listed, to **be ~** *110* in die engere Auswahl kommen
to **show sb around** *39T* jdn herumführen
showcase *99* Schaufenster
shy *115T* schüchtern
to **sign** *46* unterschreiben, unterzeichnen
to **sign off** *18* einen Brief beenden
signal *70* Zeichen
to **signal** *29* signalisieren
signature *27* Unterschrift
similar *96* ähnlich
simplicity *70* Einfachheit
sincere *85* aufrichtig
to **sink into the ground** *60* in den Boden sickern
sizeable *47* beträchtlich, (ziemlich) groß
slide *69* Dia
slightly *77* etwas, ein wenig
slip *96* Zettel
to **slow down** *14* langsamer werden
small-sized company *47* Kleinunternehmen
smart *115T* *(Kleidung:)* schick, elegant
to **socialize with sb** *110* sich mit jdm treffen, mit jdm ausgehen
socket *100* Steckdose
solid *59* massiv; *60* fest
solution (to sth) *82* Lösung (für etw)
to **solve** *82* lösen
to **sort** *31* sortieren, einsortieren
to **sort sth out** *84* etw in Ordnung bringen
source *47* Quelle
special offer *50* Sonderangebot
to **specialize in sth** *36* sich auf etw spezialisieren
specific *14* speziell, bestimmt, Fach-; *50* konkret
specifically *11* ausdrücklich, eigens
speed *25* Geschwindigkeit
to **speed up** *77* schneller werden
to **spread** *60* sich verbreiten
spreadsheet *8* Tabellenkalkulation(sdatei/-sprogramm)
square *54* quadratisch
square metre *102* Quadratmeter
stable *54* stabil
staff *7* Personal
staff, member of ~ *7* Mitarbeiter/in
stage *72* Phase, Etappe; *89* Stufe
stainless steel *53T* rostfreier Stahl
stairs *pl* *39T* Treppe
stamped addressed envelope *30* Freiumschlag
standard *33T* Anforderung, Norm
staple *26* Heftklammer
stapler *26* Klammerhefter
start, for a ~ *33T* zunächst, zuallererst
to **start legal proceedings** *93* gerichtlich gegen jdn vorgehen, Klage erheben
state *83* Status
statement *93* Beleg, (Konto-)Auszug
stationery *8* Schreibwaren, Briefpapier
to **stay away from sth** *14* sich von etw fernhalten, etw meiden
steadily *36* kontinuierlich, stetig
steel *59* Stahl
step *34* Schritt
to **stick to sth** *31* bei etw bleiben
stiff *72T* starr, steif
stock *46* Ware(n), (Lager-) Bestand
stock, in ~ *48* am/auf Lager, vorrätig, lieferbar
stop-over *16* Zwischenlandung, -aufenthalt
storage cabinet *59* Aktenschrank
store *34* Lager
to **store** *37* lagern
straight ahead *40T* geradeaus
straight away *83* sofort, unverzüglich
strange *55* seltsam
stranger *77* Fremde/r, Unbekannte/r
to **stress** *115P* betonen, hervorheben
stressed *9T* gestresst
strict *97* streng
strike *17* Streik
strong point *9T* Stärke
to **structure** *18* strukturieren
subject (line) *15* Betreff(zeile)
substitute *32* Ersatz
to **suggest** *19* vorschlagen
suggestion *21* Vorschlag
to **suit** *21* passen
suitable *16* passend, geeignet
sum *93* Betrag, Summe
to **summarize** *29* zusammenfassen
summary *80* Zusammenfassung
superb *108* ausgezeichnet
superior *85T* Vorgesetzte/r, Chef/in
superior-grade *33T* hochwertig
supplier *44* Lieferant
to **supply** *30* zur Verfügung stellen; *36* liefern
support *7* Unterstützung, Hilfe; *36* Kundendienst
to **support** *29* unterstützen, helfen; *70* untermauern
supposed, to **be ~ to do sth** *21* etw (eigentlich) tun sollen
sure, to **make ~** *8* sicherstellen, sich vergewissern
surprising *71* überraschend
survivor *106* Überlebende/r
to **swap** *40* tauschen
sympathetic *88* einfühlsam

T

t-junction *40T* Einmündung
taboo *14* Tabu
to **tackle** *106* *(Problem usw.)* angehen
to **take a deep breath** *72T* tief einatmen
to **take a risk** *36* etwas riskieren, ein Risiko eingehen
to **take action** *84* Maßnahmen ergreifen
to **take ages** *105T* ewig dauern
to **take care of sth** *37* sich um etw kümmern
to **take legal action** *92* rechtliche Schritte einleiten, gerichtlich gegen jdn vorgehen
to **take place** *16* stattfinden
to **take precedence over sth** *52* vor etw Vorrang haben
to **take the chair** *65* die Sitzung leiten
to **take time off** *32* sich frei nehmen
to **take turns** *41* sich abwechseln
takeaway *70* etw zum Mitnehmen
to **talk down** *70* von oben herab reden
target group *100* Zielgruppe
to **target sb** *98* jdn als Zielgruppe haben
tax *102T* Steuer
technique *107P* Technik

temporary *93* vorübergehend; *109* befristet
to **tend** *33T* dazu neigen
tense *72T* angespannt
tent *106* Zelt
terms *pl* *45* Bedingungen, Konditionen
terms of delivery *pl 45* Lieferbedingungen
terms of payment *pl 45* Zahlungsbedingungen
thereafter *92* danach
therefore *93* daher
thought-provoking *71* zum Nachdenken anregend
throughout *110* durchgehend
to **tie** *106* binden
till *16* bis
time, in ~ *16* rechtzeitig
time off, to **take ~** *32* sich frei nehmen
time, on ~ *34T* pünktlich
time-line *43* Zeitleiste, Zeitstrahl
time-waster *25* Zeitfresser
times, three ~ *43* dreimal, drei Mal
tiring *100* ermüdend
tone *20* Ton
tone of voice *72* Tonfall
tool *26* Werkzeug
top floor *40* oberstes Stockwerk
top, to **come out on ~** *33T* vorne liegen, Erste/r werden
to **total** *97* (insgesamt) betragen
touch, to **get in ~ with sb** *20* sich mit jdm in Verbindung setzen
to **touch on sth** *14* etw berühren
tour *64* Rundgang
towards *42* in Richtung, auf … zu
toxic *60* giftig, toxisch
trade *49* Handel; *97* Branche
trade fair *27* Handelsmesse
trade magazine *45* Branchenzeitschrift, Fachblatt
trade-in *60* Eintausch-, Austausch-
trader *52* Händler/in
traffic lights *pl* *40T* Ampel
to **train sb** *71* jdn schulen
training *7* Ausbildung
transfer *52* Übertragung
to **transfer** *46* *(Geld)* überweisen
transit, in ~ *82* während des Transports
to **translate** *14* übersetzen
traveller *102* Reisende/r
trial order *48* Probeauftrag
to **trust** *58* (darauf) vertrauen
turn, in ~ *77* der Reihe nach
turn, to **take ~s** *41* sich abwechseln
to **turn left/right** *40T* links/rechts abbiegen
turnover *36* Umsatz
two-way *106* gegenseitig, in beide Richtungen
typical *25* typisch

U
unavailable, to **be ~** *11* *(Telefon:)* nicht zu sprechen sein
underneath *68* unten, unterhalb
underscore *15* Unterstrich
understandable *70* verständlich
underway *81* unterwegs
unfamiliar (with sth) *14* nicht vertraut (mit etw)
unfortunately *85* leider
unique *106* einzigartig
unit *74* Einheit
unlined *54* unliniert
unpaid *28* unbezahlt
update *18* Informationen über neueste Entwicklungen
to **update** *52* aktualisieren, auf den neuesten Stand bringen
up-to-date *55* auf dem neuesten Stand der Technik
up to now *80* bis jetzt, bislang
up to standard, to **be ~** *82* der Norm/den Anforderungen genügen
upstairs *39T* oben
use, to **put sth to good ~** *71* etw sinnvoll einsetzen

V
vacancy *109P* freie/offene Stelle
vacant *105T* frei
valid *50* gültig
value *57* Wert
value for money *59* Preis-Leistungs-Verhältnis
value, to **add ~ to sth** *112* aufwerten, einen Mehrwert verleihen, *hier etwa:* gut ergänzen
variety *7* Abwechslung; *106* Vielfalt
various *60* verschiedene/r/s
to **vary** *72T* variieren
VAT = value added tax *58* MwSt = Mehrwertsteuer
versatile *106* vielseitig
victim *106* Opfer
view, in full ~ *100* gut sichtbar
visa *117* Visum
visual *71* visuell
visuals pl *69* visuelle Hilfsmittel
vital *71* unerlässlich
vocabulary *14* Wortschatz
vocational college *36* Berufsfachschule
vocational school *28* Berufsschule
voice *72* Stimme
volume *77* Lautstärke
volume of sales *74T* Umsatzvolumen
voluntary *52* freiwillig, willkürlich
vote *107P* Stimme
vote (on sth) *68* Abstimmung (über etw)

W
wall bracket *54* Wandhalter
walnut *59* Walnuss
warehouse *36* Lager(halle)
warranty period *50* Gewährleistungsdauer
waste *60* Müll
to **waste** *25* vergeuden, verschwenden
waste of time *14* Zeitverschwendung
to **wave sth about** *77* mit etw herumfuchteln
weakness *115T* Schwäche
weight *54* Gewicht
white board *54* weiße Tafel, Weißwandtafel
wholesale trader *99* Großhändler
wholesaler *47* Großhändler
width *54* Breite
willing *97* bereit, willens
wind power *98* Windkraft, Windenergie
wire *106* Draht
to **withhold** *94* vorenthalten
to **wonder** *72T* sich fragen
wooden *44* Holz-, aus Holz
word processing *9T* Textverarbeitung
to **work hard** *8* fleißig sein, viel arbeiten
to **work overtime** *32* Überstunden machen
work permit *117* Arbeitserlaubnis
work placement *9T* Praktikum
working breakfast *16* Arbeitsfrühstück
workplace *7* Arbeitsplatz
worth *36* wert
to **write up** *68* ausarbeiten, erstellen

X
x-ray *79* Röntgenstrahlen, Röntgen-

Y/Z
yet *38* schon
yet, not ~ *38* noch nicht
Yours faithfully *28* Mit freundlichen Grüßen; Hochachtungsvoll
Yours sincerely *19* Mit freundlichen Grüßen

Basic office vocabulary (German–English)

Firmenorganisation – *Company organization*	
Aktiengesellschaft (AG)	Public Limited Company (plc) *BE;* open corporation *AE*
Aktie	share
Aktionär/in, Teilhaber/in	shareholder
Einzelunternehmen	sole proprietor
Gesellschaft mit beschränkter Haftung (GmbH)	Limited Company (Ltd) *BE;* closed corporation *AE*
Kommanditgesellschaft (KG)	limited partnership
Personengesellschaft, offene Handelsgesellschaft (OHG)	(general) partnership

Firmenabteilungen – *Company departments*	
Buchhaltung	accounts (department)
Einkauf(sabteilung)	purchasing (department)
Forschung(s-) und Entwicklung (sabteilung)	research and development (department, R&D)
Geschäftsführung, Vorstand	board (of directors)
Lager(halle)	warehouse
Marktforschung (sabteilung)	market research (department)
Personal(abteilung)	human resources (department, HR)
Rechnungswesen	finance (department)
Rechtswesen	legal department
Rezeption, Empfang	reception
Verkauf(sabteilung), Vertrieb	sales (department)
Vertrieb	distribution (department)
Verwaltung	administration
Zentrale	head office, headquarters

Mitarbeiter/innen – *Members of staff*	
Abteilungsleiter/in	head of department
Arbeitgeber/in, Unternehmer/in	employer
Arbeitnehmer/in, Beschäftigte/r	employee
Arbeitsplatz	workplace
Ausbildung	training
Beförderung	promotion
Buchhalter/in	accountant
Bürokaufmann/-frau	office management assistant
Empfangsmitarbeiter/in	receptionist
Gehalt	salary
Geschäftsführer/in	managing director (MD), chief executive officer (CEO)
Handelsvertreter/in	sales representative
Kollege, Kollegin	colleague
Lehre	apprenticeship
Manager/in	manager
Personal	staff
Persönliche/r Assistent/in	personal assistant (PA)
Qualifikation, Abschluss	qualification
Sekretär/in	secretary

Büromaterial – *Office supplies and equipment*	
Akte(nordner)	file
Aktenschrank	storage/filing cabinet
Beamer	projector
Bildschirm	screen
Briefumschlag	envelope
Büroklammer	paper clip
Drucker	printer
Etikette	label
Flipchart	flip chart
Fotokopierer	photocopier
Klammerhefter	stapler
Locher	hole punch
Marker	highlighter
Notizblock	notepad
Rechner	computer, PC
Schreibwaren, Briefpapier	stationery
Stift	pen

Bürotätigkeiten – *office activities*	
die **Ablage machen**	to organize files, to do the filing
etw **ausrichten**	to take a message
Berichte schreiben	to write reports
Briefe beantworten	to reply to letters
etw **faxen**	to fax sth
Mitteilungen, Vermerke, Notizen schreiben	to write memos
Post verteilen	to handle the mail
Postausgang	outgoing mail; out-tray
Posteingang	incoming mail, inbox, in-tray
ein **Telefongespräch annehmen**	to answer the telephone
Textverarbeitung	word processing
Überstunden machen	to work overtime
Unterlagen, Schriftstücke	paperwork
etw **weiterleiten**	to forward sth

Geschäftsbriefe – *Commercial correspondence*	
Absatz	paragraph
Absender	sender
Adresse	address
anhängen *(E-Mail)*	to attach sth
Anhang	attachment
Anlage	enclosure (enc)

Anrede	salutation
Antwort	reply
beifügen *(Brief)*	to enclose
Betreff(zeile)	subject (line)
Briefkopf	letter head
Datum	date
Einschreiben	registered mail/post
Empfänger/in	addressee
Entschuldigungsschreiben	letter of apology
Freiumschlag	stamped addressed envelope
Mit den besten Wünschen	Best wishes
Mit freundlichen Grüßen (Hochachtungsvoll)	Yours faithfully
Mit freundlichen Grüßen	Yours sincerely
Mit freundlichen Grüßen, Viele Grüße	Best wishes, Regards
Mit herzlichen Grüßen	Best wishes, Cordially *AE*
Porto	postage
Postleitzahl	postcode
Schlussformel	complimentary close
Unterschrift	signature
vertraulich	confidential
Zeichen	reference (ref)
zu Händen	attention (attn)

Besprechungen/Präsentationen – *Meetings/presentations*

Abwesenheit	absence
Bericht	report
Einladung	invitation
Liniendiagramm	line chart
Protokoll	minutes *pl*
eine **Rede halten**	to make a speech
Säulendiagramm	bar chart
die **Sitzung leiten**	to take the chair / to be in the chair
stattfinden	take place
Tagesordnung	agenda
Tagesordnungspunkt	item on the agenda
teilnehmen	to participate
Teilnehmer/in	participant
Termin	date
Tortendiagramm	pie chart
Verschiedenes	any other business (AOB)
Vortrag	talk; lecture
vortragen	to report; to state

Dienstreisen – *Business trips*

absagen	to cancel
Anforderung	requirement
Anschlussflug	connecting flight
Ausstellung	exhibition
etw **besuchen,** an etw **teilnehmen**	to attend sth
Bitte, Anfrage	request
einfacher Flug	one-way flight
Hin- und Rückflug	return flight
Messe	(trade) fair
Passagier	passenger
Reservierung, Buchung	reservation
stornieren	to cancel
Termin	appointment
Unterkunft	accommodation
verschieben	to postpone

Geschäftspartner und Händler – *Business partners and traders*

Einzelhändler/in	retailer
Exporteur	exporter
Großhändler	wholesaler
Importeur	importer
Käufer/in	buyer
Klient/in	client
Konkurrent/in, Konkurrenz	competitor
Konkurrenz	competition
Kunde, Kundin	customer, client
Lieferant	supplier
Spediteur	carrier; forwarding agent; freight forwarder
Verkäufer/in	seller

Geschäftsvorgänge – *Business transactions*

Anfrage	enquiry
Angebot, Kostenvoranschlag	quotation
Auftrag, Bestellung	order
einen **Auftrag erteilen**	to place an order
einen **Auftrag erledigen**	to fill an order
Auftragsbestätigung	acknowledgement/confirmation (of an order)
einen **Auftrag bestätigen**	to acknowledge an order
Bestellformular	order form
Bestellnummer	order number
Erhalt, (Waren-)Eingang	receipt (of goods)
Folgeauftrag	repeat order
Lieferbedingungen	terms of delivery *pl*
liefern	to deliver
Lieferung	delivery
Muster	sample
Probeauftrag	trial order
Reklamation, Beschwerde	complaint
eine **Reklamation bearbeiten/regulieren**	to adjust a complaint
Sendung	consignment

Basic office vocabulary (German–English)

Umsatz	turnover
Verkäufe, Umsatz	sales *pl*
Versandanzeige, Versandmitteilung	advice of dispatch
Versandpapiere	shipping documents *pl*
versenden	to ship
versenden, absenden	to dispatch
Vertrag	contract
Ware(n), (Lager-) Bestand	stock
Zahlungsanzeige	advice of payment
Zahlungsbedingungen	terms of payment *pl*

Zahlung – *Payment*	
Dokumente gegen Akzept	documents against acceptance
Dokumente gegen Zahlung	documents against payment
Dokumentenakkreditiv	documentary letter of credit
fällig, ausstehend	overdue
Konto, Kreditkonto	account
letzte Mahnung	final demand
Mahnung	reminder
MwSt = Mehrwertsteuer	VAT = value added tax
Nicht(be)zahlung	non-payment
Rabatt, Nachlass	discount
Rate	instalment
Rechnung	bill, invoice
Skonto, Barzahlungsrabatt	cash discount
überweisen	to remit, to transfer
Überweisung, Zahlung	bank transfer, remittance
Vorauszahlung, Vorkasse	cash in advance
Wechsel	bill of exchange
zahlbar bei Lieferung, per Nachnahme	cash on delivery (COD)

Verbs with *to* or *-ing*

Verb + *to*	
agree	zustimmen
arrange	vereinbaren
choose	(aus)wählen
decide	(sich) entscheiden
expect	erwarten
hope	hoffen
learn	lernen
manage	es schaffen, …
offer	anbieten
plan	planen
promise	versprechen
refuse	sich weigern; ablehnen
seem	scheinen
tend	dazu neigen
want	wollen

Verb + *to* or *-ing*	
begin	anfangen
continue	fortfahren
start	anfangen
hate	hassen
like	gern haben
love	lieben
prefer	vorziehen

Auf *would* + *hate/like/love/prefer* folgt immer *to*.

Verb + *-ing*	
avoid	vermeiden
delay	aufhalten, verzögern
dislike	ungern tun
enjoy	gern tun
finish	aufhören (mit)
give up	aufgeben
go on	weitermachen
keep (on)	weitermachen
miss	vermissen
not mind	nichts dagegen haben
postpone	verschieben
practise	üben
risk	riskieren
stop	aufhören, etw zu tun
suggest	vorschlagen

Phrases + *-ing*	
It's no use/good …-ing	Es hat keinen Sinn, …
It's (not) worth …-ing	Es lohnt sich (nicht), …
There's no point in …-ing	Es hat keinen Zweck, …

Common irregular verbs

be – was/were – been	sein
become – became – become	werden
begin – began – begun	anfangen, beginnen
break – broke – broken	brechen
bring – brought – brought	bringen
build – built – built	bauen
buy – bought – bought	kaufen
catch – caught – caught	fangen
choose – chose – chosen	wählen
come – came – come	kommen
cost – cost – cost	kosten
cut – cut – cut	schneiden
do – did – done	tun, machen
draw – drew – drawn	zeichnen
dream – dreamt – dreamt	träumen
drink – drank – drunk	trinken
drive – drove – driven	fahren
eat – ate – eaten	essen
fall – fell – fallen	fallen
feed – fed – fed	füttern, ernähren
feel – felt – felt	(sich) fühlen, empfinden
fight – fought – fought	kämpfen
find – found – found	finden
fit – fit/fitted – fit/fitted	passen
fly – flew – flown	fliegen
forget – forgot – forgotten	vergessen
get – got – got (*AE* gotten)	bekommen
give – gave – given	geben
go – went – gone	gehen, fahren
grow – grew – grown	wachsen
hang – hung – hung	hängen
have – had – had	haben
hear – heard – heard	hören
hide – hid – hidden	(sich) verstecken
hit – hit – hit	schlagen
hold – held – held	halten, festhalten
keep – kept – kept	behalten
know – knew – known	kennen, wissen
lay – laid – laid	legen
learn – learnt/learned – learnt/learned	lernen
leave – left – left	abfahren, verlassen, weggehen
let – let – let	lassen
lose – lost – lost	verlieren
make – make – make	machen
mean – meant – meant	meinen, bedeuten
meet – met – met	treffen
pay – paid – paid	bezahlen
put – put – put	setzen, stellen, legen
read – read – read	lesen
ride – rode – ridden	reiten, fahren
ring – rang – rung	klingeln; anrufen
rise – rose – risen	(an)steigen
run – ran – run	laufen, rennen
say – said – said	sagen
see – saw – seen	sehen
sell – sold – sold	verkaufen
send – sent – sent	senden, schicken
set – set – set	setzen, stellen
show – showed – shown	zeigen
shut – shut – shut	schließen
sing – sang – sung	singen
sit – sat – sat	sitzen
sleep – slept – slept	schlafen
smell – smelt/smelled – smelt/smelled	riechen
speak – spoke – spoken	sprechen
spell – spelt/spelled – spelt/spelled	buchstabieren
spend – spent – spent	ausgeben, verbringen
stand – stood – stood	stehen
steal – stole – stolen	stehlen
swim – swam – swum	schwimmen
take – took – taken	nehmen
teach – taught – taught	unterrichten, beibringen
tell – told – told	sagen, erzählen
think – thought – though	denken
throw – threw – thrown	werfen
understand – understood – understood	verstehen
wake – woke – worn	tragen (Kleidung)
wear – wore – worn	tragen
win – won – won	gewinnen
write – wrote – written	schreiben

Acknowledgements

Titelfoto: Getty Images RF, Simon Brown

Alamy: S. 44/1/Kevin Foy, S. 44/4/Ulrich Niehoff, S. 48/Ludger Paffrath
Fotofinder: S. 33/ALIMDI.NET/uwe umstaetter
Masterfile: S. 9/Masterfile, S. 10/Rolf Bruderer, S. 20/1/Orbit, S. 44/5 Masterfile
Picture Alliance: S. 43/Kay Nietfeld
Shutterstock: S. 6/1/Konstantin Chagin, S. 6/2/Yuri Arcurs, S. 6/3/Andresr, S. 6/4/StockLite, S. 7/Goodluz, S. 12/1/Andresr, S. 12/2/StockLite, S. 13/StockLite, S. 14/Goodluz, S. 15/walex101, S. 18/Dmitriy Shironosov, S. 20/2/StockLite, S. 21/Igor S. Srdanovic, S. 25/Robert Kneschke, S. S. 26/1/Planner, S. 26/2/Roman Sotola, S. 26/3/luchschen, 26/4/Alex Staroseltsev, S. 26/5/juat, S. 26/6/Freddy Eliasson, S. 26/7/Uros Kikovis, S. 26/8/kanate, S. 26/9/Lipik, S. 26/10/Kletr, S. 29/Oleg Golovnev, S. 31/Yellowj, S. 34/donvictorio@o2.pl, S. 36/vgstudio, S. 39/Stephen Coburn, S. 40/Rui Vale de Sousa, S. 44/3/Diego Cervo, S. 44/6/Dariusz Gudowicz, S. 45/Lichtmeister, S. 53/1/silver-john, S. 53/3/sixninepixels, S. 53/4/sofist, S. 53/5/Tomislav Pinter, S. 53/6/utflytter, S. 53/7/JM-Design, S. 53/8/u20, S. 55/1/cobalt88, S. 55/2/Dmitriy Shironosov, S. 56/RAGMA IMAGES, S. 60/S.Dashkevych, S. 61/1/Dmitriy Shironosov, S. 61/2/Monkey Business Images, S. 61/3/Morgan Lane Photography, S. 62/1/Viorel Sima, S. 62/2/EDHAR, S. 65/Franz Pfluegl, S. 67/zhu difeng, S. 69/1/chungking, S. 69/2/sofist, S. 69/3/cherezoff, S. 69/4/nulinukas, S. 69/5/cobalt88, S. 69/6/Goygel-Sokol Dmitry, S. 69/7/Coprid, S. 69/8/Nicemonkey, S. 70/StockLite, S. 77/Sergej Khakimullin, S. 79/Tyler Olson, S. 80/1/Elena Elisseeva, S. 80/2/Maslov Dmitry, S. 83/StockLite, S. 85/Elena Elisseeva, S. 90/Kurhan, S. 98/shyshak roman, S. 102/Liviu Toader, S. 105/Goodluz, S. 107/1/michaelkung, S. 107/2/Robert Kneschke, S. 107/3/szefei, S. 107/4/Olga Sapegina, S. 107/5/Minerva Studio, S. 108/Minerva Studio, S. 114/wavebreakmedia ltd, S. 117/Stephen Coburn
stock.adobe.com: S. 44/2/bernardbodo.com/bernardbodo